Embedded Systems and Software Validation

The Morgan Kaufmann Series in Systems on Silicon

Series Editor: Wayne Wolf, Georgia Institute of Technology

The Designer's Guide to VHDL, Second Edition
Peter J. Ashenden

The System Designer's Guide to VHDL-AMS
Peter J. Ashenden, Gregory D. Peterson, and Darrell A. Teegarden

Modeling Embedded Systems and SoCs
Axel Jantsch

ASIC and FPGA Verification: A Guide to Component Modeling
Richard Munden

Multiprocessor Systems-on-Chips
Edited by Ahmed Amine Jerraya and Wayne Wolf

Functional Verification
Bruce Wile, John Goss, and Wolfgang Roesner

Customizable and Configurable Embedded Processors
Edited by Paolo Ienne and Rainer Leupers

Networks-on-Chips: Technology and Tools
Edited by Giovanni De Micheli and Luca Benini

VLSI Test Principles & Architectures
Edited by Laung-Terng Wang, Cheng-Wen Wu, and Xiaoqing Wen

Designing SoCs with Configured Processors
Steve Leibson

ESL Design and Verification
Grant Martin, Andrew Piziali, and Brian Bailey

Aspect-Oriented Programming with e
David Robinson

Reconfigurable Computing: The Theory and Practice of FPGA-Based Computation
Edited by Scott Hauck and André DeHon

System-on-Chip Test Architectures
Edited by Laung-Terng Wang, Charles Stroud, and Nur Touba

Verification Techniques for System-Level Design
Masahiro Fujita, Indradeep Ghosh, and Mukul Prasad

VHDL-2008: Just the New Stuff
Peter J. Ashenden and Jim Lewis

On-Chip Communication Architectures: System on Chip Interconnect
Sudeep Pasricha and Nikil Dutt

Embedded DSP Processor Design: Application Specific Instruction Set Processors
Dake Liu

Processor Description Languages: Applications and Methodologies
Edited by Prabhat Mishra and Nikil Dutt

Three-dimensional Integrated Circuit Design
Vasilis F. Pavlidis and Eby G. Friedman

Electronic Design Automation: Synthesis, Verification, and Test
Edited by Laung-Terng Wang, Kwang-Ting (Tim) Cheng, Yao-Wen Chang

Embedded Systems and Software Validation
Abhik Roychoudhury

Embedded Systems and Software Validation

Abhik Roychoudhury

Department of Computer Science
National University of Singapore

AMSTERDAM • BOSTON • HEIDELBERG • LONDON
NEW YORK • OXFORD • PARIS • SAN DIEGO
SAN FRANCISCO • SINGAPORE • SYDNEY • TOKYO

Morgan Kaufmann Publishers is an imprint of Elsevier

Morgan Kaufmann Publishers is an imprint of Elsevier
30 Corporate Drive, Suite 400, Burlington, MA 01803, USA

This book is printed on acid-free paper.

Library of Congress Cataloging-in-Publication Data
Roychoudhury, Abhik.
    Embedded systems and software validation / Abhik Roychoudhury.
        p. cm. – (The Morgan Kaufmann series in systems on silicon)
    Includes bibliographical references and index.
    ISBN 978-0-12-374230-8 (hardcover : alk. paper)
1. Embedded computer systems–Design and construction. 2. Embedded computer
systems–Testing. 3. Computer software–Testing. I. Title.
    TK7895.E42R72 2009
    004.1–dc22

                                                                    2009011196

British Library Cataloguing in Publication Data
A catalogue record for this book is available from the British Library

ISBN 13: 978-0-12-374230-8

For information on all Morgan Kaufmann publications,
visit our Web site at *www.mkp.com or www.elsevierdirect.com*

Printed and bound by CPI Group (UK) Ltd, Croydon, CR0 4YY
Transferred to Digital Print 2011

To Jishnu

Contents

Acknowledgments

This book owes a lot to all my students, colleagues, and co-workers. It is by working with them over the past decade that I have discovered the issues and challenges in the field of embedded systems validation. So, first and foremost, I must thank them all.

I have written this book off and on, in the course of my teaching and research work at the National University of Singapore (NUS). Funding from a University Research Council project at NUS is gratefully acknowledged.

A leave from NUS in 2007 to the Indian Institute of Science (IISc) infused in me the energy to start writing the book. The calm environs of the IISc campus helped set the mood for writing this book.

The support of Elsevier staff was instrumental in ensuring that the book has proceeded on schedule.

Finally, playing with my 5-year-old son Jishnu allowed me to absorb the pressures of writing the book in the midst of various deadlines and commitments. Thanks, Jishnu!

Singapore
19 January 2009

Preface

This book attempts to cover the issues in validation of embedded software and systems. There are many books on this topic, as a Web search with the appropriate search terms will reveal. So, why this book?

There are several ways to answer the question. The first, most direct answer is that the current books mostly deal with the programming and/or co-design of embedded systems. Validation is often discussed almost as an afterthought. In this book, we treat validation as a first-class citizen in the design process, weaving it into the design process itself.

The focus of our book is on validation, but from an embedded software and systems perspective. The methods we have covered (testing/model-checking) can also be covered from a completely general perspective, focusing only on the techniques, rather than on how they fit into the system design process. But we have not done so. Even though the focus of the book is on validation methods, we clearly show how it fits into system design. As an example, we present and discuss the model-checking method twice in two different ways — once at the level of system model (Chapter 2) and again at the level of system implementation (Chapter 5).

Finally, being rooted in embedded software and systems, the focus of our book is not restricted to functionality validation. We have covered at least two other aspects — debugging of performance and communication behavior. As a result, this book contains analysis methods that are rarely found in a single book — testing (informal validation), model checking (formal validation), worst-case execution time analysis (static analysis for program performance), schedulability analysis (system level performance analysis), and so on — all blended under one cover, with the goal of reliable embedded system design.

As for the chapters of the book, Chapter 1 gives a general introduction to the issues in embedded system validation. Differences between functionality and performance validation are discussed at a general level.

Chapter 2 discusses model-level validation. It starts with generic discussions on system structure and behavior, and zooms into behavioral modeling notations such as finite-state machines (FSMs) and message sequence charts (MSCs). Simulation, testing, and formal verification of these models are discussed. We discuss model-based testing, where test cases generated from the model are tried out on the system implementation. We also discuss property verification, and the well-known model-checking method. The chapter ends with a nice hands-on discussion of practical validation tools such as SPIN and SMV. Thus, this chapter corresponds to *model-level debugging*.

Chapter 3 discusses the issues in resolving communication incompatibilities between embedded system components. We discuss different strategies for resolving such incompatibilities, such as endowing the components with appropriate interfaces, and/or constructing a centralized communication protocol converter. Thus, this chapter corresponds to *communication debugging*.

Chapter 4 discusses system-level performance validation. We start with software timing analysis, in particular worst-case execution time (WCET) analysis. This is followed by the estimation of time spent as a result of different interferences in a program execution — from the external environment, or from other executing programs on the same or different processing elements. Suitable analysis methods to estimate the time due to such interferences are discussed. We then discuss mechanisms to combat execution-time unpredictability via system-level support. In particular, we discuss compiler-controlled memories or scratchpad memories. The chapter concludes with a discussion on time predictability issues in emerging applications. Thus, this chapter corresponds to *performance debugging*.

Chapter 5 discusses functionality debugging of embedded software. We discuss both formal and informal approaches, with almost equal emphasis on testing and formal verification. The first half of the chapter involves validation methods built on testing or dynamic analysis. The second half of the chapter concentrates on formal verification, in particular software model checking. The chapter concludes with a discussion on combining formal verification with testing. Thus, this chapter corresponds to *software debugging*.

Apart from some debugging/validation methods being common to Chapters 2 and 5, the readers may try to read the chapters independently. A senior undergraduate or graduate course on this topic may, however, read the chapters in sequence, that is, Chapters 2, 3, 4, 5.

ABOUT THE AUTHOR

Abhik Roychoudhury received his M.S. and Ph.D. in Computer Science from the State University of New York at Stony Brook in 1997 and 2000, respectively. His research has focused on formal verification and analysis methods for system design, with focus on embedded software and systems. In these areas, his research group has been involved in building practical program analysis and software productivity tools that enhance software quality as well as programmer productivity. Two meaningful examples of such endeavors are the JSlice dynamic analysis tool for Java program debugging, and the Chronos static analysis tool for ensuring time-predictable execution of embedded software. His awards include a 2008 IBM Faculty Award. Since 2001, Abhik has been at the School of Computing in the National University of Singapore, where he is currently an Associate Professor.

Introduction

Embedded software and systems have come to dominate the way we interact with computers and computation in our everyday lives. Computers are no longer isolated entities sitting on our desks. Instead, they are nicely woven and integrated into our everyday lives via the gadgets we directly or indirectly use — mobile phones, washing machines, microwaves, automotive control, and flight control. Indeed, embedded systems are so pervasive, that they perform the bulk of the computation today — putting forward "embedded computing" as a new paradigm to study. In this book, we focus on validation of embedded software and systems, for developing embedded systems with reliable functionality and timing behavior.

Not all embedded systems are safety-critical. One one hand, there are the safety-critical embedded systems such as automobiles, transportation (train) control, flight control, nuclear power plants, and medical devices. On the other hand, there are the more vanilla, or less safety-critical, embedded systems such as mobile phones, HDTV, controllers for household devices (such as washing machines, microwaves, and air conditioners), smart shirts, and so on. Irrespective of whether an embedded system is safety-critical or not, the need for integrating validation into every stage of the design flow is clearly paramount. Of course, for safety-critical embedded systems, there is need for more stringent validation — so much so that formal analysis methods, which give mathematical guarantees about functionality/timing properties of the system, may be called for at least in certain stages of the design.

Our focus in this book is on validation methods, and how they can be woven into the embedded system design process. Before proceeding further, let us intuitively explain some common terminologies that arise in validation — *testing*, *simulation*, *verification*, and *performance analysis*.

- *Testing* refers to checking that a system behaves as expected for a given input. Here the system being checked can be the actual system that will be executed. However, note that it is only being checked for a given input, and not all inputs.

- *Simulation* refers to running a system for a given input. However, simulation differs from actual system execution in one (or both) of the following ways.
  - The system being simulated might only be a model of the actual system to be executed. This is useful for functionality simulation — check out the functionality of a system model for selected inputs before constructing the actual system.
  - The execution platform on which the system is being simulated is different from the actual execution platform. This situation is very common for performance simulations. The execution platform on which the actual system will be executed may not be available, or it might be getting decided through the process of performance simulations. Typically, a software model of the execution platform might be used for performance simulations.
- *Formal verification* refers to checking that a system behaves as expected for all possible inputs. Because exhaustive testing is inefficient or even infeasible, verification may be achieved by statically analyzing a system model (which may be represented by a structure such as a finite-state machine).
- Finally, we note that formal verification methods have conventionally been used for giving strict mathematical guarantees about the functionality of a system. However, to give strict guarantees about performance (for example, to give an upper bound on the execution time of a given software), one needs to employ mathematical analysis techniques for estimating performance. Such techniques often go by the name of *performance analysis*.

In order to see what the possibilities and opportunities are in terms of integrating validation into embedded system design flows, we can look at the automobile industry. It is widely recognized that automotive electronics is a wide market, with more and more functionalities in modern-day cars being software-controlled. Indeed, innovations in automotive software can bring about new designs, a point often articulated by car manufacturers themselves. The by-now famous quotes such as "more than 90% of the innovation in a modern-day car is from the software" stand testimony to the importance of embedded software/systems in the design of a modern-day car. Naturally, because of the importance of the various car components (brakes, airbags, etc.) functioning "correctly" during the driving of a car, rigorous validation of the hardware/software controlling these components is crucial. In other words, reliable and robust embedded system design flows that integrate extensive debugging/validation are a *must*.

To see further the importance of validation in embedded systems for automobiles, we can delve deeper into the various components of a car, which can be computer-controlled. Roughly speaking, these can be divided into three categories — engine features, cabin features, and entertainment. Clearly, the engine features are the most safety-critical and the features related to in-vehicle entertainment are the least safety-critical. The engine features include critical features such as the brake and steering wheel; usually these features involve hard real-time constraints. The cabin features include less critical (but important) features such as power windows and air conditioning. The entertainment or infotainment features include control of in-car devices such as GPS navigation systems, CD player, and in-car television, as well as communication between these devices. Clearly, the computing component controlling the engine features (such as brakes) needs very rigorous validation — to the extent that the behavior of these computing components could be subjected to formal modeling and verification. For the cabin features, we at least need modeling and extensive testing of the computing components controlling the cabin features. For the infotainment features, we need performance analysis methods to ensure that the soft real-time constraints are satisfied.

Thus, as we can see from the discussion on the specific domain of automotive software, validation of different kinds are required for a complex embedded system. For the more safety-critical parts of the system, rigorous modeling and formal verification may be needed. For the less safety-critical parts, more extensive testing may be sufficient. Moreover, for the parts of the system controlling or ensuring real-time responses to/from the environment, detailed performance validation needs to be carried out. Thus, the validation methods we employ can range from formal methods (such as model checking) to informal ones (such as testing). Moreover, the level of abstraction at which we employ the validation may vary — model-level validation; or high-level implementation validation (where we consider only the inter-component behavior without looking inside the components); or low-level implementation validation (where we also look inside the system components). Finally, the criteria for validation may also vary — we may perform validation at different levels, to check for functionality errors, timing errors, and so on.

Figure 1.1 visually depicts the intricacies of embedded system validation. In particular, Figure 1.1a shows the different levels (model/implementation) and criteria (performance/functionality) of system validation.

Figure 1.1b illustrates the complications in functionality validation. For an embedded system that we seek to construct, we may design and elaborate it at different levels of details (or different levels of abstraction). If we are seeking functionality validation, then the higher the level of detail, the lower the formality of the validation method. Thus, for system design at higher levels of abstraction, we may try out fully formal validation methods. On the other hand, as we start fleshing out the implementation details of the system under construction, we may settle for more informal validation methods such as extensive testing.

As opposed to functionality validation, the picture appears somewhat different for timing validation — see Figure 1.1c. As is well understood, embedded systems

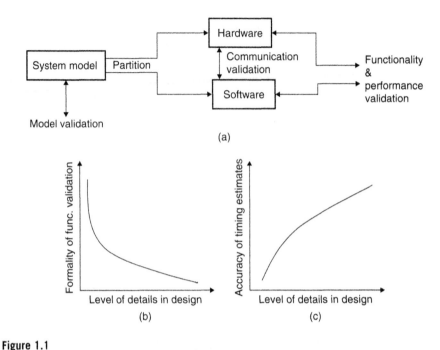

Figure 1.1

Issues in functionality and timing validation of embedded systems.

often incorporate hard or soft real-time constraints on interaction of the system with its physical environment — or, for that matter, interactions between the different components of the system. Hence, timing validation involves developing accurate estimates of the "system response time" (in response to some event from the environment). Clearly, as the details of the embedded system are fleshed out, we can develop more accurate timing estimates and, in that sense, perform more detailed timing validation.

Thus, Figure 1.1 shows the issues in validating functionality versus validating timing properties — both of which are of great importance in embedded system design flows. Two different aspects are being highlighted here:

- Formal verification of functionality is better conducted at higher levels of abstraction. As we start considering lower level details, formal approaches do not scale up, and informal validation methods such as testing come into play.
- For performance validation, as we consider lower level details, our performance estimates are more accurate.

The reader should note that other criteria along which embedded system validation may proceed, such as estimating the energy or area requirements of a system, also have certain basic similarities with timing validation. As the system design is elaborated in more detail, we can form a better idea about its timing, energy, and area requirements.

In the following chapters, we study embedded software/systems validation from various angles:

- Model-level validation (mostly functionality) — Chapter 2
- Implementation-level validation
  - High-level validation of intercomponent communication — Chapter 3
  - Low-level implementation validation
    - Performance debugging — Chapter 4
    - Functionality debugging — Chapter 5

So, let us get on with the ride — studying various debugging/validation methods for design of reliable embedded software and systems.

Model Validation

We now busy ourselves with the first step in the design process — system modeling. To describe this step, we need to clarify what a model is. Once our understanding of a system model is clear, we can also describe the role of verification and validation in the modeling phase (as far as the overall system design life cycle is concerned). Indeed, what constitutes a system model is often a major source of confusion. One of the major issues that causes this confusion is the difference between the *behavior* and the *architecture* of the embedded system being designed.

In its simplest form, *system architecture* (or *structure*) refers to the interconnection among the components, whereas *system behavior* refers to how the components change state — possibly by communicating among themselves. This understanding, although commonplace, often raises further questions because we need to clarify the notion of "components." In this book, we define the independent entities in a design as processes or active objects or components. Thus, a process has a control flow of its own and can change state possibly by executing independent actions or by communicating with other processes. System architecture then refers to the structural relationships between the system components, whereas system behavior captures how the components change state.

Let us now take a concrete example to further clarify the differences between system architecture and system behavior. Consider an air-traffic controller (ATC) that communicates with several clients. Each client could represent a tiny controller, one for each incoming aircraft, which is used to provide inputs to the incoming aircraft. The centralized controller interacts with the clients to provide important updates (such as weather information), and these updates are used as inputs by the incoming aircraft to make decisions (such as calculation of speed and trajectory). The basic system structure can be visualized as the following diagram (Figure 2.1).

Figure 2.1 shows that there is one ATC and an arbitrary number of clients (say, N). Furthermore, a subset of the clients are receiving updates from the ATC,

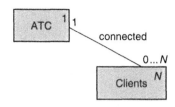

Figure 2.1

Basic system structure for an air-traffic control system.

and this is shown in the diagram as the *connected* relation (whose cardinality is thus given as $0 \ldots N$). This is what we mean by *system structure*. However, Figure 2.1 does not capture the interaction protocol between the ATC and the clients — how ATC responds to requests from clients, and how the clients make requests. This comes under system "behavior."

For readers familiar with the Unified Modeling Language or UML [54], we can offer the following analogy. System structure is described using UML class diagrams — the classes in the system, the number of objects in each class, relations across the classes, and the cardinality of the relations. On the other hand, system behavior involves state changes of the system objects due to control flow and interaction across objects. This is captured via UML state diagrams and UML sequence diagrams. Typically for each class, a state diagram will be given — showing the state changes for objects in the class. Furthermore, interaction across objects will be given as sequence diagrams.

Readers unfamiliar with UML need not worry. We will elaborate on these terms soon. But before that, we will pin down the notion of system behavior and the importance of modeling it by studying our schematic air-traffic control (ATC) example.

2.1 PLATFORM VERSUS SYSTEM BEHAVIOR

So far, we have defined behavior as the mechanism of state change via the interaction between stateful objects.[1] However, this definition is too general and does not distinguish between the system being designed and the *platform* on which the system is being implemented. It is important to clarify this difference before we proceed further.

In the case of our schematic air-traffic control application, the "system being designed" refers to the ATC and the clients. System behavior refers to the interaction

---

[1] A *stateful object* is an entity with a local state and control flow of its own.

protocol between ATC and clients. However, this does not say anything about how this interaction protocol will be implemented. It is possible that the ATC and the clients will be implemented in separate electronic control units, or ECUs, and these ECUs will communicate via a bus. Here, the bus and its access protocols (which decide who can transmit on the bus and when) form part of the platform description. Clearly the bus access protocol refers to platform behavior.

When we refer to modeling of behavior, conventionally in the formal methods or software engineering communities, this refers to behavioral modeling of the system being designed. The platform plays little or no role in the design, because the first-cut system description is supposed to be platform independent. However, the same cannot be claimed for embedded system designs, which are typically platform-aware. So, the question is how to combine platform modeling with system model when we capture behavior?

As might be expected, the combination of the platform model with system model (to form one jumbo unified model) often does not work out for scalability reasons. Instead the platform model could be validated to provide some guarantees, and these guarantees could be used in the debugging/validation of the system model.

How does this connection between platform validation and system model validation work? Suppose the system model captures distributed controllers running on different processing elements and communicating among themselves via a bus. The platform model could capture the overall platform architecture (processing elements connected via bus) and the communication behavior (in the form of the bus protocol through which the processing elements communicate). In this case, we can validate the bus protocol to derive guarantees of the following form:

- *Functionality Guarantee:*
  - The bus access mechanism never deadlocks, or
  - Each request for bus access is eventually served.
- *Timing Guarantee:* Each request for bus access is served within *n* time units (for some constant *n*).

Subsequently, these guarantees can be used (often implicitly) while debugging or validating the system model.

A schematic diagram showing the interaction between platform and system behavior is shown in Figure 2.2. Here the system has four threads of control, marked as T1, T2, T3, and T4, which are running on three different processing elements. In particular, T1 and T2 share the same processing element and receive input data from the environment (via sensors). As far as the communication patterns in the system model are concerned, the schematic diagram captures the following:

- T1 and T2 communicate data to T3. Because the data is accumulated from different sensors, T3 presumably performs some fusion of the data.
- T3 communicates data to T4.

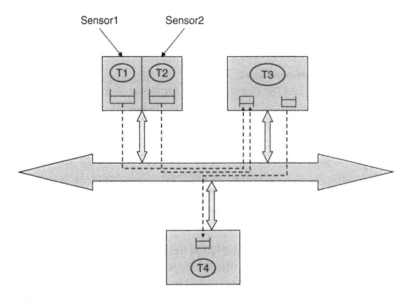

Figure 2.2

Schematic interaction among environment, system, and platform.

However, the foregoing communication behavior is implemented in a complex way. In particular, we see that T1 and T2 share the same processing element — so there has to be some decision (possibly taken by the scheduling policy in the processing element) on who will communicate over the bus. The key issue is that in embedded system design, the system models cannot be oblivious of such platform-dependent issues as processor communication and scheduling within a processing element. This is particularly so because the system models can also be used to give performance guarantees (apart from guarantees on system functionality).

We will discuss the timing analysis of the platform's communication mechanisms in Chapter 4. In this chapter, we discuss debugging and validation of the system models. However, the same (or similar) modeling formalisms can be used for describing system behavior as well as platform behavior. In particular, we can certainly use finite-state machines (FSMs) for modeling platform behavior and the model-checking technique for validating platform behavior.

2.2 CRITERIA FOR DESIGN MODEL

Usually, the formal modeling of behavior starts from informal requirements that are given as English documents. Requirements documents are varied in nature, differing from one application domain to another. The behavioral requirements could be given as rules (written informally in English). Alternatively, the requirements can be represented visually in the form of diagrams. One common example of representing requirements visually is the use of *timing diagrams* for hardware circuits where the evolution of various signals is shown in a clock-cycle by clock-cycle fashion.

For systems with a software component (such as most embedded systems would have!), the use of visual requirements is a bit more elaborate and complicated. In particular, the UML provides various types of diagrams for depicting behavior — state diagrams, sequence diagrams, and activity diagrams, to name a few. There is a tremendous amount of research work on the formal semantics of these individual diagrams. For our purposes, we are willing to accept a design model if it provides a *complete modeling of behavior* of the system under construction *using notations which are incorporated into an existing well-understood standard* (such as UML). The reason for making this choice is obvious. We do not want to make the task of modeling behavior so arduously complex that no design engineer will care to attempt it! Nor do we want design engineers to prove theorems on formal semantics of the UML diagrams before they can use these diagrams.

Our view of modeling is a pragmatic one: It is one of clarifying the English requirements into a description (the model) that can then be analyzed for debugging purposes. Furthermore, because one of the most common analysis methods involve running simulations on the model (i.e., exploring the possible runs), we usually require the model to be equipped with an understanding of the execution semantics. Thus we articulate the following criteria for acceptable design models.

Definition 1 (Criteria for Design Model) *Our view of a design model (of an intended embedded system) is that it should have the following properties.*

- Complete — *The model should be a complete description of system behavior.*
- Based on well-accepted modeling notations/standards — *We depend on these standards for the model's semantics, rather than dabbling in semantic issues ourselves.*
- Preferably executable — *We prefer that the model be naturally equipped with an execution semantics, so that simulations can be run on the model itself.*

The notion of a model being "complete" (or not) also needs further explanation. Often the requirements may refer to many system variables which are not crucial to the logic of the system design. To illustrate this point, let us refer back to our schematic air-traffic control example (Figure 2.1) where the centralized ATC provides weather updates to the clients. Now, when we model the system we essentially model the *protocol* through which the ATC and the clients interact so that weather information can be exchanged. Because the purpose of modeling is mainly to debug this interaction protocol, there is no need to model real weather information within the model — indeed, it would not be of much use! To concretize the issue further, let us consider a hypothetical session between the centralized ATC and the clients:

- Client1 sends "connect" request to ATC.
- Client2 sends "connect" request to ATC.
- ATC sends weather information to Client1, Client2.
- ...

If the clients (in this case Client1, Client2) do not make any decisions based on the weather information, then there is no need to represent the weather information concretely — just the protocol involving the propagation of the weather information is modeled. What if the system being modeled does make decisions based on the weather? Suppose the clients send different signals to the aircraft depending on whether the ambient temperature is greater than or less than 10°C. Even then we do not need to maintain the exact temperature as a system variable. Instead we can simply maintain a boolean variable $Temp_{10}$ that is true if the temperature is greater than 10°C.

To give the readers another example, this time from platform modeling, let us consider a bus communication protocol. Processors hooked to the bus need to negotiate bus access by following this protocol. Now, if our aim is to model and debug the protocol, we do not need to model in detail the actual data that is transmitted on the bus once a processor is granted bus access. All of these tricks form the various state abstractions that we will define more formally later in this section.

In summary, while doing behavioral modeling, we may abstract different system variables that are mentioned in the requirements. Thus, when we say that a model is "complete," we mean "complete at the corresponding level of abstraction." In other words, whatever processes and system variables are modeled, their complete behavior (and not just behavioral snippets as are captured in UML sequence diagrams) is described.

Our goal in enunciating the foregoing criteria is to make sure that the task of modeling does not become burdensome, yet the models are still useful for debugging/validation in early stages of the system life cycle.

2.3 INFORMAL REQUIREMENTS: A CASE STUDY

At this stage, we have presented the notion of behavior and what we want in a design model. Soon, we will be introducing the modeling notations, too. But before we do so, let us get a feel for what real-life informal requirements look like, and how to grapple with these informal requirements to construct a formal model.

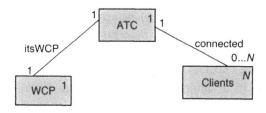

Figure 2.3

System structure for CTAS weather-update controller case study.

The case study we have in mind is the air-traffic control system mentioned earlier. We are going to model a weather-update controller that manages the communication of weather information between a centralized controller and several clients (where each client sends input or keeps in touch with an incoming aircraft as already mentioned). The weather-update controller is a part of the Center TRACON Automation System or CTAS [21]. The CTAS is a set of tools developed at NASA to aid air-traffic controllers in managing high volumes of air-traffic flows at large airports. Various processes such as TS (Trajectory Synthesizer) and RA (Route Analyzer) that make up the CTAS system require the latest weather updates for their functioning.

The weather update controller involves three classes of objects — the weather-aware clients, a centralized air-traffic controller (abbreviated ATC), and a weather control panel (abbreviated WCP). The system structure is a slight modification of Figure 2.1 and is given in Figure 2.3. Both WCP and CM are also part of the CTAS system. We refer to various processes requiring the weather updates simply as clients. Thus, we consider the CTAS system to be consisting of three classes of processes: (i) WCP and (ii) ATC classes with one object each, and (iii) a client class consisting of multiple client objects.

In our system, the latest weather update is presented by the weather control panel to various connected clients, via the controller. This update may succeed or fail in different ways; furthermore, clients get connected/disconnected to the ATC by following an elaborate protocol. It is the formalization of this protocol that we are concerned about when we talk of behavioral modeling. Our main purpose here is to illustrate that subtle errors can be easily missed at the level of informal requirements. In the later sections of this chapter, we show how the same errors can be found by analyzing the formal model.

2.3.1 **The Requirements Document**

The requirements document for the CTAS weather controller is available from `http://scesm04.upb.de/case-study-2/requirements.pdf`.

We encourage the reader to go through the requirements document from this website at this stage. We should remind the reader that in this example, the requirements document is reasonably well structured as a collection of rules. Each rule essentially specifies what response is to be provided when a particular action is encountered.

Even then, with these simple well-structured requirement rules, they are too voluminous to be reproduced here so that we can even try to understand the intricacies in modeling. Our aim here is *not* to impress upon the reader that informal requirements of real systems can be huge and can take a human a lot of time to comprehend — I believe most of us would agree with that statement. Instead, we want to illustrate at a micro level how subtle errors can be missed even in simple well-structured requirements. This serves as a motivation for studying and using all the material we will present on system modeling thereafter. With this aim, we have simplified the requirements of the CTAS weather controller system. We produce them as a separate subsection (Section 2.3.2) for the benefit of the reader. The requirements would appear comprehensible to design engineers even at a quick glance.

2.3.2 Simplification of the Informal Requirements

- **Initial States**

  Initially, the WCP is enabled for manually weather updating, the ATC is at its idle status, and all the clients are disconnected. Two standard behaviors of this system are as follows.

- **Client Initialization Phase**

  1. A disconnected weather-aware client can establish a connection by sending a connection request to the ATC.
  2. If the ATC's status is idle when the connection request is received, it will set both its own status and the connecting client's status to preinitializing and disable the weather control panel so that no manual updates can be made by the user during the process of client initialization.

     Otherwise (ATC's status is not idle), the ATC will send a message to the client to refuse the connection, and the client remains disconnected.
  3. When the ATC is preinitializing, it will send a message to instruct the newly connected client to get the new weather information, and then set both its own status and the client's status to initializing.
  4. If the client reports success for getting the new weather, the ATC will send another message to inform the client to use the weather information, and then set both its own status and the client's status to postinitializing.

     Otherwise, if obtaining the new weather information fails, the ATC will disconnect the client and set its own status back to idle.

5. If the client reports success in terms of using the new weather information, the initialization process is completed. The ATC will set both its own status and the client's status to idle and reenable the WCP so that manual weather update is allowed again.

   Otherwise, if using the new weather information fails, the ATC will disconnect the client, reenable the WCP, and set its own status back to idle.

- **Communicating Weather Updates**

1. Users can manually update new weather information only when the WCP is enabled. Clicking the update button on the WCP sends an update message to the ATC.

2. When the ATC is idle and receives update request from the WCP, it will set its own status and all the connected weather-aware clients' status to preupdating and disable the WCP from any further update requests before the completion of the current update.

3. When the ATC's status is preupdating, it will send messages to instruct all connected clients to get the new weather information, and then set its own status and the clients' status to updating.

4. If all the clients report success for getting the new weather information, the ATC will send messages to inform the clients to use the new weather information, and then set its own status and the clients' status to postupdating.

   Otherwise, if any of the connected clients report failure in terms of getting the new weather information, the ATC will send messages to all clients to use their old weather information, and then set its own status and the clients' status to postreverting.

5. When ATC's status is postupdating, if all the clients report success in terms of using the new weather information, the updating is completed. The ATC will set its own status and the clients' status to idle and reenable the WCP.

   Otherwise, if any of the connected clients reports failure in terms of using the new weather information, the ATC will disconnect all connected clients, reenable the WCP, and set its own status back to idle.

6. When ATC's status is postreverting, if all the clients report success in terms of using the old weather information, the reverting is completed. The ATC will set its own status and the clients' status to idle and reenable the WCP.

   Otherwise, if any of the connected clients report failure in terms of using the old weather information, the ATC will disconnect all connected clients, reenable the WCP, and set its own status back to idle.

Comment

The simplified requirements in the preceding give the feel for the requirements document of a real system, albeit on a very small scale. This specification is certainly comprehensible, and yet we cannot use it directly to find errors in it. It turns out that the informal specification just given has a deadlock *error — the system can reach a state from where no action is possible. We now go on to study modeling notations and checking procedures (working on those notations) that can detect and even help correct such errors.*

2.4 COMMON MODELING NOTATIONS

The most well-known and often the most popular behavioral modeling formalism is that of a *finite-state machine* or a *finite-state transition system*. Throughout this book, we will use these terms interchangeably, and we will use the abbreviation FSM for both of these terms.

2.4.1 Finite-State Machines

At the most vanilla level, a finite-state machine can be described as a structure

$$M = (S, I, \rightarrow)$$

where S is a finite set of states, $I \subseteq S$ is the set of initial states, and $\rightarrow \subseteq S \times S$ is the transition relation. Thus, a finite-state transition system captures a conventional bubble-and-arrow diagram with the bubbles denoting the states, and the arrows denoting the transition from one state to another. In Figure 2.4, we show a trivial finite-state transition system and its states, initial states, and transitions.

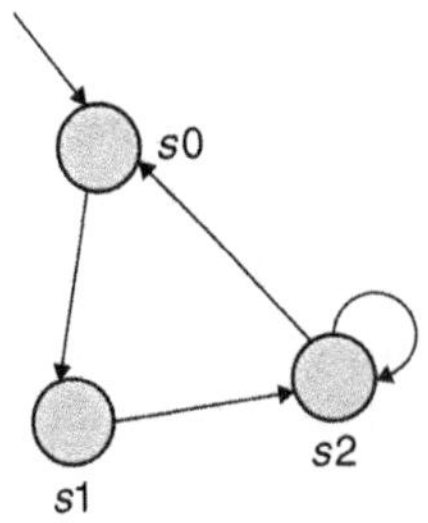

$S = \{s0, s1, s2\}$

$I = \{s0\}$

$\rightarrow = \{(s0, s1), (s1, s2), (s2, s2), (s2, s0)\}$

Figure 2.4

Example finite-state transition system.

We now explain some of the important concepts behind system modeling via finite-state machines, namely:

- *Unit step:* How much computation denotes a single transition in the finite-state machine?
- *Hierarchy:* How do we construct or visualize a finite-state machine model at different levels of granularity?
- *Concurrency:* How do we compose the behaviors of concurrently running subsystems, each of which is modeled as a finite-state machine?

Unit Step

Inherent in the FSM modeling formalism is the notion of a system progressing by discrete steps. Thus, starting from an initial state, the system moves in steps by executing transitions. This naturally raises the question: What will the states and transitions be capturing in the first place? We say:

- A *state* denotes a specific valuation of the system variables, and
- A *transition* denotes a change in the valuation of system variables.

With this interpretation, it is reasonable to ask whether a transition is simply an abstraction of a time unit: in other words, when the actual system is implemented, what time the different transitions in the model take up, and whether they take up equal amounts of time. We emphasize to our readers that the transition system is merely a system model, so exactly what the transitions in the model correspond to in the actual system implementation depends to some extent on what meaning is ascribed to the transitions during modeling. Typically, when the transition system serves as a model of a clocked synchronous system (a system driven by a common clock, say a sequential circuit), then a transition is used to denote a clock-cycle-wise evolution of the signals in the system. In this case, a transition takes place every clock cycle (possibly leading back to the same state if none of the system signals changed its value). Because the system signals cannot change state without a new clock cycle emerging, it is enough to observe the system state every clock cycle.

However, for asynchronous systems (such as software systems), we can denote a transition as the execution of a minimal block of code that is atomically executed — say, a statement or an instruction. In this case, we do not make the system model platform-dependent, dependent on the platforms on which the system will be executed. Hence we do not know how much time each statement will take. But again, it can be argued that because the system state will not change without a statement/instruction being executed, it is enough to model state change for every statement/instruction. We also wish to note that whether we choose a statement or an instruction as the unit step in the modeling also depends on the designer — at what level (s)he intends the modeling and verification to be carried out. For programming languages endowed with a virtual machine (such as Java), it is also customary to model/verify a program at the level of bytecodes. Of course, the smaller the unit step, the more accurate is the model (meaning closer to the implementation). At the same time, a more accurate FSM model can be more troublesome to verify via search procedures, because it contains more detail and the size of the model *blows up*.

Hierarchy

Related to the issue of resolving what is a unit step in an FSM, there are other issues in using an FSM for system modeling. Intuitively, it is possible to draw each FSM hierarchically, reducing the visual blow-up. In other words, each state in a local FSM can denote a complicated FSM, and so on. Such hierarchical modeling corresponds to understanding the FSM model of a system at different levels of granularity. Clearly, corresponding to the different levels of hierarchy, the notion of *unit step* also changes. We now illustrate this issue with the help of an example.

An example FSM is shown in Figure 2.5. In this diagram we show the FSM for a light controller. At its most basic level, the FSM has only two states — off and on. However, when the light is on, this state can be elaborated by the brightness of the light, shown by the substates, dim and bright. Furthermore, when the light is brightly lit, it can be "stable" or, depending on some controls, it may turn "flashing." This is shown as another hierarchy level in Figure 2.5. Thus, the basic idea in hierarchical

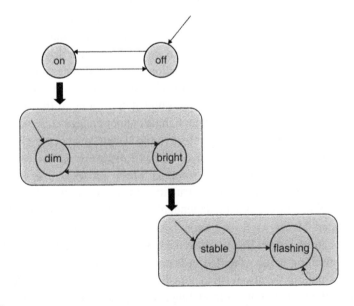

Figure 2.5

Hierarchy levels in FSM-based modeling.

modeling is that different system variables can be modeled at different levels of the hierarchy. In our example, we may assume at least three internal variables of the light controller — mode (whether the light is off or on), brightness (whether the light is dim or bright when it is on), and stability (whether the light is stable or flashing when it is bright). These three variables are modeled at different levels, allowing us to visualize the light controller at progressively higher levels of detail.

At the topmost or first level of the hierarchy (Figure 2.5), there are only two states — "on" and "off." Transition from the "on" state to the "off" state is an example of a unit step at this level. However, if we elaborate the "on" state and go to the next lower level of hierarchy, we see that the "on" state becomes elaborated by the "dim" and "bright" substates. Thus, a transition from "dim" to "bright" is a unit step at the second hierarchy level in Figure 2.5, but it does not qualify as a unit step in the first hierarchy level. This example illustrates how the unit step changes as we consider different hierarchy levels of a hierarchically modeled FSM.

Concurrency

Apart from resolving what is a unit step in a finite-state transition system, there are other difficulties in using an FSM for system modeling. Typically the system being modeled consists of a number of processes running concurrently (and communicating from time to time). For example, the air-traffic control system discussed in this chapter is a concurrent composition of a centralized air-traffic controller (ATC), several client processes, and a weather-control panel (WCP) process. So how do we model all these disparate processes when we try to model the air-traffic control system? Usually one would construct at least three FSMs, one for each *class* of processes — FSM_{ATC}, FSM_{Client}, and FSM_{WCP}. Note that the system being modeled might have many many client processes. However, the behavior of all these clients might be specified by a single FSM. For a system with three clients, the system model will be

$$FSM_{ATC} \times FSM_{Client} \times FSM_{Client} \times FSM_{Client} \times FSM_{WCP}$$

where $\times$ denotes the *concurrent composition* of two FSMs. We define the concurrent composition operation as follows.

Definition 2 (Basic FSM Composition) *Given two FSMs $M_1 = (S_1, I_1, \rightarrow_1)$ and $M_2 = (S_2, I_2, \rightarrow_2)$, we have*

$$M_1 \times M_2 = (S_1 \times S_2, I_1 \times I_2, \rightarrow)$$

where for any $s, s' \in S_1$ and $t, t' \in S_2$ we have $((s,t),(s',t')) \in \rightarrow$ iff $(s,s') \in \rightarrow_1$ or $(t,t') \in \rightarrow_2$. Stated otherwise, we have a transition from state (s,t) to state (s',t'), that is, $(s,t) \rightarrow (s',t')$, if and only if either $s \rightarrow_1 s'$ or $t \rightarrow_2 t'$.

Describing a system model as a concurrent composition of the FSMs of the participating processes is standard practice. It allows us to avoid constructing the global state machine corresponding to the concurrent composition. Instead we model the local FSMs for the individual processes and simply say that the global FSM of the entire system can be obtained by composing these local FSMs.

Thus, for a system with two processes whose local FSMs each have 20 states, we draw only $20 + 20 = 40$ states, as opposed to a global FSM with up to $20 \times 20 = 400$ states. The reader should note that we even though we are drawing only $20 + 20 = 40$ states, they implicitly *represent* all the 400 states. We could have also explicitly drawn these 400 states. However, the notation of describing a global FSM as a composition of local FSMs allows us to avoid drawing all those 400 states — we draw only $20 + 20 = 40$ states to represent all the $20 \times 20 = 400$ states!

Thus we view a system as a concurrent composition of processes where the control flow in each process is encoded as an FSM. The overall control flow of the system is obtained by any arbitrary *interleaving* of the control flows of the constituent processes. Interleaving is implicitly integrated into the definition of FSM composition — a composite state (s, t) makes a transition if and only if either s or t makes a transition in their local FSMs. In a broad sense, having a notion of interleaving integrated in the process composition is a useful thing to do. In particular, consider the system implementation as implementing the local FSMs in a distributed fashion. In this case, the local FSMs will be running at different speeds depending on the platform on which they are run. Because we do not want to make any assumptions about the relative speeds of the platforms on which the FSMs are run, an interleaving semantics is safe to assume. Note that even if all the local FSMs are implemented on a single processor, we still cannot assume anything about the scheduling policy running on the processor. In such cases, the local FSMs will be run as threads on a single processor, and the scheduling policy will determine which thread will proceed. Again, without making specific assumptions about the scheduling policy, the interleaving semantics (which allows any enabled process to proceed) will capture all possible behaviors. This underscores the purpose of a system model in embedded system design: It is intended to capture all possible behaviors that may emerge in system implementations — possibly more behaviors than will be observed in the actual implementations, but *never fewer*.

2.4.2 Communicating FSMs

At this stage, we have given the FSM as a basic system model and defined the composition of FSMs. However, the FSM model we have presented so far is too simplistic for general usage. Let us examine why. The local FSMs denote individual threads of control, and their composition is defined by interleaving. However, we have built no mechanism for the threads of control to communicate. In general, the processes in a system design are bound to communicate. Indeed, it is the communication that is the centerpiece of the process interaction. Without inter-process communication, there would hardly be any subtle bugs that need to be found by modeling and validating the system. We have not discussed inter-process communication across FSMs at all, and we proceed to do now.

How do we add communication to our basic FSM model? The simplest way is to label the transitions with "action" names. Thus, each FSM is now defined as $M = (S, I, \Sigma, \rightarrow)$, where S is a finite set of states, $I \subseteq S$ is the set of initial states, Σ is a collection of actions also called the *action alphabet*, and $\rightarrow \subseteq S \times \Sigma \times S$ is the transition relation. Composition of FSMs is now defined as follows.

Definition 3 (Composition of Communicating FSMs) *Given two FSMs*

$$M_1 = (S_1, I_1, \Sigma_1, \rightarrow_1) \text{ and } M_2 = (S_2, I_2, \Sigma_2, \rightarrow_2)$$

their composition is defined as

$$M = (S_1 \times S_2, I_1 \times I_2, \Sigma_1 \cup \Sigma_2, \rightarrow)$$

Here $S_1 \times S_2$ is the set of states, $I_1 \times I_2$ is the set of initial states, and $\Sigma_1 \cup \Sigma_2$ is the action alphabet. The transition relation $\rightarrow$ is defined as follows. Given action $a \in \Sigma_1 \cup \Sigma_2$, states $s, s' \in S_1$ and $t, t' \in S_2$, we have $((s,t), a, (s', t')) \in \rightarrow$, also written as $(s,t) \xrightarrow{a} (s', t')$, if and only if any one of the following conditions holds:

- $a \in \Sigma_1 \cap \Sigma_2$ *and* $(s, a, s') \in \rightarrow_1$ *and* $(t, a, t') \in \rightarrow_2$
- $a \in \Sigma_1 - \Sigma_2$ *and* $(s, a, s') \in \rightarrow_1$
- $a \in \Sigma_2 - \Sigma_1$ *and* $(t, a, t') \in \rightarrow_2$

Let us now examine the foregoing definition. First of all, we add action labels to all transitions in our finite-state transition systems or FSMs. Now, when we compose two FSMs M_1 and M_2, if their action alphabets are completely disjoint, the composition will proceed as before, by arbitrarily interleaving transitions from the local FSMs. However, if the intersection of the action alphabets of M_1, M_2 is nonempty, the composition of M_1, M_2 proceeds *differently*. For action labels that are common to M_1 and M_2, we require both of the FSMs to make a move together on these common actions. On the other hand, for action labels that are local to M_1 (M_2), it is sufficient for only M_1 (M_2) to make a move. In other words, we make FSMs M_1 and M_2 communicate on the common actions.

Let us examine the example in Figure 2.6. We have shown two local FSMs, each with two states conveniently marked as "idle" and "busy." If we ignore the action labels on the transitions and compose the two FSMs as per our earlier definition, we get a global FSM with four states (idle, idle), (idle, busy), (busy, idle), and

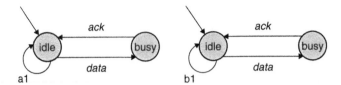

Figure 2.6

Basic communication across FSMs (common actions marked in italics).

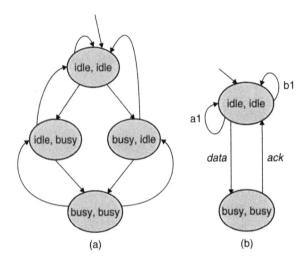

(a)   (b)

Figure 2.7

Global FSM by composing the local FSMs in Figure 2.6 (a) without considering action labels and inter-process communication, (b) after considering action labels and communication.

(busy, busy). This FSM is shown in Figure 2.7a. On the other hand, if we consider the action labels, we require both the local FSMs to make a joint move on the common actions "data" and "ack" (marked in italics in Figure 2.6). Thus, the action "data" here *summarizes* a communication across the two processes. In this case, the global FSM obtained by composing the two local FSMs has only two states; it is shown in Figure 2.7b.

One may seriously question the purpose of such a communication — after all, what do the local FSMs communicate to each other? Usually, while modeling an embedded system, we expect the various system components to communicate data among themselves. In this case, our inter-process communication via common actions simply denotes some sort of a handshake or synchronization. The important issue here is that this is a mechanism for two or more processes to communicate via a common action. If we want to model data communication across processes, this can be achieved by allowing actions that go beyond simple symbols. Thus, instead of having simple action symbols a, b, c in our FSM, each action symbol can be a complex structure with one or more parameters. Once we have a basic mechanism of communication across FSMs, such extensions to model data communication can be easily added. Typically, such extensions are achieved by (a) making the occurrence of any common action a communication between exactly two processes (multiparty communication is ruled out), and (b) assigning explicit sender and receiver roles for a common action. The sender role is typically denoted by an exclamation mark or !, whereas the receiver role is denoted by a question mark or ?. Using these notations we have modified the diagram of Figure 2.6 into Figure 2.8.

Now, let us examine the local FSMs in Figure 2.8. One of the processes, called the sender process, executes $data(5)$. The action label $data$ being a common action, this involves the other process (also called the receiver process) to execute its action $data(X)$ along with it. Here X is a local variable of the receiver process. As a result of this joint move, we achieve:

- Synchronization of the two processes as before, and
- Passing of the value 5 to variable X (data communication).

Having such *value-passing* in our models is important for capturing data communication. However, to capture the directionality of the value passing (i.e., which process sends the value, and which process receives it), we explicitly mark the sending and receiving of values via ! and ? symbols.

What if the sender process wants to send the value stored in one of its local variables (irrespective of what the value is)? If the local variable is Y, this can be denoted by an action label of the form $!data(Y)$. When this action is executed, Y should be instantiated to a concrete value that is then propagated to the receiver side.

Note that our communication involves the sender and the receiver to come together in the form of a handshake. In the concurrency theory literature, this is often referred to as "blocking send," because the sender cannot send data unless the receiver is ready. This corresponds to synchronous communication — because, in a way, the sender and receiver synchronize.

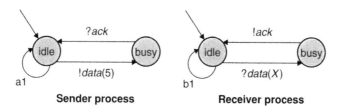

Figure 2.8

Data communication across FSMs: ! denotes send, ? denotes receive.

The alternative is to have a *nonblocking send*, where the sender can proceed even if the receiver is not ready. This is only possible if there is an underlying message buffer storing messages that have been sent but have not been received. The presence of such buffers will no doubt alter the definition of global system state.

Consider a system with two processes p, q with local FSMs FSM_p and FSM_q. Let there be two message buffers, $Buf_{p!q}$ for storing messages sent from p to q and $Buf_{q!p}$ for storing messages sent from q to p. The local FSM of $Buf_{p!q}$ is given by the schematic in Figure 2.9, where N is the capacity of the buffer. Here we have shown only the number of filled slots of the buffer, and not the messages stored in the buffer. In most implementations the message buffers supporting nonblocking sends will be *queues* enforcing a first-in-first-out (FIFO) discipline.

For the sake of understanding, Figure 2.9 also shows a sample p and q process. Here p sends to q infinitely, while q receives from p infinitely. Now, let us examine Figure 2.9 more closely. The send action $p!q$ is supposed to be a communication between processes p and q. However, in the presence of the stateful buffer process, it is a communication involving p and buffer. Similarly, $q?p$ is now a communication involving the buffer process and q process. Interpreted in this way, we can see that the composition of p, q and buffer allows p to send messages without q receiving them, provided there are at most N messages that have been sent but not received. Here N denotes the capacity of the buffer that is modeled by the buffer process $Buf_{p!q}$. The global FSM is then given by composing FSMs of processes with the FSMs of the buffers. Thus, for a system consisting of two processes p and q, the global FSM is

$$FSM_p \times FSM_q \times FSM_{Buf_{p!q}} \times FSM_{Buf_{q!p}}$$

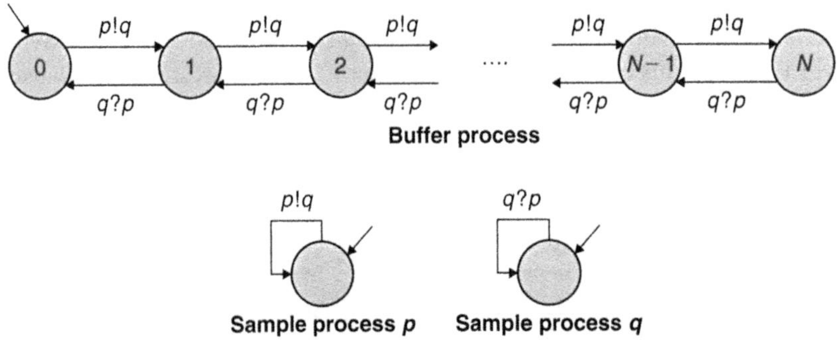

Buffer process

Sample process p   **Sample process q**

Figure 2.9

FSM of a buffer to store messages from process p to process q. Sample p and q processes are also shown for the reader's understanding.

For systems with more processes, there will be more buffers, and the global state will be modified accordingly. Referring back to the example in Figure 2.9, we note that q never sends any messages to p in our example, so we have not shown $FSM_{Buf_{q!p}}$, the buffer for storing messages from q to p.

Connection to State and Class Diagrams

The communicating FSMs we have presented capture hierarchy, concurrency, and communication. Thus, they have all the essential ingredients of the State Diagrams in the Unified Modeling Language (UML). The Statecharts model, also called the State Diagrams in the Unified Modeling Language (UML), is based on communicating FSMs. Statecharts were developed by David Harel [34] for reactive systems and have subsequently been integrated into UML as one of the major diagram types. Statecharts build on FSMs by integrating OR-states and AND-states. An OR-state encodes hierarchy, presenting a FSM at different levels of details. An AND-state allows us to show the different concurrently running processes in a system as separate state machines, rather than constructing their concurrent composition. Indeed, this is what we emphasized while discussing concurrency modeling via FSMs. Statecharts allow OR- and AND-states to be intermixed arbitrarily. Apart from AND/OR-states, statecharts allow for communication among processes in a system via broadcast. The semantics of statecharts' broadcast communication is best described operationally. In Section 2.6.1, we discuss simulation of state diagrams — where we clarify broadcast communication in state diagrams.

Regarding system modeling via class and state diagrams, one other point deserves explicit mention. When we model an embedded system, it is common to have multiple processes with the same behavior. Thus in our running example of the air-traffic control system, all the clients are behaviorally similar. Following the standard UML-based object-oriented design methodology, it is common to specify such processes together as a client *class*. The behavior of any object of this class will be captured by a single state diagram. The structural relationship or associations across classes will be captured by a UML class diagram. The class diagram shows the classes, multiplicities of objects in each class, relations across classes, and cardinality of these relations. The class diagram for our air-traffic control case study was earlier given in Figure 2.3. It shows that there is one centralized controller ATC, one weather control panel WCP, and N clients. It also shows the relations across these three classes, such as the *connected* relation that keeps track of the clients connected to the ATC. As we can see from this example, the designer can specify names of relations across the system classes in a class diagram. In addition, the class diagrams allows some special relationships across classes such as subclass relationship and part-of relationship (e.g., in automotive control, a cruise-controller class has a part-of relationship with the car class).

Toward Message Sequence Chart-Based Models

One subtle point needs to be brought out before we wrap up our discussion on FSMs. For the sake of modeling nontrivial data communication across FSMs, we assigned explicit sender and receiver roles, making all communication binary. Strictly speaking, this restriction is not necessary. We can have a common action appearing in several processes' local FSMs. This common action need not be restricted to two processes, and it does not need to be an atomic action. Instead it can be a complex protocol snippet involving several processes. This allows us to dream of a system in two levels. First we describe the local FSMs of each process at a high level where we describe the protocols in which the process participates in (and in what order it does so). Later on, we proceed to describe or elaborate each of these protocols. As a simple example, in Figure 2.10 we describe a producer-consumer style example consisting of three kinds of processes — producer(s), a medium (for passing the data), and consumer(s). Such systems are common in embedded system design — for example, consider the producer to be a processor's bus interface, the medium to be a bus controller, and the consumer to be a memory unit attached to the bus. At a high level, we can simply design a producer to (a) produce data, (b) request bus access until it is granted, and then (c) transfer the data. Similarly, the medium could simply (a) process requests from producer(s), then (b) allow transfer of data. The consumer could (a) get data via transfer over medium, and (b) consume the data. At this high level, we can describe the producer, medium, and consumer as the simple FSMs in Figure 2.10. The action labels are `get_data`, `request`, `transfer` and `put_data`; out of these, `get_data` and `put_data` are local actions, `request` involves communication of two processes, and `transfer` involves communication of three processes. However, the action labels here need not be atomic actions. Instead they can denote protocol snippets that need to be modeled and presented in the next level of system modeling.

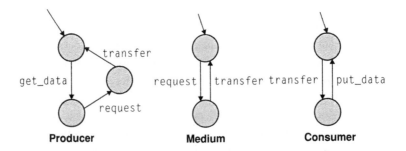

Figure 2.10

A high-level FSM where the actions may denote complex protocols.

There are various ways of describing such protocol snippets. One popular way is to describe them via Message Sequence Charts, also known as Sequence Diagrams in UML. Indeed, some recent papers describe system models where the common actions in communicating FSMs can be described via message sequence charts [31, 77].

We now proceed to describe message sequence charts (MSCs). We first mention how MSCs can be used to complement an FSM-like system model. We then describe how, with the help of MSCs, new intercomponent style system models can be developed.

2.4.3 Message Sequence Chart–Based Models

FSMs highlight intraprocess control flow while suppressing inter-process communication to send-receive actions. We will now discuss system models that highlight the inter-process communication while suppressing the intraprocess control flow or computation. The basic building block of such system models is a message sequence chart (MSC).

Message sequence charts [102] have traditionally played an important role in software development. MSCs describe scenarios for system behaviors. These scenarios are constructed prior to the development of the system, as part of the requirements specification phase. MSCs can be used to depict the interaction between different components (objects) of a system, as well as the interaction of the system with the external environment (if the system is reactive). Syntactically, an MSC consists of a set of vertical lines, each vertical line denoting a process (or a system component). Computations within a process are shown via internal events, and any communication between processes is denoted by a unidirectional arrow (typically labeled by a message name). Figure 2.11 shows a simple MSC with two processes; $m1$ and $m2$ are messages sent from p to q.

Semantically, a MSC denotes a set of events (message send, message receive, and internal events corresponding to computation) and prescribes a partial order over these events. This partial order is the transitive closure of (a) the total order of the

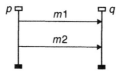

Figure 2.11

A schematic MSC.

events in each process[2] and (b) the ordering imposed by the send-receive of each message.[3] The events are described using the following notation. A send of message m from process p to process q is denoted as $\langle p!q, m \rangle$. A receive event by process q to a message m sent by process p is denoted as $\langle q?p, m \rangle$. An internal event x executed by process p is denoted as $\langle p, x \rangle$. As mentioned earlier, the message m as well as the processes p, q can contain variables. Variables transmitted via messages can appear in internal events as well.

Consider the chart in Figure 2.11. Using the foregoing notation, the total order for process p is $\langle p!q, m1 \rangle \leq \langle p!q, m2 \rangle \leq \langle p, a \rangle$ where $e1 \leq e2$ denotes that event $e1$ "happens-before" event $e2$. Similarly, for process q we have $\langle q?p, m1 \rangle \leq \langle q?p, m2 \rangle$. For the messages we have $\langle p!q, m1 \rangle \leq \langle q?p, m1 \rangle$ and $\langle p!q, m2 \rangle \leq \langle q?p, m2 \rangle$. The transitive closure of these four ordering relations defines the partial order of the chart. Note that it is *not* a total order because from the transitive closure we cannot infer that $\langle p!q, m2 \rangle \leq \langle q?p, m1 \rangle$ or $\langle q?p, m1 \rangle \leq \langle p!q, m2 \rangle$. Thus, in this example chart, the send of $m2$ and the receive of $m1$ can occur in any order.

We now formally define an MSC. The vertical lines in an MSC are the concurrently running processes whose interaction we capture. In MSC terminology, these vertical lines are also called *lifelines*.

Definition 4 (MSC) *An MSC m can be viewed as a partially ordered set of events $m = (L, \{E_l\}_{l \in L}, \leq)$, where L is the set of lifelines in m, E_l is the set of events lifeline l takes part in m, and $\leq$ is the partial ordering relation over the occurrences of events in $\{E_l\}_{l \in L}$ such that*

- *$\leq_l$ is the linear ordering of events in E_l, which are ordered top-down along the lifeline l,*
- *$\leq_{sm}$ is an ordering on message send/receive events in $\{E_l\}_{l \in L}$. If $e_s = p!q, m$ and the corresponding receive event is $e_r = q?p, m$, we have $e_s \leq_{sm} e_r$.*
- *$\leq$ is the transitive closure of $\leq_L = \bigcup_{l \in L} \leq_l$ and $\leq_{sm}$, that is, $\leq \; = (\leq_L \cup \leq_{sm})^*$*

In our MSC semantics, we consider the send and receive of a message as separate events. In other words, the sends are "nonblocking": A send event can proceed without waiting for the corresponding receive event. As mentioned in Section 2.4.1, this requires the presence of message buffers. In particular we may assume that for a MSC with n processes, each process has $n - 1$ message buffers to store incoming messages from the other $n - 1$ processes. However, we may also consider MSCs

---

[2] Time flows from top to bottom in each process.
[3] The send event of a message must happen before its receive event.

where each message passing is a handshake between the sender and the receiver. In other words, the sends can be blocking. Under the handshaking semantics, the partial order corresponding to an MSC m will certainly respect the partial order of m constructed by assuming nonblocking sends. In fact, the partial order under the handshaking semantics can be obtained by constraining the partial order constructed by assuming nonblocking sends. We simply require all send events to occur at exactly the same time as their corresponding receive. As an example, consider the chart in Figure 2.11. Assuming that the sends are nonblocking, we have

$$\langle p!q, m1 \rangle \leq \langle p!q, m2 \rangle \qquad \langle q?p, m1 \rangle \leq \langle q?p, m2 \rangle$$

$$\langle p!q, m1 \rangle \leq \langle q?p, m1 \rangle \qquad \langle p!q, m2 \rangle \leq \langle q?p, m2 \rangle$$

In the case of blocking sends we have only

$$\langle p!q, m1 \rangle \leq \langle p!q, m2 \rangle \qquad \langle q?p, m1 \rangle \leq \langle q?p, m2 \rangle$$

Furthermore, we know that $p!q, m1$ and $q?p, m1$ happen together, as do $p!q, m2$ and $q?p, m2$.

Use of MSCs in System Modeling

At this stage, we have illustrated the basics of MSC syntax and semantics. However, we have not elaborated the usage of MSCs — how they are actually *used* in system modeling. Conventionally, MSCs are used to denote snippets or scenarios of system behavior. For this reason, in the literature, MSC-based modeling has often been referred to as "scenario-based modeling." Depending on whether we view the system as an open system or a closed system, MSCs are used for depicting snippets of interaction between system and environment (open-system view) or for depicting snippets of interaction between system components (closed-system view). Let us elaborate both of these points with the help of our running example from the air-traffic control domain. With the open-system view, we can simply view the "system" as the centralized controller ATC, while the clients and weather control panel form the environment of the system, interacting with the ATC. With the closed system view, the system consists of ATC, WCP and clients — interacting with each other. Whatever the view, the MSCs in this case will be used for depicting sample interactions between the ATC and the Clients/WCP. A sample MSC from our air-traffic control example is shown in Figure 2.12. It shows a client seeking a connection from the ATC. The ATC updates its internal records, sets the client's status accordingly, and disables the WCP.

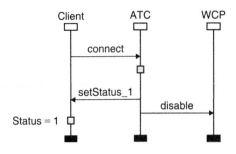

Figure 2.12

An MSC from our air-traffic control system.

The Problem with MSCs

An MSC describes only one scenario that *may* happen in system execution. It simply denotes an interesting protocol snippet that may or may not occur during system execution. In our running example of air-traffic control, we have shown an MSC showing a client connecting to the MSC in Figure 2.12. But, this by no means shows the complete behavior of the system — not all execution traces are required to exhibit the MSC (e.g., consider the pathological case where no client connects to the ATC). Compared to the model of FSMs that we learned earlier, this indeed sounds like a very weak form of requirement. While modeling a system using FSMs, we made the following statement: "A system model should capture all possible behaviors that may emerge in system implementations, possibly more behaviors than will observed in the actual implementations, but *never fewer*." In this sense, is MSC is a good system model? The answer is no. An MSC does not give a complete description of system behavior at any level of abstraction, and hence it does not meet the very first criterion of design models we had enunciated in Definition 1. We now proceed to explain how this problem with MSCs can be alleviated.

MSC-Graphs and HMSC

To alleviate the foregoing problem, the model of MSC-graphs has been proposed. An MSC-graph is simply an FSM where each state of the FSM denotes an MSC. The behaviors allowed by an MSC-graph can be obtained by finding the traces of the MSC-graph starting from an initial state. This leads to traces of infinite length. Sometimes, one or more nodes of the MSC-graph may also be marked as a "final" node. In such cases, the MSC-graph generates traces, each of which is obtained by *concatenating* finitely many MSCs. An example of an MSC-graph (and its constituent

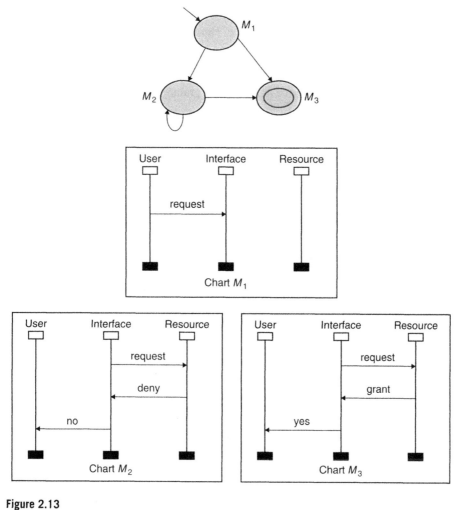

Figure 2.13

An example MSC-graph.

MSCs) is shown in Figure 2.13. Because this graph has a final state, it can be seen as a finite-state automaton representing the collection $M_1 \circ (M_2)^* \circ M_3$. That is, the graph represents one execution of chart M_1, followed by zero or more (but finitely many) executions of chart M_2, followed by M_3 getting executed exactly once.

Let us now study the example of Figure 2.13. It shows interactions among a user, an interface, and a resource. The user requests resource access via the interface. The interface forwards this request to the resource. Depending on whether the resource is occupied or not, the user's request is granted/denied and this decision is communicated to the user via the interface. Here we have

- Chart M_1 denoting a resource access request by the user,
- Chart M_2 denoting resource access being denied to the user, and
- Chart M_3 denoting resource access being granted to the user.

The behaviors of the system, summarized by $M_1 \circ (M_2)^* \circ M_3$ thus denotes resource access request by the user, followed by zero or more failed attempts to get the resource, followed by an eventual granting of resource access. Thus, any sequence of MSCs of the form $M_1 \circ (M_2)^* \circ M_3$ is a behavior allowed by the MSC-graph. Now what does it mean for a concrete sequence of MSCs, say $M_1 \circ M_2 \circ M_3$, which is in fact captured by the expression $M_1 \circ (M_2)^* \circ M_3$, to be an allowed behavior of an MSC-graph? To answer this question, we will need to study the issue of MSC concatenation.

There are two popular ways of concatenating MSCs. The first one, called *synchronous concatenation*, stipulates that for a concatenation of two MSCs, say $M_2 \circ M_3$, all events in M_2 must happen before any event in M_3. In other words, it is as if the participating processes synchronize or handshake at the end of an MSC. On the other hand, *asynchronous concatenation* performs the concatenation at the level of lifelines (or processes). Thus, for a concatenation of two MSCs, say $M_2 \circ M_3$, any participating process (say Interface) must finish all *its* events in M_2 prior to executing any event in M_3. The partial orders resulting from synchronous and asynchronous concatenation will be very different.

As an example, let us try to construct the partial orders for $M_2 \circ M_3$ (where M_2 and M_3 refer to the MSCs in Figure 2.13) under synchronous and asynchronous concatenation. In particular, is the receipt of the "no" message by the user (the event $\langle user?interface, no \rangle$) required to occur before the send of "request" by interface in chart M_3 (the event $\langle interface!resource, request \rangle$ in chart M_3)? The reader may refer to Figure 2.14 for a visual depiction of the MSC concatenation $M_2 \circ M_3$. We see that under synchronous concatenation $M_2 \circ M_3$, all events in chart M_2 take place before all events in chart M_3. Therefore, the receipt of the "no" message by the user (the event $\langle user?interface, no \rangle$ in chart M_2) is required to occur before the send of "request" by interface in chart M_3 (the event $\langle interface!resource, request \rangle$ in chart M_3). However, under asynchronous concatenation $M_2 \circ M_3$, only events of each process in chart M_2 are required to occur before the events of the corresponding process in chart M_3. Therefore, the receipt of the "no" message by the user process (the event $\langle user?interface, no \rangle$) is only required to occur before events of the user process in chart M_3. Therefore, $\langle user?interface, no \rangle$ (an event of the user process in chart M_2) can occur *after* $\langle interface!resource, request \rangle$ (an event of a different process, the interface process, in chart M_3). In fact, in the example of Figure 2.14, under asynchronous concatenation $M_2 \circ M_3$, the interface and resource processes

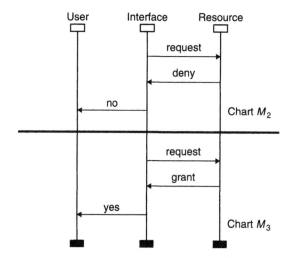

Figure 2.14

Concatenation of two MSCs (see Figure 2.11 for the constituent MSCs).

could even complete all their events in chart M_3, while the user process might still not have finished M_2. The interested reader might want to double-check this claim.

Given the two notions of concatenation, let us now go back to what an MSC-graph means in terms of behavior. To do this, we will need the notion of *linearization* of an MSC.

Definition 5 (MSC Linearization) *A linearization of an MSC m is a sequence of events σ where (a) each event of MSC m appears exactly once, and (b) the order of occurrence of events in σ respects the partial order of the MSC m. The set of all linearizations of an MSC m will be denoted as $\mathcal{L}in(m)$.*

Now, an MSC-graph can be seen as a generator of MSC sequences: That is, given a sequence of MSCs, we can test whether the MSC-graph allows the sequence or not. For every allowed sequence of MSCs, if we adopt asynchronous concatenation, a sequence of MSCs also produces an MSC. Then, any sequence of events obtained by linearizing the partial order of this resultant MSC is an allowed behavior.

If we adopt synchronous concatenation, for every allowed sequence of MSCs, we simply linearize the partial order of the individual MSCs and concatenate these linearizations to get allowed behaviors. Let us take an example (Figure 2.13) to illustrate this point. Clearly $M_1 \circ M_2 \circ M_3$ is an allowed sequence of MSCs for this MSC-graph. From the allowed sequence of MSCs of an MSC-graph, which traces (i.e., sequence of events) can we conclude to be allowed behaviors of the MSC-graph in Figure 2.13? Under asynchronous concatenation, $M_1 \circ M_2 \circ M_3$ is an

MSC, so all traces in $\mathcal{L}in(M_1 \circ M_2 \circ M_3)$ are allowed behaviors of the MSC-graph. Under synchronous concatenation, $\mathcal{L}in(M_1) \circ \mathcal{L}in(M_2) \circ \mathcal{L}in(M_3)$ are the allowed execution traces.

Finally, just as we added hierarchy to FSMs, the model of MSC-graphs can also be endowed with hierarchy. Such a model is popularly called a high-level MSC or HMSC. Thus, each node of an HMSC is either an MSC or (recursively) an HMSC. *Clearly, every MSC-graph is an HMSC, but not vice versa.*

Before we wrap up our discussion on MSC-graphs, we raise a pragmatic issue. The schematic in Figure 2.13 is simply capturing the interactions of the interface and the resource with one sample user. However, in a real system implementation there could be *many* users. Can we think of modifying the MSC-graph model so that we can capture interactions of interface/resource with many users without duplicating the same MSCs over and over again? This is left as an exercise for our readers.

Executable Models

The model of MSC-graphs and HMSCs that we presented here can be used to provide a complete system description. However, it still does not meet one of the important criteria that we had enunciated for design models in Definition 1 — they are *not* executable. In other words, we cannot simply synthesize the code[4] for each process by following through their lifelines in the sequence of MSCs allowed by the MSC-graph. This is because whether we follow synchronous or asynchronous concatenation, moving from one node to another in the MSC-graph involves a decision about the "next step." Now if there is a node M_1 with two outgoing edges to nodes M_2, M_3 (as in the example shown in Figure 2.13), what if some of the processes participating in MSC M_1 move to M_2, while some other processes move to M_3? Clearly, this is not a legal behavior allowed by the MSC-graph, yet it is possible if we generate code in a local, per-process fashion. At this point, our reader may be wondering why we should care at all about inter-process style notations such as MSCs, if ultimately we want to generate code in a per-process fashion from the models? The answer to this question is a pragmatic one — MSCs are extremely popular among system designers, and they are closer to the informal system requirements. On the other hand, FSM models are closer to system implementations. Hence FSM models are more suitable for code generation.

Other MSC-Based Models

The main appeal of MSCs is their simplicity in describing interaction protocols. Yet, as we can see, building even complete system descriptions from MSCs involves a

---

[4] The term *synthesis* here refers to generating an implementation from a specification.

bit of work. One of the reasons for studying MSC-graphs/HMSCs is that often the requirements document contains sample interactions given as MSCs, and it might be (relatively) easy for the system designer to build a formal model by combining the MSCs into a graph structure. This formal model can then be used for simulations, debugging, and checking early in the system life cycle.

Apart from the model of MSC-graphs, there are other ways of integrating MSCs to build a complete system model. In the last decade, several system models have been proposed directly based on MSCs. One prominent attempt in this direction is the formalism of *live sequence charts* (LSCs) [22, 36]. Live sequence charts build on the MSC notation to describe properties of the system behavior. It involves a different, rather non-operational way of thinking while modeling or dreaming about the system to be designed. For example, for the system in Figure 2.13, the designer might start with the following guarantee:

Whenever the user requests the interface, the request is eventually granted.

Note that this property does not require the designer to think about the operational method for satisfying the user's request — the interface requesting the resource, and if the resource says no then requesting again — none of it. The designer only has in mind the above property from a user's perspective that (s)he wants the system to satisfy.

The good thing about the LSC model is that it allows such properties to be specified, visualized, and even checked. As the user can think of more such properties, the system behavior becomes more constrained. The LSC formalism provides an execution engine (called the Play Engine) to check whether a collection of such properties are "conflicting." This is to prevent the designer from specifying inconsistent properties that no system can possibly satisfy.

In the LSC language, there are two kinds of charts — universal and existential. Existential charts are just like MSCs, so we leave them out of discussion. Any universal chart is a synchronous concatenation of two MSCs — a pre-chart and a body-chart. As per the notational convention of LSCs, a pre-chart is always shown inside a dashed hexagon. Now, consider a universal chart *Pre ◦ Body* where *Pre* is the pre-chart, ◦ denotes synchronous concatenation, and *Body* is the body-chart. A system implementation satisfies the universal chart *Pre ◦ Body* if and only if from every reachable state a linearization of *Pre* is executed, it must be *eventually* followed by a linearization of *Body*. Thus, for any execution trace of the system, if a linearization of *Pre* is encountered, it must be eventually followed by a linearization of *Body*. In Figure 2.15a we show the LSC universal chart for the requirement "Whenever the user requests the interface, the request is eventually granted." Note that the chart only constrains the order of messages appearing in the chart; messages not appearing in the chart can occur in any order. Thus the MSC shown in Figure 2.15b, which indeed is a legal behavior of the original MSC-graph shown in Figure 2.13, is also allowed by the LSC of Figure 2.15a.

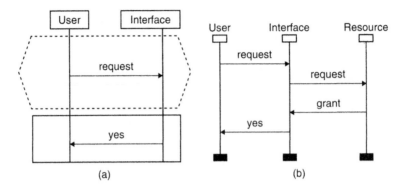

Figure 2.15

(a) An LSC for Figure 2.13, and (b) an MSC run satisfying the LSC property.

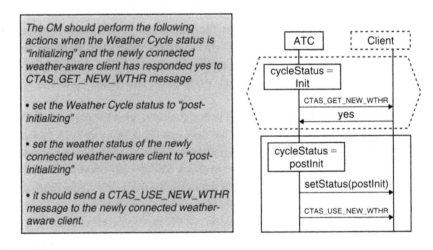

Figure 2.16

LSC encoding a requirement from our air-traffic control system.

In the preceding, we mention a universal LSC as a property or a requirement against which we can check a system implementation. However, pragmatically speaking, we can also use LSCs as a system modeling language — if we can specify enough properties of the system under construction to constrain the system behavior. The reader who delves into the official requirements document of our air-traffic control example in this chapter (see page 14, available at `http://scesm04.upb.de/case-study-2/requirements.pdf`) will find that such requirements are readily expressed as LSC universal charts. In Figure 2.16 we show an actual requirement from the informal requirements document and its straightforward LSC translation. The client is enclosed within a dashed box — indicating this is an interaction of the ATC with *any* client. A collection of such requirements becomes a collection of LSC universal charts readily yielding an executable system model directly from requirements.

2.5 REMARKS ABOUT MODELING NOTATIONS

At this point, we have familiarized ourselves with a host of modeling notations. The purpose of all these notations is to help us express the system model from different viewpoints. One may ask why have so many modeling notations — why not have a unified model? In this context, we would like to remind the reader that the well-known Unified Modeling Language (UML) also accommodates specification of system behavior from different viewpoints — state diagrams (close to FSMs) supporting the intracomponent view, and sequence diagrams (close to MSCs) supporting the intercomponent view. In some sense, the intra- and intercomponent views form two dual views of system behavior — each having its distinct advantages.

The intracomponent modeling via FSMs highlights the computation steps *inside* each process while suppressing the inter-process communication. It leads more directly to code generation for the individual processes of the system — bringing the model closer to implementation. However, when the designer is trying to get a handle on the system behavior at the very early stages, starting from the informal requirements written in English, it is easier for the designer to start by drawing some sample scenarios in the form of MSCs. The MSCs highlight inter-process communication while suppressing the computation steps inside each process. These MSCs can then be combined to a MSC-based system model such as HMSC. In other words, the intercomponent view of modeling is useful for synthesizing system models from informal requirements, whereas the intracomponent view is useful for synthesizing system implementations from system models.

A natural question then is whether MSC-based models such as HMSCs can be translated into FSM-based system models. Thus, say, starting from an HMSC model of a system, is it possible to straightforwardly synthesize the behavior of each process in the system as an FSM? The answer to this question is unfortunately, no. In Figure 2.17a, we give an MSC-graph (or HMSC, since every MSC-graph is an HMSC but not vice versa). The MSC-graph has an initial state but no final states. Now, the most natural way of generating code from this model[5] is as follows — for each process, we simply follow its role in the MSC sequences allowed

---

[5] Generating code from model here refers to generating a mixed hardware/software implmentation from the model.

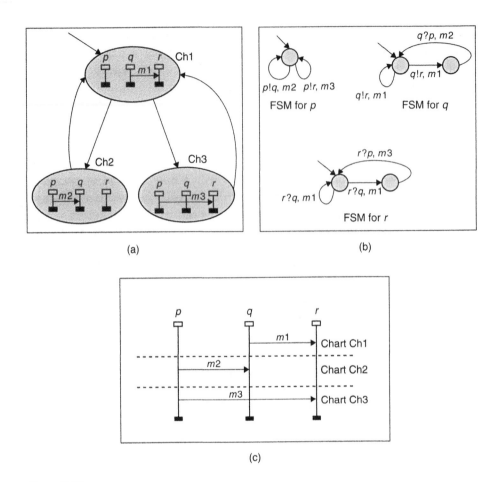

Figure 2.17

(a) An MSC-graph, (b) local FSMs for the processes participating in the MSC-graph, and (c) an unintended behavior or "implied" scenario obtained by composing the local FSMs.

by the MSC-graph. This produces the local FSMs of the processes as shown in Figure 2.17b.

The MSC-graph only allows MSC sequences of the form

$$(M_1 \circ (M_2 + M_3))^{\omega}$$

that is, infinitely many executions of "M_1 followed by either M_2 or M_3."

Clearly, by composing the local FSMs in Figure 2.17b, we will allow the behavior $M_1 \circ M_2 \circ M_3$, shown in Figure 2.17c. In the modeling literature, these scenarios are often called as "implied scenarios" [93] — scenarios that were not intended behaviors in the MSC-based system model, but get included once we construct local FSMs. It is the presence of these implied scenarios that makes the automated translation of MSC-based system models to FSMs hard.

Thus, pragmatically speaking, the embedded system designer often resorts to UML-based system modeling in two steps. First, aided by the informal requirements in English, the designer envisions the system model in terms of MSCs. At this point, the designer may or may not build a complete system model, that is, (s)he might simply draw a collection of MSCs. Of course, it can be more advantageous to draw a complete MSC-based system model (e.g., MSC-graphs or HMSCs) because it can then be used for other purposes, such as test generation from the MSC-graphs. Test generation from MSC-graph models is typically driven by a test-purpose MSC — we unroll the MSC-graph to find paths in the graph whose behavior is "similar" to the given test-purpose MSC.

Once the designer has a better handle on the system (having drawn a complete or incomplete system specification using MSCs), the designer can then develop an FSM-style description of the individual processes in the system in the second step of modeling. Of course, if the system designer can quickly generate the local FSMs of the processes from the informal requirements (this depends on how the requirements document is structured), then the step involving MSC construction can be bypassed.

The overall flow in terms on UML-based system modeling is summarized in Figure 2.18. As we can see, the designer may completely bypass the generation of an MSC-based system model such as HMSC. However, generating the FSMs directly from MSCs without constructing an HMSC may involve a leap in understanding of the intended system behavior. Of course, even if we generate HMSCs and then generate FSMs, the generation of FSMs from HMSCs is typically not automated because of the presence of implied scenarios (as articulated by the example of Figure 2.17). Also, if the MSC-based system model is created, test cases can be directly generated from the MSCs. These test cases can be tried out on the FSM-based model, or (with some effort) even on the system implementation.

2.6 MODEL SIMULATIONS

At this point, we have introduced the different modeling notations (mostly UML-based ones) and discussed the roles they play in system modeling. Let us now step back and try to recall the original purpose of system modeling. Modeling is primarily meant to clarify the thoughts of the embedded system designer, in terms of deciding what the intended behaviors of the system under construction are. Certain design flows for embedded systems assign an ambitious role to the system model — typically these flows envision that the system implementation will be generated from the system model semiautomatically with the propagation of the design constraints

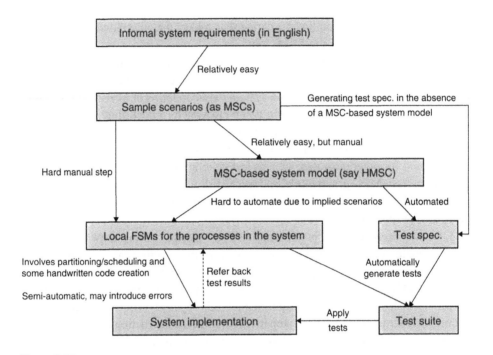

Figure 2.18

The steps in UML-based modeling of embedded system behavior.

from the system model to the implementation. In reality, we feel that the system model serves as a useful guideline for designing/constructing the system, but not a definitive guide from which the system implementation can be automatically generated. Thus, we do not see the model simply as a documentation (of intended system behavior) that is completely divorced from the system construction steps. On the other hand, it might be too much to expect correct-by-construction system design directly (and automatically) from the model.

Primarily the model's role is to clarify and understand system behavior in the early stages of system design. This is not done in one step; rather, it is an iterative process. In this iterative process, the designer gradually comes to understand the intended system behaviors. Once an initial model is created, one of the major weapons the system designer can use for understanding intended system behaviors is model simulations. Simulating the model can uncover "unexpected" behaviors. This is primarily because of the heavy usage of concurrency/communication in any embedded system. Even though the designer may well understand the intended behaviors of the individual processes, it might be hard to manually find out whether unintended behaviors creep in when the processes are composed together. Once the designer finds "unexpected" traces by simulating the system model, (s)he can consult the informal requirements document (written in English) to find out whether these traces are indeed unintended. If they are unintended, the model could be refined to exclude such traces.

It should be noted here that model simulations are typically carried out for the prominent use cases, that is, the most common ways in which the system-under-construction could be used. Going back to our air-traffic control example, if we want to simulate the behaviors of the centralized controller ATC, we may run simulations for the common ways in which the clients may use the ATC. Note that here the ATC is the system-under-construction, and the clients are the environment (they use the system). Thus, the use cases will be defined from the clients' viewpoint, because they are the users of the system (in this case the ATC), and we seek to model/implement the ATC in such a way that it faithfully captures the requirements. The common use cases might be (i) request connection from ATC, (ii) request weather update from ATC, (iii) attempt to disconnect from ATC, and so on.

By simulating a model for prominent use cases, we are primarily testing out the common cases in which the system will be used. Sometimes, model simulations can be used to achieve more ambitious goals. Multiple simulations can be carried out through a systematic exploration of the model, possibly ensuring some sort of structural coverage of the model. By such multiple simulations we can generate a suite of execution runs or test cases that give a clear idea about the set of behaviors captured by the model.

2.6.1 FSM Simulations

Simulating one single FSM representing global system behavior is not particularly difficult. After all, an FSM naturally comes equipped with execution semantics, and we can exploit this execution semantics to guide our simulation. Starting from an initial state, the simulation simply moves from a state to one of its successor states. Which successor is chosen may depend on the criterion being used to guide the simulation.

However, when the system description is given as a composition of local FSMs, the simulation needs to take into account the communication across the local FSMs. If the model of communication supports inter-process communication via atomic action labels (as discussed in Section 2.4.1), we simply need to keep track of the following during simulation: (a) local states of the individual processes, and (b) action labels that are common to multiple processes. For example, if the model of communication is a handshake on common action labels, and one of the processes is ready to execute an action label a that appears in multiple processes, it will be blocked until another process is also ready to execute a.

We can of course provide more structure for the action labels. An action label appearing in the FSM of a process p may be of the form $p!q, m$ — meaning, send message m to process q. This action in process p is targeted toward a *specific* process. Thus, it cannot be executed until process q is also ready to execute the corresponding dual action $q?p,m$.

Simulating UML State Diagrams

In the case of statecharts (also adopted as UML state diagrams), the communication mechanism is much more complicated. As mentioned earlier, different processes in the system (which are running concurrently) may be depicted as AND-states. That is, we can draw the local FSMs of the processes, and put them in an AND-state to show that they are running concurrently. However, the method of communication across these processes is via a complex broadcast mechanism. Each action label in a local FSM is typically of the form

$$Trigger/Action$$

If a process is at state s, which has an outgoing transition with label t/a, this transition will be activated when trigger t arrives. As a result of taking the transition, instantaneously action a will be executed. Because action a can serve as the trigger of some other action label for another transition (possibly in another FSM), this may cause further transitions to be executed. Thus, when we model a reactive system (a system in ongoing interaction with an external environment) using state diagrams, a single trigger from the external environment will cause a *super-step*, where a sequence of transitions are executed. The super-step will terminate when none of the processes in the system have an enabled transition. A super-step essentially constitutes the system response to an external trigger. At the conclusion of a super-step, the system is basically waiting for another trigger from the external environment. Note that a super-step is executed *atomically*.

To explain the state management needed for state diagram simulation, let us study a simple but concrete example. Consider a system consisting of a processor and a bus controller. Every now and then, the program running on the processor encounters memory accesses. In our example, for simplicity let us only consider memory write accesses. Once the program running on the processor encounters a write-memory access, the processor's bus interface requests the bus controller for bus access. The request may be either accepted or denied. If the request is accepted, the processor sends the relevant information for the memory write (such as the address to which to write, and the data to be written). If the request is denied, the processor makes a renewed request for bus access. Here the system model consists of the processor and the bus controller. The environment is captured by the program running on the processor.

Sample MSCs showing the response of the system to a write request from the environment are shown in Figure 2.19a. The state diagram for the system is shown

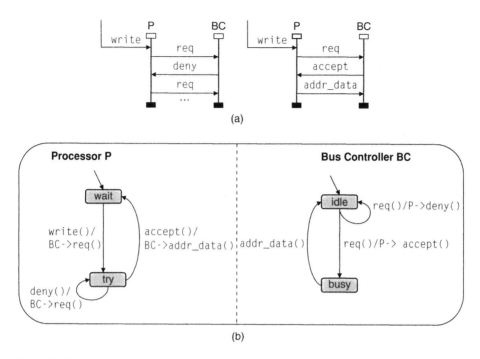

Figure 2.19

(a) Sample MSCs showing a processor seeking bus access for a memory write. (b) State diagrams for processor and bus controller.

in Figure 2.19b. It uses an AND-state to show the concurrent composition of the processor and bus-controller. Each action label on the transitions of the processor and bus-controller is of the form *trigger/action*. In Figure 2.19b, message passing across processes has been implemented via method calls. Thus the sender of a message calls a method of the receiver, which is immediately executed by the receiver. To avoid visual clutter, we have not shown the parameters of the methods in Figure 2.19b.

Let us examine the simulation of the state diagram in Figure 2.19b. Initially, the system is in the state (wait, idle), that is, the processor is in "wait" state and the bus controller is in "idle" state. If a `write` request comes from the environment (the program running on the processor), the processor will execute a transition from the "wait" state, and thereby invoke the `req()` method of the bus controller (the action of the transition). This will trigger one of the two outgoing transitions from the "idle" state of the bus-controller and so on. As a result of a "write" request from the environment, the sequence of method calls executed will be of the form

```
write,req,(deny,req)*,accept,addr_data
```

Note that all of these method calls will be executed as *one atomic step* (also called a *super-step*), and only then will the system reach a stable state. Thus, whenever a trigger is generated by the external environment, a simulator for state diagrams must compute a super-step in the manner we just described. The simulator has to check for termination of the super-step by checking that none of the processes are in such a state, that the trigger of an outgoing transition is enabled.

The implementation of a single communication across processes (analogous to the send-receive of a message in MSCs) also deserves mention. In Figure 2.19b, we have shown implementation via method calls, which essentially results in synchronous or handshake communication. Considering the processor's transition marked `write()/BC->req()` in Figure 2.19b, we see that this translates to a method call `BC->req()` within the code of the processor class.

It is also possible to implement message passing across processes, where the sender generates an event, the event is put into a system queue, and the receiver retrieves messages from the system queue. In such an asynchronous implementation, the state diagram simulator also needs to manage the system queue. There are various issues here, such as how many queues to maintain in the system (each process might have its own queue). An even more serious issue is that several processes might be enabled to receive an event, in which case the simulator has to decide which process will act as the receiver. This is particularly the case when the state diagram describes *classes* of processes, as we now discuss.

Object-Oriented Designs with Classes

In many realistic embedded system designs, it might be convenient to borrow basic notions of object-oriented programming to specify *classes* of processes. For example, consider a multiprocessor system-on-chip with many processors hooked on the bus. While specifying the design it might be convenient to define a class of processors, and then describe the behavior of any object in the processor class as a single state diagram.

Specifying processes with the same behavior via a class is important. We can avoid repeating the same behavioral specification for every object in the class. This, of course, leads to concise system specifications. However, during simulation of the system model (say, given as a state diagram), we will maintain the state of *every* process in the system. Thus, in our running example of the air-traffic control system (Section 2.3), while simulating the centralized controller for finding subtle bugs, we might simulate it with a large number of clients, say 100. Simulating the system model will require us to maintain the local states of each of the 100 client objects. However, this is completely unnecessary. Because the behavior of all 100 client objects is given by the same FSM, we can simply enumerate the states in that FSM (say $\{s_1, s_2, s_3\}$) and simply maintain in each step of the simulation the *number* of client objects in each of these states (say 50 objects in state s_1, 20 objects in state s_2, and 30 objects in state s_3 — total 100 objects).

To illustrate in more detail how such an abstract simulation works, we fall back on our state diagram in Figure 2.19b. Consider a system with n processors and a single bus controller. Initially, all the processors are idle, so the state of the processor objects is simply captured via the mapping

$$wait \rightarrow n, \ try \rightarrow 0$$

This simply means that n processor objects are in the "wait" state and no processor object is in the "try" state. Now, if a processor attempts to request bus access (owing to a "write" trigger from the environment), the state of *all* the processor objects simply changes to

$$wait \rightarrow n - 1, \ try \rightarrow 1$$

The simulation thus progresses by simply maintaining the number of processor objects in "wait" and "try" states. This is as opposed to maintaining the local state of each individual processor object (e.g., processor $1 \rightarrow$ *wait*, processor $2 \rightarrow$ *try*, ..., processor $n \rightarrow$ *wait*). Performing process abstractions in this manner gives us many benefits in simulation:

- First of all, it reduces the time and memory overhead for simulation. In certain situations, we may have designs with very large number of objects (e.g., consider a telecom system with millions of phones and switches).
- We should also remember that system modeling and simulation is carried out long before system implementation and deployment. Consequently, during system modeling/simulation, the designer may *not* have a clear idea about the exact number of objects in a class. To understand this point, let us refer back to our air-traffic control system (Section 2.3), where a centralized controller interacts with many clients; each client corresponds to an incoming aircraft. Of course, while designing the controller, it is impossible for the designer to guess the maximum number of clients the controller will ever be interacting with once it is deployed. Indeed, the number of clients the controller will interact with in a real-life situation is finite, but *unbounded*— we do not know how many aircraft may ever try to arrive at the same time! By abstracting the states of the individual clients, we can simulate the controller with a very large number of clients without worrying about the costs of simulation.
- By abstracting the individual process states, we group together many concrete system states into one abstract state. Thus, in our processor-bus example of Figure 2.19, the abstract state

$$wait \rightarrow n - 1, \ try \rightarrow 1$$

groups together all of the following concrete states:

processor 1 → *try*, processor 2 → *wait*, ..., processor *n* → *wait*

processor 1 → *wait*, processor 2 → *try*, ..., processor *n* → *wait*

...

processor 1 → *wait*, processor 2 → *wait*, ..., processor *n* → *try*

Thus by simulating the model along sequences of abstract states, we effectively simulate many "similar" concrete traces at one go. Hence we are more likely to encounter unintended and unexpected system behaviors by conducting such a simulation, as compared to a random simulation of concrete traces.

2.6.2 Simulating MSC-Based System Models

We now briefly discuss the issues in simulating MSC-based system models to uncover sample system behaviors. In an FSM-based model, the design style is intraprocess, as mentioned earlier. This means that the computation happening inside the processes (the intraprocess control flow) is given emphasis. The communication across processes is suppressed as atomic actions. Thus, the send and receive of a message may appear as atomic actions inside the sender and receiver processes. On the other hand, the MSC-based system models emphasize the inter-process communication while suppressing intraprocess control flow. Thus, the focus here is on the communication patterns across processes. The MSC notation is a convenient way of capturing these communication patterns.

Because we have already discussed simulation of FSM-based models, what are the new issues in simulating MSC-based system models? In simulating an FSM-based model (such as a UML state diagram), we might monitor the local states of the processes and update these local states during simulation. We can do so because the global system state is simply the composition of local states. Thus, by updating the local states, we update the global system state.

In an MSC-based system model, such a per-process update of the local states will be difficult. This is exemplified by the difficulty in generating per-process FSM-style code from MSC-graphs, primarily due to implied scenarios. The reader is referred back to the discussion in Section 2.5, in particular Figure 2.17.

A model such as the MSC-graph captures the possible sequences of MSCs that may happen during system execution. Thus, the system execution simply maintains the sequence of MSCs executed so far, and the progress in the current MSC. The progress made in the current MSC is captured through the notion of an MSC cut.

Definition 6 (MSC cut) *Consider an MSC m = (L, {E$_l$}$_{l \in L}$, ≤), where L is the set of lifelines in m, E$_l$ is the set of events in which lifeline l takes part in m, and ≤ is the partial ordering relation over the events in {E$_l$}$_{l \in L}$. A cut in MSC m is a mapping where each lifeline l is mapped to an element from E$_l$ ∪ {end}. The symbol "end" denotes the situation where all events in the corresponding lifeline have been executed.*

For a lifeline *l* in an MSC, the events E_l in which the lifeline *l* takes part occur in a strict sequence. Thus, by mapping the lifeline *l* to an event $e \in E_l$, we simply denote that all events prior to *e* have been executed in lifeline *l*. As mentioned in the preceding, when all events have been executed in a lifeline *l*, we map *l* to a special symbol "*end.*" Figure 2.20 shows an MSC cut in a visual manner, for an MSC in our air-traffic control example. It shows the situation where:

- Client has sent the *connect* message, but has not received *setStatus_1*,
- ATC has sent *setStatus_1*, but has not sent *disable* message, and
- WCP has not executed any events.

During simulation, maintaining the MSC cut allows the simulator to remember how much of the current MSC has been executed. The question is how to advance the cut, that is, given a cut, what constitutes a legal simulation step? To answer this question, we can define the notion of a minimal event.

Definition 7 (Minimal Event) *Given an MSC m = (L, {E$_l$}$_{l \in L}$, ≤), and cut of this MSC c$_m$: L → {E$_l$}$_{l \in L}$ ∪ {end}, a minimal event of the MSC w.r.t. the cut is an event e such that e ∈ {E$_l$}$_{l \in L}$, e = c$_m$(l) for some lifeline l, and for all events e′ ∈ {E$_l$}$_{l \in L}$ where e′ ≤ e, event e′ has already occurred according to the cut c$_m$.*

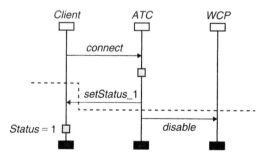

Figure 2.20

An MSC cut, shown via dashed lines.

Given an MSC cut, we can have several minimal events. For example, in Figure 2.20, *Client?ATC, setStatus*_1 and *ATC!WCP, disable* are minimal events. Simulation now progresses by executing any one of the minimal events.

It is worth noting that all events appearing in an MSC cut are not minimal events. In Figure 2.20, the cut maps the lifeline WCP to the event *WCP?ATC, disable*. However, as per the definition of minimal event (Definition 7) we do not allow the MSC simulation to execute this event in order to progress the cut. This is simply because there exists at least one event (in this case the send of the *disable* message) as per the MSC partial order, which has not been executed yet.

We have now discussed the simulation of a single MSC. We start with a cut where all processes have not executed any event. At any step the cut progresses by executing a minimal event, thereby leading to a new MSC cut. This is repeated until the cut maps all the MSC lifelines to *end*.

So far, we have discussed the simulation of a single MSC. When we simulate an MSC-graph, if we follow synchronous concatenation of the nodes in the graph, we simply simulate one node (and hence one MSC) at a time. If we follow asynchronous concatenation of the nodes in the MSC-graph, different processes in the system may be executing in different nodes at some point of time during simulation. Hence we may need to maintain a cut across MSCs. To illustrate this point, let us refer back to the MSC-graph shown in Figure 2.13. Consider a simulation run executing the sequence of MSCs M_1, M_2, M_3. Under asynchronous concatenation of MSCs, the Interface process can go ahead and execute node M_3 after having finished its part in node M_2, even when other processes (such as User) have not finished their part in node M_2. Thus, a cut can span across MSCs, because at a given point in time, different processes might be executing different MSCs.

Figure 2.21 shows such a cut spanning across two MSCs. Note that in this cut, the *Resource* process has finished its part in node M_3, while the *User* process has not even finished its part in node M_2. Thus, there are two issues to be considered while simulating a sequence of MSCs in an MSC-graph.

- All the processes should be guided through the same sequence of MSCs. This is trivial under synchronous concatenation because after each node of the MSC-graph, processes synchronize. Under asynchronous concatenation, we may maintain an extra thread that tells any process, when it finishes its part in a node, which is the next node to visit. Because all processes get their input from this extra thread, we can make them execute the same sequence of MSCs.
- Under asynchronous concatenation, we may need to maintain a cut across MSCs during simulation. Of course this requires the simulator to remember not just the current MSC, but previous MSCs as well. It is possible that in certain situations, the simulator may need unbounded memory, because one process may arbitrarily get ahead of another. Figure 2.22a shows such an example. For

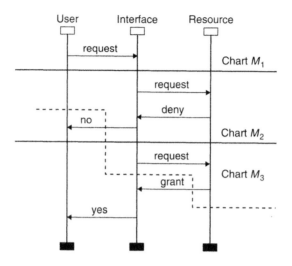

Figure 2.21

Cut across MSCs, shown via dashed lines.

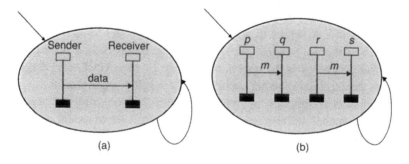

Figure 2.22

MSC-graphs whose simulation involves unbounded memory under (a) asynchronous message passing and (b) synchronous message passing.

the sequence $M_1, M_1, \ldots, M_1$, the sender process may get arbitrarily ahead of the receiver process because the sender may keep on sending messages without the receiver ever receiving them. This problem can be dealt with in two ways.

1. *Solution 1:* During simulation of MSCs, we maintain event queues for the processes. The length of these event queues place a bound on how much a process can overtake another. This is because, during sending, the sender needs to check whether the queue is full.

2. *Solution 2:* Solution 1 does not take care of all MSC-graphs where unbounded memory may be required for simulation. Figure 2.22b shows

such an example — processes p,q can get arbitrarily ahead of processes r,s in the sequence of MSCs $M_1, M_1, \ldots, M_1$. In that case, we can simply disallow MSC-graphs where such unbounded memory is required for simulation. Indeed, it is uncommon to have such unbounded MSC-graphs in real-life situations. Fortunately, a criterion for checking whether an MSC-graph is "bounded" (that is, requires bounded memory for simulation) also exists. The interested reader is referred to [3, 78].

This concludes our discussion on model simulations, which help us validate the system model against requirements. We now discuss model-based testing that can help us validate the system implementation against the system model.

2.7 MODEL-BASED TESTING

Simulating a model can uncover unexpected behaviors. This is particularly so when the simulation is not random. In fact, given a system model, we can guide the simulation along the prominent use-cases and try to find out whether the model behaves "as expected." Indeed, this is one of the primary ways in which model simulation is used. It serves as a validation of the model vis-à-vis the informal requirements — that is, whether the system requirements (stated in English) have been faithfully captured in the system model (say, given as UML state diagrams). It also allows the designer to better understand the English requirements.

Although model simulation helps tighten the link between informal requirements and the system model, we also need a link between the system model and the mixed hardware-software implementation of the system. The question is how this link can be established. We seek to do so by test generation. Basically, we are concerned with building pragmatic methods to bring the system implementation as close as possible to the informal requirements. Because it is infeasible to automatically generate implementations from requirements, we are looking at mechanisms that can at least tighten this correspondence. The three layers of system description are summarized in Figure 2.23. We show that the system model is validated against the requirements via model simulation, whereas the system implementation is validated against the model via test application. Generating test cases from the model and then trying the test cases on the implementation often goes under the name of model-based testing [8].

The key idea in model-based testing is to develop an explicit behavioral model of the system from informal requirements (using popular design notations such UML state diagrams). The design model forms a precise specification of intended system behaviors. The model is searched to generate a test suite or a set of test cases. These test cases are tried on the system implementation (which might have been

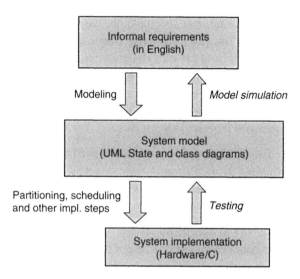

Figure 2.23

The three main layers in model-based system development.

constructed manually or semiautomatically) to check the system's behaviors and match them with the intended behaviors as described by the model. This allows us to connect up the system implementation with the system model.

There are two popular methods for generating test cases from the system model: (a) generating a suite of test cases to ensure structural coverage of the model, and (b) generating test cases from the model based on some test specification. The first method simply generates a set of test cases such that for each state/transition of a state diagram model, at least one test case goes through it. In the testing literature, this often goes by the name of coverage criteria–based test generation.

In the following we concentrate on the second method, which, in the testing literature, often goes by the name of test purpose–based test generation. These methods allow a more targeted description of unintended/intended usages of the system-under-construction. The description of the unintended or intended usage may itself be the test specification. Often this test specification is described via a message sequence chart or UML sequence diagram.

The test generation mechanism searches the state diagram model to find trace(s) satisfying the test specification. The goal is to generate tests that avoid the unintended behaviors specified and exhibit intended behaviors.

The overall flow for model-based testing as discussed here was summarized in Figure 2.18. As shown in the figure, if an MSC-based system model (say, an HMSC) is available, test specifications can be obtained by traversing the HMSC. Thus, by traversing the HMSC model we synthesize various test specifications, each of which is an MSC. For each test specification, we use the corresponding MSC to drive the generation of test cases (concrete traces satisfying the partial order of the test specification MSC) from the state diagram description of the system model. The test cases are employed on the system implementation, and the test results can sometimes be referred back to the state diagram model.

At this stage, we need to clarify what a test specification means. Usually test specifications are grouped into two categories.

- *Positive Test Specifications:* These denote desired or intended behaviors that should be exhibited by the system.
- *Negative Test Specifications:* These are undesirable behaviors which should *not* be exhibited by the system.

Tests satisfying negative test specifications are typically used to refine the system model, and thereby enhance our understanding of the system being constructed. Tests satisfying positive test specifications can be tried out on the system implementation.

Turning to our running example from air-traffic control, we give an example of a positive and negative test specification. These are shown in Figure 2.24 in the Message Sequence Chart notation. The positive test specification says that it is possible for the weather control panel (WCP) to request the centralized controller (ATC) to initiate an update; if the weather update is successfully completed for all connected clients, the ATC enables the WCP. The negative specification says that it is *not* possible for a client to successfully get a weather update from the centralized controller (ATC), and yet get disconnected from the ATC.

We have now defined the syntax of a test specification (MSC notation), and their meaning (positive/negative specification). However, when do we say that an execution trace of the model satisfies a given a test specification? There are at least two ways of defining this notion, as shown in the following. The notion of MSC linearization was introduced earlier; see Definition 5. Basically, a linearization of

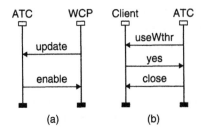

Figure 2.24

Test specifications from our air-traffic control example. (a) Positive test specification, (b) negative test specification.

an MSC m represents a total order over the events of m that respects the partial order of m.

- A trace σ is said to satisfy a positive test specification MSC m, if σ contains at least one linearization of m as a *contiguous subsequence*; similar definition for negative test specifications.
- A trace σ is said to satisfy a positive test specification MSC m, if σ contains at least one linearization of m as a *subsequence*; similar definition for negative test specifications.

In the preceding, we have used the notion of a subsequence. This is a standard concept, which we recapitulate for the convenience of the reader.

Definition 8 (Subsequence) *A string σ' is a subsequence of σ if and only if σ' is obtained from σ simply by deleting a finite number of symbols in σ.*

Thus, the string bde is a subsequence of the string $abcde$, but the string bdc is not a subsequence of string $abcde$ because the order of symbols has been reversed.

Formally, let Σ be the set of all events appearing in the system model. According to the first notion in the preceding, we say that an infinite trace σ over Σ in the system model satisfies a test specification MSC m, if

- $lin_m \in \mathcal{L}in(m)$ is a linearization of m, and
- σ is of the form $\Sigma^* lin_m \Sigma^\omega$.

According to the second notion in the preceding, we say that an infinite trace σ over Σ in the system model satisfies a test specification MSC m, if

- $lin_m \in \mathcal{L}in(m)$ is some linearization of m,
- $lin_m = \sigma_1^m, \sigma_2^m, \ldots, \sigma_k^m$ that is lin_m is a sequence of k events and σ_i^m is the ith event in lin_m for all $1 \leq i \leq k$,
- σ is of the following form, where $\Sigma \backslash lin_m$ denotes the set $\Sigma - \{\sigma_1^m, \sigma_2^m, \ldots, \sigma_k^m\}$:

$$(\Sigma \backslash lin_m)^* \sigma_1^m (\Sigma \backslash lin_m)^* \sigma_2^m \ldots (\Sigma \backslash lin_m)^* \sigma_k^m (\Sigma \backslash lin_m)^\omega$$

Thus, the events $\sigma_1^m, \sigma_2^m, \ldots, \sigma_k^m$ appear in this order in trace σ but possibly interspersed by other events that do *not* appear in the linearization lin_m. Figure 2.25 shows a test trace in a system with two clients satisfying the test specification of Figure 2.24a. Note that it also contains the Client processes, which are not mentioned in the test specification.

Whichever notion we employ, we need an underlying search procedure working on FSMs or state diagrams that seeks to find an execution trace satisfying the test specification. The simplest such search procedure can be a generate-and-test

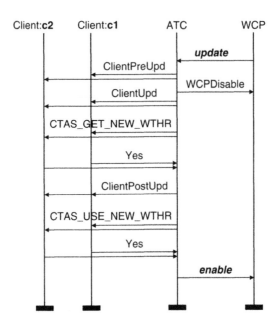

Figure 2.25

Test trace satisfying specification in Figure 2.24a.

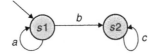

Figure 2.26

FSM with infinitely many traces.

procedure — generate the traces in the model one by one, and check each generated trace against the test specification and stop when you find a trace satisfying the test specification. Such a strategy will not work, simply because the number of traces in an FSM can be infinite, for example, consider the FSM in Figure 2.26. In this FSM, one trace is a^ω, which loops forever in state $s1$. There are also infinitely many traces of the form a^*bc^ω, that is, traces of the form

- bc^ω (c^ω denoting c repeated forever)
- abc^ω
- $aabc^\omega$
- ... , and so on.

The infiniteness here stems from the fact that a trace could loop in state $s1$ any number of times before exiting to state $s2$. Thus, we can see that a simple generate-and-test search procedure will not work for generating witness traces satisfying a test specification MSC. In Section 2.8, we will present a well-known search procedure called *model checking* that can efficiently generate witness traces corresponding to a given test specification.

Test Generation versus Test Execution

Let us now step back and recall what we are trying to accomplish via testing. We are checking the following: When the system-under-test implementation is triggered by the environment with a particular sequence of inputs, does it respond with the desired sequence of outputs? In this context, we have the following:

- The *test specification* describes for a particular choice of triggering inputs —— (a) what are the desirable outputs, and (b) what are the undesirable outputs.
- The *generated test* describes a sequence of input/output actions derived from the model where on receiving the triggering inputs given in the test specification, the system-under-test model responds with desirable outputs.
- Using the test specification and the generated test, we can develop a test harness that automatically drives the system implementation along a predetermined sequence of input/output actions, compares the actual outputs with desired outputs, and automatically delivers a "verdict" about whether the test is passed. This step corresponds to *test execution*. Thus, test execution involves running the generated test on the actual system implementation.

More on Test Execution

Given a test case or a test trace (satisfying a test specification), we now describe how it can be executed in a distributed control system. We first partition the lifelines in the test case MSC into two groups —— those constituting the implementation-under-test (IUT) and the remaining processes (which we call the *tester processes* or *tester components*).

To obtain the tester components from a test case MSC, one can follow a distributed tester synthesis approach (e.g., [41]). The test case MSC is viewed as a partial order $\langle E, \leq \rangle$ over various events E appearing in it. The partial order $\leq \equiv (\leq_l \cup \leq_m)^*$ is the transitive closure of $\leq_l$ and $\leq_m$, where $\leq_l$ is the linear ordering of events from top to bottom along all lifelines, and $\leq_m$ represents the ordering between a message send e_s and its corresponding receive e_r, s.t. $e_s \leq_m e_r$. A sample test-case MSC and its corresponding partial order are shown in Figures 2.27a and 2.27b. Note that a send (receive) event corresponding to a message m is shown as $!m$ ($?m$) in Figure 2.27.

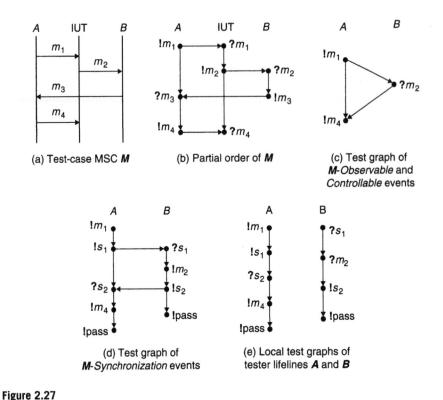

(a) Test-case MSC *M*

(b) Partial order of *M*

(c) Test graph of
M-*Observable* and
Controllable events

(d) Test graph of
M-*Synchronization* events

(e) Local test graphs of
tester lifelines *A* and *B*

Figure 2.27

Generation of tester components from a test-case MSC.

For generating the tester components, a reduced partial order $\langle E_T, \leq_T \rangle$, called a *test graph*, is obtained from the test-case MSC's partial order. It contains only controllable and observable events E_T ($\subseteq E$) with respect to the IUT components in test case MSC, and a partial ordering $\leq_T$ over them such that, $\forall e, e' \in E_T, e \leq_T e'$ iff $e \leq e'$. For the test-case example shown in Figure 2.27a, where lifelines[6] *A* and *B* represent the tester lifelines, the test graph is shown in Figure 2.27c. In the next step, *synchronization* messages are introduced in the test graph to preserve the causality constraints between the events appearing along the distinct tester lifelines. For a direct ordering between two events appearing along different lifelines, a synchronization send is introduced after the first event along its lifeline, and the corresponding receive is added before the second event along its lifeline. Further, after the last event along

---

[6] Recall that the terminology *lifeline* refers to a vertical line in an MSC. A lifeline denotes an active process with its own control flow.

each tester lifeline in the test graph, sending of a *pass* message is also added. These messages are received by the master tester (not shown here), based on which it gives test verdicts. The test graph for the foregoing example, with synchronization messages (s_1 and s_2), and *pass* verdicts, appears in Figure 2.27d. From the resulting test graph detailed in the preceding, a *local* test graph for each tester lifeline is derived by taking a projection over the events appearing along that lifeline (shown in Figure 2.27e). A *tester component* is then derived as a sequential automaton from each local test graph. Further, in these tester components, from each state with an outgoing transition labeled with a receive event $?e_r$, two outgoing edges labeled with θ and $?\neg e_r$ respectively, are added. Here θ represents a timeout event, which occurs if no input is received within a given timeout value. It results in the sending of an *inconclusive* verdict. On the other hand, $?\neg e_r$ represents the receipt of a test-case event other than e_r and results in the sending of a *fail* verdict. The tester components for tester lifelines A, B are shown in Figure 2.28.

Test Verdicts Resulting from Test Execution

The final test verdict is given based on the test verdicts received from various tester-components during test execution. Possible verdicts are:

- **Pass** The *pass* verdict is given by the master tester if it receives a pass verdict from *all* tester components.
- **Fail** A *fail* verdict is given by the master tester if any of the tester components sends a fail verdict.
- **Inconclusive** An *inconclusive* verdict is given if some tester components reply with an inconclusive verdict, with none of them sending a fail verdict.

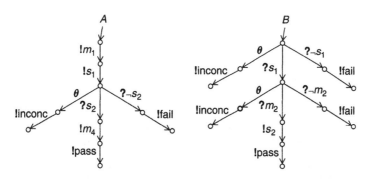

Figure 2.28

Generated tester components for test-case MSC shown in Figure 2.27a.

2.8 MODEL CHECKING

So far, we have discussed how test specifications will be described and how generated tests will be executed on the system implementation. However, we have not discussed the test-generation procedure. Clearly, we cannot simply generate the execution traces in the system model and check for each one of them whether it satisfies the test specification. This is because the number of traces in the system model may be infinite, as shown in the example of Figure 2.26.

In this section, we describe a search procedure that can be used to generate tests corresponding to a test specification from a system model. In fact, our search procedure is much *more general* and can be used for property verification of the system model. In other words, we can state desirable properties in a property specification language and automatically check (via search) whether the property holds for the model. Furthermore, if the property does not hold for the model, our search procedure will generate counterexample evidence that tells the designer why the property does not hold. The counterexample evidence can be used to debug and possibly rectify the model.

Thus, the search procedure we are going to talk about has applications beyond test generation. It is a property verification procedure that can be used to debug the model. The bugs thus found could point to one of the two following possibilities: Either the model does not faithfully capture the requirements, or the requirements do not satisfy some desirable property (and hence the requirements should be rectified).

The general formulation of the model checking problem is simple — it seeks to find whether a given FSM satisfies a property. The question really is what kind of properties we are talking about, and whether these properties can be automatically checked. In particular, the property specification language should be general enough to describe our test specifications. As we will see, linear-time temporal logics (the property specification language we describe now) can describe test specifications and much more.

2.8.1 Property Specification

The property specification language in model checking is based on temporal logics. As the name suggests, *temporal* logics should have something to do with the evolution of *time*. In particular, they talk about how the system-being-checked should evolve over time. Thus, a temporal logic property constrains the order in which events can happen in the system-being-checked. However, temporal logic properties do not incorporate an explicit notion of time. Thus, one *cannot* state properties such as

On June 1, 2007, I am writing a section on temporal logics, after which I shall write a section on model checking on June 2, 2007.

The foregoing is a temporal constraint on *my* "behavior." So if *I* represent the system-being-checked, the foregoing puts constraints on my behavior. The verification procedure (model checking) is supposed to check that these constraints do indeed hold, by efficiently checking "all possible behaviors" of the system-being-checked.

The only problem with the foregoing property is that it refers to time in an *explicit* fashion — writing about temporal logics occurring on June 1, 2007, and so on. Temporal logics only describe properties that constrain the *ordering* of events in system execution. However, temporal logic properties do not constrain events to occur at specific time stamps or time intervals. Thus, they may specify the following:

> *Writing a chapter on temporal logics occurs before*
> *writing a chapter on model checking.*

A property may even specify that "writing a chapter on temporal logics" occurs *immediately before* "writing a chapter on model checking." However it cannot specify that "writing a chapter on temporal logics" occurs on June 1, whereas "writing a chapter on model checking" occurs on June 2. Nor can a property specify that "writing a chapter on temporal logics" occurs *one day* before "writing a chapter on model checking."

In other words, any quantitative notion of time is not supported in our property specification language. However, properties about relative ordering of events can be represented.

We assume that the system-being-checked is represented as a finite state machine $M = (S, I, \rightarrow)$, where S is the set of states, $I \subseteq S$ is the set of initial states, and $\rightarrow$ is the transition relation. A behavior is simply an *execution trace* of the FSM, an infinite sequence of states (and actions) starting from an initial state. With the foregoing notion of behavior, it is clear what we mean by "all possible behaviors." It is the set of all execution traces of the FSM.

Note that an execution trace is potentially infinite in length even when the set of states in the FSM is finite. In Figure 2.29, the FSM contains only three states {*red, yellow, green*} — but the only execution trace $(green, yellow, red)^{\omega}$ is infinite in length.

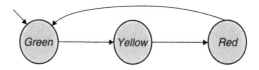

Figure 2.29

A crude FSM-based description of a traffic-light controller.

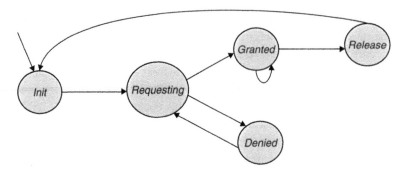

Figure 2.30

A crude FSM capturing interactions between a client and a controller.

The reader should recall that the number of execution traces in an FSM can also be infinite. Consider the schematic FSM in Figure 2.30, which captures the interactions between a client and a controller. What are the traces of this FSM?

- $init(requesting,denied)^{\omega}$
- $init(requesting,denied)^*granted^{\omega}$
- ...

An execution trace of the FSM may visit the *denied* state $0,1,2,\ldots,\omega$ times — leading to infinitely many execution traces (each of which is of infinite length).

When we want to check a property against a system model (possibly given as FSM), we check that the property for all the execution traces of the system. If we find that it does not hold for some execution trace, we report back that trace as counter-example evidence.

Before proceeding to give a formal definition of our property specification language, let us understand it informally via a very simple example. Figure 2.29 shows a very simple FSM representing a traffic-light controller. It simply shows that the traffic light changes color from green to yellow to red — repeating forever. It is a good example of a reactive system, a system in continuous interaction with its environment. In this simplified modeling of the controller, we do not show the detailed interaction between the controller and its environment (the traffic flow, for example) but only show that the controller shuffles the color of the light forever. Now, given this FSM model, our property specification language may state properties such as the following:

- The light is *always* green.
- Whenever the light is red, it *eventually* becomes green.
- Whenever the light is yellow, it becomes green *immediately after.*
- Whenever the light is green, it remains green until it becomes yellow.

The reader is probably getting a feel for the kind of operators our property specification language contain. These are marked in italics in the preceding — *always*, *eventually, immediately after*, and so on. These refer to certain "primitive properties" (such as the light being green) being true/false, and the ordering in which these properties may become true/false along the execution traces in the system model. Note that the properties we stated earlier are not necessarily true for our crude traffic-light controller in Figure 2.29. In fact, the very first property — the light is always green — is not true. Model checking is simply a checking procedure which automatically (and efficiently) checks such properties against a FSM system model. Thus it has to check that the given property is true for *all* the traces in the system model, *without* enumerating the traces (because there can be infinitely many traces).

At this stage, let us try to make our traffic-light controller more sensitive to the flow of traffic. Instead of shuffling between green, yellow, and red, the controller can stay green for a longer time if traffic is coming. Similarly, if there is no traffic, the controller can stay red instead of turning back to green. If we want to model the behavior of the controller for all possible traffic flows, it will be the FSM shown in Figure 2.31. There are several observations we can make about this controller.

- First of all, the controller could stay red forever, so properties such as "whenever the light is red, it eventually becomes green" are not true for this controller.
- Once the light becomes green, it may move from green to yellow after 1 time unit, 2 time units, 3 time units, and so on. This leads to infinitely many execution traces in the FSM. All of them need to be considered for checking a given temporal property.

We are now ready to present our property specification language. We need to remind ourselves of the following key points:

- Our properties are interpreted over infinite-length execution traces. Given a property φ and an infinite-length execution trace σ, we can ask the question whether $\sigma \models \varphi$, that is, whether σ satisfies φ. Of course, we need to use the semantics of our property specification language to find out whether the answer to the question is yes or no.

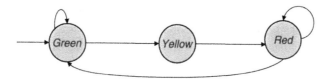

Figure 2.31

Another FSM-based description of a traffic-light controller.

- Even though our properties are interpreted over infinite-length execution traces, *we can also verify terminating programs*. In that case, we can convert the finite traces of the program to an infinite one, by simply letting the program loop at its end state forever.
- Given an FSM system model M, we say that M satisfies a property φ if and only if *all* execution traces of M satisfy φ.

Our specification language is called *linear-time temporal logic*, abbreviated as LTL. It is called *temporal* logic because it captures properties about how systems will evolve over time. Once again we remind the reader that temporal logics do not capture time in an explicit fashion, that is, we cannot state properties of the form "at time $t = 5$ seconds, event e will occur" or "whenever event e occurs within 2 seconds, event e' must occur." Instead, it is possible to say properties about the ordering in which states change/events occur. Thus, we can say "eventually event e occurs" or "whenever event e occurs, it is eventually followed by event e'." We note that our property specification language is called *linear-time* temporal logic, because the properties are interpreted over execution traces of the system that have a *linear* view of how the system progresses over time.

The syntax of our property specification language is defined recursively as follows. Here *Prop* denotes the set of atomic propositions (or primitive formulae):

$$\varphi = true \mid false \mid Prop \mid \neg\varphi \mid \varphi \vee \varphi \mid \varphi \wedge \varphi \mid X\varphi \mid G\varphi \mid F\varphi \mid \varphi U\varphi \mid \varphi R\varphi$$

In the preceding, *true* and *false* are two special formulae corresponding to logical truth and falsehood. The formula *true* is always true and the formula *false* is never true. Further, the atomic propositions form the basic building blocks of the formula. A formula is constructed using the following:

- Atomic propositions
- propositional logic operators $\wedge$ (and), $\vee$ (or), $\neg$ (not)
- temporal logic operators X (next), G (globally), F (finally), U (until), R (release).

Let us now examine the role of each of these. The set of atomic propositions is a set of primitive formulae, each of which can be interpreted over a state in an FSM. Given an atomic proposition p and a state s, we can determine whether p is true in s. To give a simple example, let us consider our traffic-light controller (Figure 2.31). Consider an atomic proposition g that stands for "the light is green." Then, as per the intended meaning inherent in our FSM modeling, we can say that g is true in the state marked green in Figure 2.31, whereas it is false in the other two states of Figure 2.31.

The inclusion of the propositional logic operators in our property specification language means that we are building our specification language on top of propositional logic. In other words, propositional logic will be used to describe property about states. Thus, we can state properties such as "the color is green *or* yellow." However, such properties are interpreted over states, that is, given a state in the FSM being checked, we can determine whether such a property is true or false. Properties about *evolution* of states are given by the temporal operators — which constrain the execution traces of the FSM being checked.

We now clarify the formal semantics of the temporal operators. First let us present the notion of a *suffix*.

Definition 9 (Suffix of a String) *A suffix of a string σ is obtained from σ by deleting the first k symbols of σ from σ where k is a nonnegative finite integer, that is, $k \geq 0$.*

Thus, the suffixes of the string *abcde* are the strings *abcde*, *bcde*, *cde*, *de*, *e*, and ϵ (the empty string). Because a suffix is obtained by deleting a finite number of symbols from the beginning of the string, a suffix of an infinite string must also be an infinite string.

We have five temporal operators in our property specification language: X, F, G, U, and R. All of them are used to describe properties of infinite-length execution traces. Unlike propositional logic operators, which can be used to describe properties of states, these operators are used to describe properties of *infinite sequences* of states. Thus, they try to constrain how the states change along any execution trace of the system being checked.

In Figures 2.32 to 2.36, we pictorially present the semantics of the five temporal operators in LTL, namely X, F, G, U, and R, respectively. As shown in Figure 2.32, an execution trace $\sigma = \langle s_0, s_1, s_2 \ldots \rangle$ satisfies $X\varphi$ (where φ is any arbitrary LTL

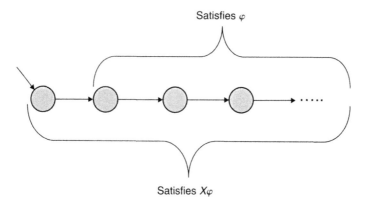

Satisfies φ

Satisfies $X\varphi$

Figure 2.32

Pictorial description of X (next-state) operator in LTL.

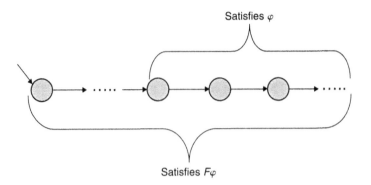

Figure 2.33

Pictorial description of F (finally or eventually) operator in LTL. A trace σ satisfies $F\varphi$ if and only if some suffix of σ satisfies φ.

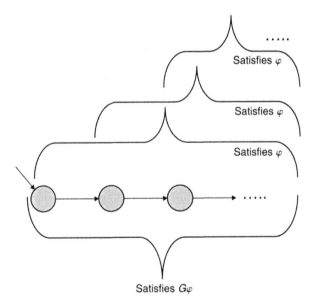

Figure 2.34

Pictorial description of G (globally) operator in LTL. A trace σ satisfies $G\varphi$ if and only if all suffixes of σ satisfy φ.

formula) if and only if the execution trace $\langle s_1, s_2, \ldots \rangle$ starting from the next state satisfies φ. Note that this gives the meaning or semantics of the X operator. In other words — given a trace σ, to check whether σ satisfies an LTL formula $X\varphi$, we need to see whether φ holds in the trace starting from the second state of σ.

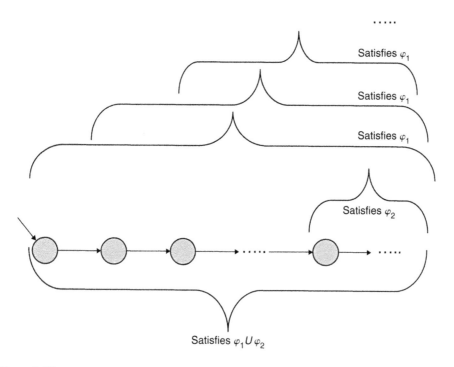

Figure 2.35

Pictorial description of U (until) operator in LTL. A trace σ satisfies $\varphi_1 U \varphi_2$ if and only if some suffix of σ satisfies φ_2, and all prior suffixes of σ satisfy φ_1.

The pictorial description of the F (finally) operator appears in Figure 2.33. It shows that an infinite-length trace $\sigma = \langle s_0, s_1, s_2 \ldots \rangle$ satisfies $F\varphi$ if and only if there exists some suffix of σ which satisfies formula φ. Similarly, Figure 2.34 captures the meaning of the G (globally) operator of LTL. It shows that an infinite-length trace σ satisfies $G\varphi$ if and only if *all* the suffixes of σ satisfy formula φ. Clearly, by the definition of the operators we have

$$F\varphi \equiv \neg\neg F\varphi \equiv \neg G\neg\varphi$$

that is, $\neg F\varphi \equiv G\neg\varphi$. This is not difficult to see, because the fact that a trace σ satisfies $\neg F\varphi$ means that there does not exist any suffix of σ that satisfies φ. This means that all suffixes of σ satisfy $\neg\varphi$, that is, σ must satisfy $G\neg\varphi$. Note that in a similar way, we can also derive

$$G\varphi \equiv \neg F\neg\varphi$$

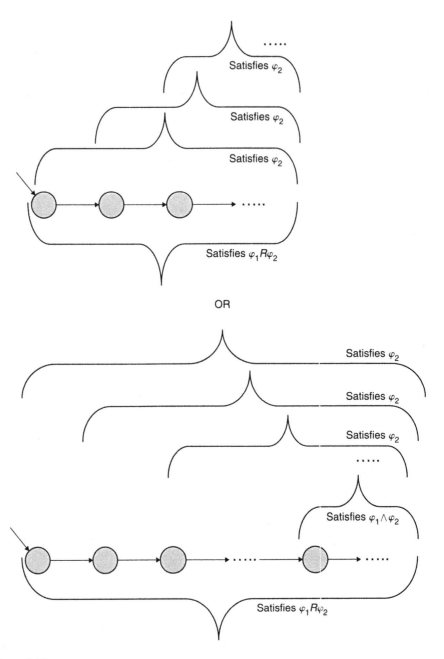

Figure 2.36

Pictorial description of R (release) operator in LTL.

Linear-time temporal logic has two other operators — U (until) and R (release). Intuitively, the formula $\varphi_1 U \varphi_2$ is satisfied by an infinite trace σ if and only if (i) there exists a suffix σ' that satisfies φ_2, and (ii) all suffixes of σ "prior to" σ' satisfy φ_1. Note that the suffix σ' which satisfies φ_2 need not satisfy φ_1. The key to understanding this intuitive definition are the two words "prior to." The reader can now refer to Figure 2.35 for a pictorial explanation. It shows that an infinite trace σ satisfies $\varphi_1 U \varphi_2$ if and only if

- φ_1 holds for all suffixes of σ *until* φ_2 holds, and
- φ_2 *eventually* holds for some suffix of σ.

We can also rephrase the preceding as φ_2 holds in some suffix σ' of σ and φ_1 holds for all suffixes of σ which strictly contain σ'.

Thus, by definition of the operator U, we have the equivalence

$$F\varphi \equiv (\textit{true } U \ \varphi)$$

for any LTL formula φ. This is because the formula *true* is satisfied by any trace (just as the formula *false* is not satisfied by any trace).

The last operator we discuss is the release operator. Just as the F and G operators are dual of each other, that is,

$$F\varphi \equiv \neg G \neg \varphi \qquad G\varphi \equiv \neg F \neg \varphi$$

the U (until) and R (release) operators are also dual of each other. In other words,

$$\varphi_1 R \varphi_2 \equiv \neg(\neg\varphi_1 U \neg\varphi_2) \qquad \varphi_1 U \varphi_2 \equiv \neg(\neg\varphi_1 R \neg\varphi_2)$$

for any LTL formulae φ_1, φ_2. Thus, $\varphi_1 R \varphi_2$ is true for an execution trace if and only if σ does *not* satisfy $\neg\varphi_1 U \neg\varphi_2$. Now, let us employ the definition of the U (until) operator we discussed just now. A trace σ satisfies $\neg\varphi_1 U \neg\varphi_2$ if and only if

- $\neg\varphi_1$ holds for all suffixes of σ *until* $\neg\varphi_2$ holds, and
- $\neg\varphi_2$ *eventually* holds for some suffix of σ.

Thus, a trace σ does *not* satisfy $\neg\varphi_1 U \neg\varphi_2$ (i.e., it satisfies $\varphi_1 R \varphi_2$) if and only if

- $\neg\varphi_1$ does not hold for some suffix σ' of σ where $\neg\varphi_2$ only holds in a suffix after σ' (i.e., in a suffix σ'' of σ where σ'' is also a suffix of σ'), or
- $\neg\varphi_2$ never holds for some suffix of σ.

In other words, a trace σ satisfies $\varphi_1 R \varphi_2$ if and only if

- φ_1 holds for some suffix of σ' of σ, and for all suffixes up to and including σ', the formula φ_2 also holds, or
- φ_2 holds for all suffixes of σ.

These two cases are pictorially illustrated in Figure 2.36. Thus, a trace σ satisfies $\varphi_1 R \varphi_2$ if and only if the occurrence of a suffix satisfying φ_1 *releases* the requirement for φ_2 to hold. Of course, if we never encounter a suffix of σ that satisfies φ_1, the formula φ_2 must hold forever (for all the suffixes).

At this stage, we have presented the syntax and semantics of all the operators of our property specification language. The reader may wonder at the need for five distinct temporal operators, when they can all be expressed using two operators — X (next-state) and U (until). In fact, as discussed in the preceding, the until operator (along with the operators of propositional logic $\neg, \vee, \wedge$) can represent F (finally), G (globally) and R (release) as derived operators.

$$F\varphi \equiv (true\,U\,\varphi)$$

$$G\varphi \equiv \neg F \neg \varphi \equiv \neg(true\,U\,\neg\varphi)$$

$$\varphi_1 R \varphi_2 \equiv \neg(\neg\varphi_1\,U\,\neg\varphi_2)$$

However, we discuss and present all the operators here for the sake of completeness. The redundancy in the property specification language is intended to help the designer specify properties more easily.

Interpreting Other Operators and Atomic Propositions

One important issue needs to be mentioned to complete our discussion on LTL semantics. In the preceding, we described the semantics of LTL in a recursive fashion. Thus, the semantics of a formula $\varphi_1 U \varphi_2$ is defined using the semantics of φ_1, φ_2 and so on. This exercise is done for all the temporal operators — X, F, G, U, R. What about operators that are not temporal, namely the propositional logic operators $\vee$, $\wedge$, $\neg$? This issue is easy to solve; we simply say that for an infinite execution trace π,

- $\pi \models \varphi_1 \vee \varphi_2$ if and only if $\pi \models \varphi_1$ or $\pi \models \varphi_2$,
- $\pi \models \varphi_1 \wedge \varphi_2$ if and only if $\pi \models \varphi_1$ and $\pi \models \varphi_2$,
- $\pi \models \neg\varphi$ if and only if $\neg(\pi \models \varphi)$.

Also, for the two constants *true* and *false*, we say that *true* holds for any execution trace, whereas *false* does not hold for any execution trace.

Finally, we need to deal with atomic propositions. Consider any atomic proposition $p \in Prop$ (recall that *Prop* is the set of all atomic propositions). How do we determine whether $\pi \models p$ for a given execution trace? The problem here is that an atomic proposition is inherently a property of a state — it either holds or does not hold in a *state*. However, we are trying to find out whether an atomic proposition holds or not in a *trace* (a sequence of states). This dilemma is solved by saying that an execution trace $\pi = \langle s_0, s_1, \ldots \rangle$ satisfies an atomic proposition p, if and only if p

is true in the initial state s_0 of the trace. That is,

$$\pi = \langle s_0, s_1, \ldots \rangle \models p \text{ iff } s_0 \models p$$

Simple Examples

To get more comfortable with the semantics of LTL, let us work out a few concrete examples. Consider the traffic-light controller FSM in Figure 2.37. It is the same as Figure 2.31, except that we have named the three states as $s0, s1, s2$.

Let us examine the temporal properties we had earlier stated informally:

- The light is *always* green.
- Whenever the light is red, it *eventually* becomes green.
- Whenever the light is yellow, it becomes green *immediately after*.
- Whenever the light is green, it remains green until it becomes yellow.

To encode these properties, we first decide on the atomic propositions. We choose three atomic propositions — *green*, *yellow*, *red* — with obvious meanings. In other words, the proposition *green* is true in a state if and only if the color of the traffic light is green, and so on. Thus, *green* is true only in state $s0$ and is false in states $s1, s2$. Similarly, *yellow* is true only in state $s1$ and red is true only in state $s2$. These evaluations of the atomic propositions are also shown clearly in Figure 2.37; in each state we write down only the atomic proposition(s) that are true in that state.

Using these atomic propositions we can now formalize the aforementioned four properties in LTL:

- $G(green)$
- $G(red \Rightarrow F\ green)$
- $G(yellow \Rightarrow X\ green)$
- $G(green \Rightarrow (green\ U\ yellow))$

At this stage, we have only encoded the properties in LTL; they need not be true for our traffic-light controller FSM. Note that for a property to be true, it *must* be true for all the execution traces of the FSM. Let us take the first property $G(green)$.

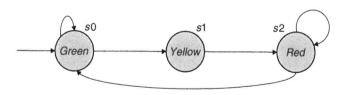

Figure 2.37

FSM-based description of a traffic-light controller (repeated for convenience of the reader).

Is it satisfied by all the execution traces of Figure 2.37? The execution traces of Figure 2.37 are (i) the trace $(s0)^\omega$, and (ii) the infinitely many traces $(s0)^*$ $s1$ $(s2)^\omega$. Clearly the trace $(s0)^\omega$ satisfies G $green$, because the atomic proposition $green$ is true in state $s0$. However, the property does not hold for $(s0)^*$ $s1$ $(s2)^\omega$, simply because $green$ is not true in state $s1$. Thus, the property $G(green)$ is not true for the FSM in Figure 2.37. Note that the manual reasoning we went through to determine the truth/falsehood of $G(green)$ in Figure 2.37 achieves the same purpose as model checking — we checked whether a given temporal property holds for a given FSM. However, we did so by enumerating the traces. Model checking is an algorithmic verification technique that will precisely avoid such trace enumeration.

The reader may try to determine whether the other three properties hold for the FSM in Figure 2.37. These are left as an exercise for the reader.

Encoding Test Specifications

We embarked on the discussion on model checking with a specific goal. We intended to use model checking as an automatic procedure for generating test cases (or witnesses) corresponding to a given test specification. However, apart from this specific usage of model checking, we should note that it has found acceptance in the industry as an automated verification procedure. In the electronic design automation (EDA) industry or in processor design companies, model checking is regularly used for unit verification — for formally validating parts of the design. In the recent past, model checking has been extensively used by software giant Microsoft for systematically debugging device driver software [12]. Thus, model checking should truly be seen as a general-purpose automated verification procedure for finite-state systems. Given an LTL property φ and a finite-state system M, it checks

$$M \models \varphi$$

If φ is true for all execution traces of M, the procedure returns $true$, meaning that the property φ has been verified to be true. If φ does not hold for all execution traces of M, then model checking returns $counterexample$ $evidence$ — an execution trace of M that does not satisfy φ.

Now let us recall our original goal for discussing model checking — using it as a search procedure for generating test witnesses corresponding to a test specification. For this purpose, we will need to describe test specifications in our property specification language. As discussed earlier, the test specification is usually a message sequence chart — a partial order of events. Given an MSC m, this is how we can automatically construct an LTL property φ_m that when model checked will produce a witness for m.

- Construct all linearizations (Definition 5) of MSC m. Let this set of all linearizations be $\mathcal{L}in(m)$.
- For each linearization $\sigma \in \mathcal{L}in(m)$, let σ be the finite string $\langle e_1, e_2, \ldots, e_k \rangle$. Because an MSC is a partial order of events, $e_1, \ldots, e_k$ must be events. Corresponding to the string σ, we construct the LTL property

$$\psi_\sigma = F(e_1 \wedge X(e_2 \wedge X(\ldots X(e_k)\ldots)))$$

- Corresponding to the MSC, we construct the property

$$\varphi_m = \neg \left(\bigvee_{\sigma \in \mathcal{L}in(m)} \psi_\sigma \right)$$

Thus, the constructed property φ_m states that none of the linearizations of MSC m is witnessed. Model checking will try to prove this property. If a test case satisfying one of the linearizations of MSC m indeed exists, our checked property will be false, and the model search will provide this test case as counterexample evidence. Thus, the counterexample trace returned will be the desired witness test case for our test specification MSC.

Note that we had earlier outlined two notions of test specification satisfaction, for a given test specification MSC. In the preceding, we constructed the LTL property corresponding to the first notion — where we deem a test trace as a witness of a given test specification MSC if and only if the test trace contains at least one linearization of the MSC as a *contiguous subsequence*. The other, weaker notion of test specification satisfaction we discussed involves generating a test trace that contains one linearization of the test specification MSC as a *subsequence* (Definition 8). For this notion we can construct the LTL property from a given test specification MSC m as follows:

- Construct all linearizations (Definition 5) of MSC m. Let this set of all linearizations be $\mathcal{L}in(m)$.
- For each linearization $\sigma \in \mathcal{L}in(m)$, let σ be the finite string $\langle e_1, e_2, \ldots, e_k \rangle$, where $e_1, \ldots, e_k$ are events. Then corresponding to the string σ, we construct the LTL property

$$\psi_\sigma = (\varphi_\sigma \ U \ (e_1 \wedge X(\varphi_\sigma \ U \ (e_2 \wedge X(\varphi_\sigma \ U \ \ldots(e_{k-1} \wedge X(\varphi_\sigma \ U \ e_k))\ldots)))))$$

where φ_σ is true in a state if none of $e_1, \ldots, e_k$ are enabled, that is,

$$\varphi_\sigma = \neg(e_1 \vee e_2 \vee \ldots \vee e_k)$$

■ Corresponding to the MSC we construct the property

$$\varphi_m = \neg \left(\bigvee_{\sigma \in \mathcal{L}in(m)} \psi_\sigma \right)$$

Once again, φ_m represents the property which states that *none* of the linearizations of MSC m is witnessed. A counterexample of the property will be a witness test for MSC m.

The reader is probably intimidated by the LTL formulae we constructed corresponding to a test specification. However, note that the LTL formula will be constructed from the test specification MSC *automatically*. Thus, the designer only needs to describe the test specification at the level of MSCs, an intuitive UML-based notation.

Property Templates and PSL

In general designers may find it hard to write down the properties they have in mind via LTL. For this reason, there has been a great deal of recent effort in coming up with common "property templates." This is to help designers write common LTL properties. Such templates are useful because model checking has uses beyond test generation. Indeed, it is a general-purpose automated verification procedure for finite-state systems. As mentioned earlier, model checking has been extensively used for processor verification (by companies such as Intel), hardware verification (by several CAD giants), and embedded software verification (by companies such as Microsoft).

Given the widespread use of model checking, it is important to develop user-friendly languages that enable the designer to write LTL properties. One such industry-adopted language is PSL, an abbreviation for *Property Specification Language* [70]. It was developed by Accellera and can be used to describe properties of designs written in standard languages such as Verilog, VHDL, and SystemC. PSL has two distinct layers — the boolean layer and the temporal layer. The boolean layer can be used to describe propositional logic properties about the design-being-verified. These properties may contain expressions in the hardware description language (HDL) in which the design is described.

The temporal layer essentially presents the temporal operators we discussed for LTL, albeit with syntactic sugar. It essentially gives understandable names to the LTL operators — for example, G is called as always, X is called as next, and so on. In addition, it presents several derived operators that the designers can conveniently use. These operators can also be defined in LTL, albeit in a convoluted fashion. One example of such an operator is the before operator. Intuitively, the property

$$\varphi_1 \text{ before } \varphi_2$$

means that if φ_2 holds in the future, φ_1 must hold strictly before φ_2. This is a rather intuitive description in English, which can be formalized by the LTL formula

$$F(\varphi_2) \Rightarrow ((\neg\varphi_1 \wedge \neg\varphi_2)U(\varphi_1 \wedge XF\varphi_2))$$

Clearly, the designer would like to use the `before` operator of the industry-adopted standard PSL rather than writing this complicated LTL formula! PSL is truly an important development that has enabled more acceptance of formal techniques such as temporal logics and model checking. Readers interested in this property specification language may refer to [70].

2.8.2 Checking Procedure

Going back to our air-traffic control case study, recall that the informal requirements in Section 2.3.2 allowed a deadlock scenario — where no process can make progress. We can formalize the absence of deadlocks in LTL as $G\neg p$, where the atomic proposition p is true only in those states that have no enabled actions. The informal requirements have to be modeled as FSMs, one for each process — clients, centralized ATC, and the weather control panel (WCP).

Thus, model checking will check that all execution traces of the system-being-verified satisfy $G\neg p$. In other words, all reachable states have enabled actions — thereby proving the absence of deadlocks. If indeed there is a deadlock in the system-being-verified, model checking will produce *counterexample evidence* in the form of an execution trace that does not satisfy $G\neg p$, the property being verified. This trace will satisfy $\neg G\neg p$, that is, Fp. In this trace, the system reaches a deadlocked state, thereby showing the presence of deadlocks.

We now describe the checking procedure. Recall that we are trying to check

$$M \models \varphi$$

where M is a *finite-state* transition system and φ is a formula written in the linear-time temporal logic (LTL) specification language. As mentioned earlier, LTL formulae are constructed out of atomic propositions (the set of all atomic propositions is denoted as *Prop*), propositional logic operators (and, or, and not) and temporal operators (next, until, eventually, globally, and release). To form a connection between the formula-being-checked and the system-being-checked, we say M is of the form

$$M = (S, I, \rightarrow, L)$$

where, as before, S is the set of states, $I \subseteq S$ is the set of initial states, and $\rightarrow \subseteq S \times S$ is the transition relation. In addition, we have the labeling function

$$L : S \rightarrow 2^{Prop}$$

where 2^{Prop} is the powerset of *Prop*, that is, the set of all subsets of *Prop*. If *Prop* = $\{p,q\}$ we have $2^{Prop} = \{\phi, \{p\}, \{q\}, \{p,q\}\}$. Thus, the labeling function maps each state s in the FSM to a subset of atomic propositions — the atomic propositions that are true in state s. Given an FSM and a set of atomic propositions *Prop*, the labeling function tells us for each state in the FSM which atomic propositions in *Prop* are true.

Note that the atomic propositions appearing in φ (the LTL formula being checked) are also drawn from *Prop*. Thus, the atomic propositions in *Prop* act as the bridge between the system-being-checked and the formula-being-checked. Indeed, without the labeling function for the FSM-being-checked, we would be unable to interpret an LTL formula over an execution trace of the FSM.

Given that the atomic propositions form the link between the system model M and the property φ, how do we settle the question $M \models \varphi$? The broad steps in the checking procedure are as follows.

1. Take the negation of the LTL property being verified $\neg\varphi$; none of the execution traces of M should satisfy $\neg\varphi$.
2. Construct a *finite-state automaton* corresponding to this negated property; call it $A_{\neg\varphi}$.
3. *Compose* the system-being-checked M with the automaton $A_{\neg\varphi}$, to produce a product automaton $M \times A_{\neg\varphi}$.
4. *Check* whether any execution trace σ of M is still a legal execution trace of the product automaton $M \times A_{\neg\varphi}$.
   - If yes, it constitutes a violation of φ in M; report σ as counterexample evidence.
   - If no, property φ holds for *all* execution traces of M.

We now elaborate each of these steps. In particular, we clarify (i) the association of LTL properties with finite-state automata, (ii) the notion of composition used for constructing $M \times A_{\neg\varphi}$, and (iii) the check employed on the product automaton in the last step. We will see that by converting LTL properties to FSMs, we get a very simple and elegant search procedure for checking LTL properties. Indeed, by converting LTL properties to FSMs, we will see that model checking of arbitrary LTL properties will be accomplished via simple depth-first-search!

From LTL Property to Finite-State Automaton

Let us first clarify the notion of finite-state automaton. A finite-state automaton is defined as $A = (Q, \Sigma, Q_0, \rightarrow, F)$, where Q is a finite set of states, Σ is a finite collection of symbols (also called the *alphabet*), $Q_0 \subseteq Q$ is the set of initial states, $\rightarrow \subseteq Q \times \Sigma \times Q$ is the transition relation, and $F \subseteq Q$ the set of final states. The main change from a transition system to an automaton is this set of final sets that capture which strings are *accepted* by the automaton. Thus, each automaton can be associated with a collection of strings (whose symbols are drawn from Σ), also called the *language* of the automaton.

The foregoing only describes the syntax of a finite-state automaton. What about its semantics? In other words, how do we define the set of strings that are accepted by the automaton? Different possible notions of acceptance are possible, giving different kinds of automaton. Here we present two notions of string acceptance that are well known and relevant for our discussion.

- *Regular languages:* An automaton $A = (Q, \Sigma, Q_0, \rightarrow, F)$ accepts a string σ with symbols from Σ if and only if (i) σ is a finite-length string, that is, $\sigma \in \Sigma^*$, and (ii) by running σ from some initial state $i \in I$, we end up in some final state $f \in F$.
- *ω-regular languages:* An automaton $A = (Q, \Sigma, Q_0, \rightarrow, F)$ accepts a string σ with symbols from Σ if and only if (i) σ is an infinite-length string, that is, $\sigma \in \Sigma^\omega$, and (ii) by running σ from some initial state $i \in I$, we visit at least one final state $f \in F$ infinitely often.

In both cases, the set of strings accepted by a finite-state automaton A is called the language of the automaton, denoted $L(A)$. The first notion is very well known and is useful for representing (a possibly infinite) collection of finite-length strings. The second notion allows us to use a finite-state automaton to represent (possibly infinite) collections of infinite-length strings. Such finite-state automata over infinite strings are also known as *Büchi automata*.

To illustrate the difference between the two notions, we take a simple example. Figure 2.38 shows a finite-state automaton where the final states are marked with two concentric circles. The alphabet of symbols is $\Sigma = \{a, b\}$. Note that the automaton is nondeterministic, that is, from a given state there may be several transitions on a given symbol. Using the first notion of acceptance in the preceding, we say that the automaton accepts all finite-length strings that end in a nonzero run of *b*s. However, using the second notion of acceptance, we deem the automaton to accept all infinite-length strings with *finitely* many *a* symbols. This is because the automaton makes only moves on *b* once it reaches the accepting state, and because the accepting state

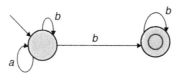

Figure 2.38

An example finite-state automaton over the alphabet $\Sigma = \{a, b\}$.

must appear infinitely often in any accepted string — therefore, there can be only finitely many occurrences of a.

Now, let us consider the purpose these finite-state automata serve in our model-checking procedure. We intend to convert the LTL property-being-verified to a finite-state automaton (and then compose this resultant property automaton with the FSM being verified). Recall that LTL properties are interpreted over infinite-length execution traces, because the execution traces of an FSM (the system being verified) are in general of infinite length. Consequently, the property automaton for a given LTL property φ should represent a *collection* of infinite-length strings — precisely those execution traces that satisfy φ. In other words, if an LTL property φ is converted to a Büchi automaton A_φ, we have

$$L(A_\varphi) = \{\sigma \mid \sigma \in \Sigma^\omega, \sigma \models \varphi\}$$

Thus, any string in the language of A_φ satisfies φ as per LTL semantics, and vice versa. Formally, a Büchi automaton is defined as follows.

Definition 10 (Büchi Automaton) *We define a Büchi automaton as*

$$A = (Q, \Sigma, Q_0, \rightarrow, F)$$

where Q is a finite set of states, Σ is a finite alphabet, $Q_0 \subseteq Q$ is the set of initial states, $\rightarrow \subseteq Q \times \Sigma \times Q$ is the transition relation, and $F \subseteq Q$ is the set of accepting states.

The language $L(A)$ of the automaton A just defined is the following set of infinite strings over the alphabet Σ:

$$L(A) = \{\sigma \mid \sigma \in \Sigma^\omega \text{ and } \sigma \text{ has a } \mathbf{run} \ r \text{ in } A \text{ such that } inf(r) \cap F \neq \varnothing\}$$

A $\mathbf{run}$ r of a string σ in A is an infinite sequence of states of A obtained by running σ from an initial state. That is, $r[0] \in Q_0$ and for all $i \geq 0$, $r[i] \xrightarrow{\sigma[i]} r[i + 1]$. Also, for a run r, $inf(r)$ is the set of states appearing infinitely often in r.

To summarize, given an LTL property φ which we seek to verify for a given model M, we first construct the Büchi automaton $A_{\neg\varphi}$ corresponding to $\neg\varphi$. The language of $A_{\neg\varphi}$ (the set of strings accepted by $A_{\neg\varphi}$) is the set of execution traces that satisfy $\neg\varphi$, that is, the set of execution traces which do not satisfy φ.

As an example, suppose we are trying to verify $GF\ p$ for a given FSM where p is an atomic proposition. The negation of $GF\ p$ is $FG\neg p$, the property being true for all traces where p only occurs finitely many times. The (nondeterministic) Büchi automaton corresponding to this property is shown in Figure 2.39. We may imagine this property automaton as an observer that watches every move made by the FSM

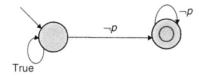

Figure 2.39

Büchi automaton for the LTL property $FG\neg p$.

being verified and makes moves in parallel with the FSM. Note that the automaton is essentially similar to Figure 2.38 (which accepts all strings with finitely many a symbols; the reader may wish to compare the two figures) with one important difference. The annotations on the transitions are formulae over the atomic propositions appearing in the LTL property. Thus, we read Figure 2.39 as follows. Whenever the system-being-verified reaches a state where $\neg p$ holds, the transition from the initial state to the accepting state of the property automaton in Figure 2.39 is enabled.

Indeed, there exists an automatic procedure for translating any LTL property φ to a Büchi automaton over an alphabet containing formulae over the atomic propositions in φ. The details of the construction are quite technical and of little consequence to our understanding of model checking as a verification procedure. The interested reader is referred to [94]. For our understanding, it suffices to understand the following: (a) the notion of Büchi automata as a mechanism for accepting a set of infinite strings, and (b) any LTL property φ can be converted to a Büchi automaton that accepts only those execution traces which satisfy φ. Even though we do not discuss the automatic procedure for converting LTL properties to Büchi automata, we have discussed here the semantic link between LTL properties and Büchi automata — an LTL property φ is converted to a Büchi automaton that accepts only those traces which satisfy φ. So, even though we have not discussed the automatic procedure for converting LTL properties to Büchi automata, we know how to manually construct the Büchi automaton corresponding to a given LTL property.

Composing System with Property

Let us again recall the steps for checking a system model M against an LTL property φ.

- Construct Büchi automaton $A_{\neg\varphi}$ corresponding to the LTL property $\neg\varphi$.
- Compose M with $A_{\neg\varphi}$ to get a product automaton $M \times A_{\neg\varphi}$.
- Check whether any trace of M is accepted by $M \times A_{\neg\varphi}$.

We have already elaborated (a) the notion of Büchi automata and (b) the semantic link between LTL properties and Büchi automata. For composing the system model with property automata, we adopt *synchronous composition* — that is, every transition of the system model is coupled with a corresponding transition in the property automaton (if one is enabled). Given a system model

$$M = (S, I, \rightarrow_M, L)$$

where L is a mapping $S \rightarrow 2^{Prop}$ (*Prop* is the set of atomic propositions), and the property automaton $A_{\neg\varphi}$

$$A_{\neg\varphi} = (Q_{\neg\varphi}, Bool(Prop), Q0_{\neg\varphi}, \rightarrow_{\neg\varphi}, F_{\neg\varphi})$$

where *Bool(Prop)* is the set of propositional logic formulae over the set of atomic propositions *Prop*, we define

$$M \times A_{\neg\varphi} = (S \times Q_{\neg\varphi}, Bool(Prop), I \times Q0_{\neg\varphi}, \rightarrow, S \times F_{\neg\varphi})$$

Thus, the product $M \times A_{\neg\varphi}$ is also a Büchi automaton. The set of states of the product automaton is $S \times Q_{\neg\varphi}$ — the cartesian product of the set of states of the system model/property automaton. In other words, if the set of states of the system model is $S = \{s1, s2\}$ and the set of states of the property automaton is $Q_{\neg\varphi} = \{q1, q2\}$; the set of states of the product automaton will be the set of pairs $S \times Q_{\neg\varphi} = \{(s1, q1), (s1, q2), (s2, q1), (s2, q2)\}$. Similarly, the set of initial states is the cartesian product of the set of initial states of the system model/property automaton. The set of final states is $S \times F_{\neg\varphi}$. Thus a state in the product automaton is considered accepting whenever the product automaton reaches a final state. The intuition here is simple — the product construction enables the property automaton to watch and record the moves of the system model. We consider a state in the product automaton as accepting if it contains an accepting state of the property automaton. The alphabet of the product automaton is the same as that of the property automaton — propositional logic formulae over a predefined set of atomic propositions *Prop*. The transition relation of the product automaton is constructed as follows. We have $(s, q) \xrightarrow{\psi} (s', q')$ if and only if

- $s \rightarrow_M s'$, where $s, s' \in S$, that is, states in the system model M
- $q \xrightarrow{\psi}_{\neg\varphi} q'$ where q, q' are states of the property automaton $A_{\neg\varphi}$ and ψ is a propositional logic formula over a predefined set of atomic propositions *Prop*. That is, there should be a transition on formula ψ from state q to state q' in the property automaton $A_{\neg\varphi}$
- The formula ψ is true is state s as per the labeling function of the system model M.

To concretely understand how the composition works, let us take an example. Figure 2.40 shows a system model M and a property automaton A (corresponding to the LTL property $FG\neg p$ as shown earlier in Figure 2.39). The labeling function of

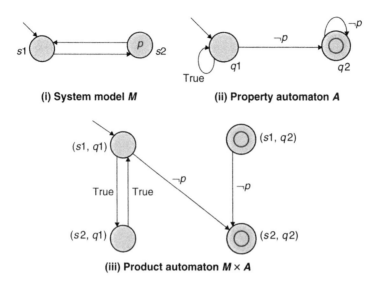

Figure 2.40

Product automaton construction.

the system model is indicated in Figure 2.40. In this case, there is only one atomic proposition p which is false in state $s1$ and true in state $s2$ of system model M.

The product automaton is also shown in Figure 2.40. To understand the product automaton construction, consider any transition in it, say the transition

$$(s1, q1) \overset{\neg p}{\to} (s2, q2).$$

This transition appears because $s1 \to s2$ is a transition in the system model, $q1 \overset{\neg p}{\to} q2$ is a transition in the property automaton, and $\neg p$ holds in $s1$ as per the labeling function of system model M. Similarly, we can argue that $(s2, q1) \overset{\neg p}{\to} (s1, q2)$ should *not* be a transition in the product automaton because although $s2 \to s1$ in the system model and $q1 \overset{\neg p}{\to} q2$ in the property automaton, we note that $\neg p$ does not hold in $s2$ as per the labeling function of the system model M.

We see that there cannot be any trace visiting any of the accepting states in the product automaton of Figure 2.40 infinitely often. Therefore, using the notion of acceptance in Büchi automata, the language of the product automaton is empty. In other words, none of the traces of the system model satisfy $FG\neg p$. So, *all* the traces in the system model satisfy $\neg FG\neg p = GFp$. This amounts to a *verification* of the linear-time temporal logic property GFp against the system model M shown in Figure 2.40. Indeed, we expect that GFp will hold for the system model in Figure 2.40 because (a) GFp signifies that p holds infinitely often, and (b) for the only trace

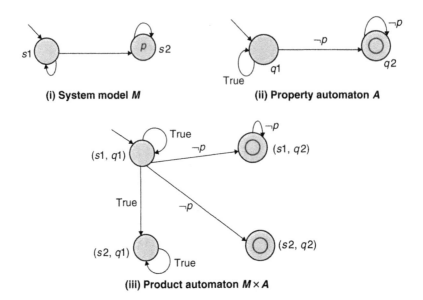

(i) System model *M*   (ii) Property automaton *A*

(iii) Product automaton *M* × *A*

Figure 2.41

Another product automaton construction.

in the system model of Figure 2.40, the proposition *p* is alternately true and false (and thus holds infinitely often).

In Figure 2.41 we show another product automaton construction. Here the system model is chosen so that it does *not* satisfy *GFp* — there are traces in which proposition *p* does not hold infinitely often. The property automaton is as before — it represents *FG¬p*, the negation of the LTL property *GFp*. We see that the product automaton's *language* is nonempty. Thus, there are traces of the system model that satisfy *FG¬p*, that is, violate *GFp*. These traces can be obtained from the strings that are accepted by the product automaton. In Figure 2.41, the only string accepted by the product automaton is

$$(s1,q1),(s1,q2),(s1,q2),(s1,q2),\ldots$$

By projecting this string w.r.t. the states in the system model (that is, leaving out the property automaton's states), we get the trace

$$s1,s1,s1,s1,\ldots$$

that is, the self-loop at state *s1* in the system model of Figure 2.41. Indeed, this is a trace of the system model that does not satisfy *GFp*, thereby giving us counterexample evidence of why the LTL property *GFp* is not true in the system model of Figure 2.41.

Emptiness Check

We again recall the steps for checking a system model M against an LTL property φ:

- Construct Büchi automaton $A_{\neg\varphi}$ corresponding to the LTL property $\neg\varphi$.
- Compose M with $A_{\neg\varphi}$ to get a product automaton $M \times A_{\neg\varphi}$.
- Check whether any trace of M is accepted by $M \times A_{\neg\varphi}$.

We have described the first two steps so far, and we now proceed to describe the last step — algorithmically checking whether any trace of M is accepted by $M \times A_{\neg\varphi}$. This amounts to checking whether the *language* of $M \times A_{\neg\varphi}$ is empty. If indeed the language of $M \times A_{\neg\varphi}$ is empty, we know that no trace of M is accepted by $M \times A_{\neg\varphi}$. Thus, no trace of M satisfies $\neg\varphi$, and hence φ is satisfied by all traces of M — thereby amounting to a verification of property φ on system model M.

How can we check whether the language of $M \times A_{\neg\varphi}$ is nonempty? As per the notion of acceptance of Büchi automata, an (infinite) string is accepted by the automaton if it visits an accepting state infinitely often. Because the number of states is finite, this is only possible if one or more accepting states are visited within a loop, as shown in Figure 2.42. Such loops are also called "accepting cycles." Thus, to check whether the language of an automaton $M \times A_{\neg\varphi}$ (i.e., whether it accepts any string), we only to have to check for the presence of at least one accepting cycle. As we can see from Figure 2.42, this amounts to answering the following question: *Starting from an initial state s_0, is there a path to an accepting state s_{acc} s.t. s_{acc} is reachable from itself ?*

The foregoing question can be answered algorithmically as follows.

1. Perform depth-first search from the initial state(s) until you reach an accepting state s_{acc}.
2. Whenever you reach an accepting state s_{acc}, remember s_{acc} (in a global variable) and start a nested depth-first search from s_{acc}. This nested search will stop whenever s_{acc} (which was remembered in a global variable) is reached.
3. If no accepting cycles are found in the previous two steps, report "yes" (the LTL property being checked is true).

Figure 2.42

An accepting cycle starts from an initial state and loops in one or more accepting states.

Otherwise, if an accepting cycle is found, report "no" (property being checked is false). Furthermore, concatenate the stacks of the two depth-first searches to report "counterexample evidence."

Now, let us walk through each of the steps mentioned in the preceding. The first step finds a path π from an initial state to an accepting state s_{acc}. Furthermore, this path is captured in the stack maintained by the depth-first search. The second step finds another path π' from state s_{acc} to state s_{acc}; again this path is captured in the stack of the depth-first search. In the final step, we check whether any accepting cycles are found, and if one is found, we simply concatenate π, π' to report the accepting cycle. This amounts to *evidence* of why the property being checked is not true in the system model. The designer can then look through the concatenated path $\pi \circ \pi'$ (a path in the system model) to *debug* the system model. The path $\pi \circ \pi'$ is a counterexample trace for the LTL property being verified.

The checking procedure outlined in this section has been implemented inside the SPIN model checker [37]. We now briefly describe the SPIN toolkit — primarily in an effort to entice our readers to get hands-on with some of the techniques we are describing.

2.9 THE SPIN VALIDATION TOOL

For reliable development of embedded systems, model development and debugging serves as a crucial first step. In this chapter, we have so far presented a variety of modeling and validation approaches along these lines, namely state machine–based modeling, sequence diagram–based modeling, model-based testing, and model checking.

We now describe an open-source modeling/validation tool that supports some of these. Historically, the SPIN tool was developed in Bell Laboratories around the 1980s and has been distributed as open-source software since 1991.[7] The SPIN tool supports state machine–based modeling of concurrent systems and model checking of linear-time temporal logic properties. If the property is not satisfied (by the system being checked), the counterexample trace is given. Because the counterexample trace involves interaction between multiple processes, it is displayed as a message sequence chart that highlights the interaction across processes.

In addition, SPIN has a number of other nice validation features such as random simulation and user-guided simulation. Thus, if a counterexample trace is found by model checking of a given LTL property, the designer can perform user-guided simulation along the counterexample trace to uncover the error source.

---

[7] http://spinroot.com/spin/whatispin.html.

The modeling language for the SPIN tool is called Promela — an abbreviation for *protocol meta-language*. It supports many language features for modeling sequential or distributed software/protocols, namely:

- *Concurrency*, in the form of allowing multiple processes in a system model,
- *Communication* across processes, in the form of message passing (synchronous message passing in the form of handshake or asynchronous message passing via channels) and/or shared variables,
- *Nondeterminism* within a process, to support the situation where all the details of a process may not be captured in the Promela model, and
- *Standard C-like syntax* within a process supporting assignments, switch, while, and other control constructs.

Details of the Promela modeling language appear in the SPIN manual. Instead of giving details of Promela, we give in Figure 2.43 a very simple example to illustrate some of modeling/validation features of SPIN.

In this example, two concurrent processes *node1* and *node2* are communicating via two channels *data* and *ack*. Because the channels have a nonzero capacity, the sends can be nonblocking, that is, the sending process can send and continue even though the message is not received on the other side. However, the channel capacity is 1, which means that there can only be one outstanding message in each channel. In Figure 2.44, we illustrate possible behaviors allowed by the system in Figure 2.43. In particular, Figure 2.44a shows a situation where a message sent is immediately picked up on the receiving side, whereas Figure 2.44b depicts a situation where the channels have one outstanding message.

```
chan data, ack = [1] of bit;

proctype node1() {              proctype node2() {
do                              do
:: data!1;                      :: ack!1;
:: ack?1;                       :: data?1;
od                              od
}                               }

init{ atomic{
        run node1(); run node2();
    }
}
```

Figure 2.43

A trivial communication mechanism modeled in SPIN.

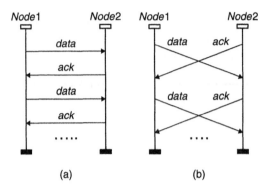

Figure 2.44

Two interleavings, both allowed by the system model in Figure 2.43.

Let us now illustrate a simple bus-based communication in SPIN's modeling language Promela. Consider a system with two processors hooked to a bus, each trying to access a memory unit; access to the bus is controlled by a bus arbiter. We can model it as per the schematic in Figure 2.45. Here we have three process definitions — processor (applies to both the processors in the system), memory (applies to the single memory unit), and arbiter (applies to the bus arbiter). The schematic model illustrates inter-process communication by shared variables as well as by message passing. In particular, the bus arbiter conveys its decision on who will access the bus by setting a shared variable. On the other hand, the processor that accesses the bus communicates with the memory unit by sending messages over a channel, the channel resembling the actual system bus.

Note that the do...od denotes an infinite loop where in each iteration any one of the enabled choices is executed nondeterministically; a choice is considered to be enabled when its corresponding guard is true. Thus, if both processors request bus access, our model allows the access to be given to any one of them. This means that we have not modeled specific bus-scheduling algorithms, and the validation results are applicable to all bus-scheduling algorithms (provided the algorithm grants bus access to one of the requesting processes, which is always the case).

To explain the execution semantics in SPIN, we should note that its notion of time is discrete, that is, the timeline is divided into discrete time units. Overall, the SPIN tool supports *asynchronous* composition of processes executing concurrently. What this means is that, at any time unit, only one of the processes in the system makes a move. Of course, in any particular time unit, more than one process may be "enabled" (i.e., ready to make a move). SPIN constructs and explores all possible behaviors resulting from different interleavings of the processes.

As far as formal verification is concerned, SPIN supports model-checking of LTL properties. The LTL property is negated and converted into a Büchi automaton that is

```
bit grant; chan bus = [1] of {byte}; bit request[2];

proctype Processor(bit id){ byte data;
        do
        :: request[id] = 1->
                if
                :: grant == id->bus!data;
                :: else;
                fi;
        :: request[id] = 0
        od;
}

proctype Arbiter()
{
        do
        :: request[0] == 1 -> grant = 0;
        :: request[1] == 1 -> grant = 1;
        od;
}

proctype Memory() {byte data;
        do
        :: bus?data; /* process the "data" */
        od;
}

init{
    atomic{ run Processor(0); run Processor(1); run Arbiter(); run Memory(); }
}
```

FIGURE 2.45

Modeling of bus access mechanism in SPIN.

composed with the transition system being checked. The model-checking problem is then reduced to checking whether the set of traces accepted by the composed automaton is empty. This is accomplished by a simple depth-first search procedure. In other words, the core model-checking algorithm employed in SPIN is similar to the technique we have elaborated in Section 2.8.2.

One may think that because of its asynchronous composition, SPIN is unsuitable for modeling clocked systems — systems that are driven by a common clock. However, it is possible to describe such systems by modeling the clock as a separate process and using the clock process's events (the ticks) to drive/enable the other processes. The reader may wish to modify Figure 2.45 to achieve bus-based communication in a clocked setting in SPIN. This is left as an exercise for our readers.

Clearly, instead of trying to program clocked systems within the framework of asynchronous composition of concurrent processes, it is more convenient to model systems directly in a synchronous composition framework. We now discuss the SMV validation tool that supports synchronous concurrent composition and has been widely used for hardware modeling/validation.

For modeling and validation of clocked systems, SMV might be more suitable than SPIN. On the other hand, for modeling and validation of asynchronous software/protocols, SPIN might be easier to use than SMV.

2.10 THE SMV VALIDATION TOOL

SMV stands for Symbolic Model Verifier. The tool was developed initially in Carnegie Mellon University in 1980s and 1990s. Currently the tool has several versions, such as CMU-SMV, Cadence-SMV, and NuSMV — distributed as open-source software from various institutions.

The modeling language of the SMV tool is relatively low-level and supports synchronous concurrent composition of processes. Each process is described as a module that has its own private signals and also receives signals from other modules as parameters. Thus, each module is able to read certain signals from other modules in every time unit. In each time unit, every module will change state (synchronous composition). The state transition in each module is described on a per-signal basis, that is, for each signal we describe how its value will change from the current time unit to the next time unit. In other words, there is no notion of *control flow* within each module (as compared to SPIN, which describes each process as a C-style program).

To illustrate how the modeling works, let us try to describe a simple bus-based communication in SMV (similar to the exercise we tried out in SPIN). Again, we consider two processors (contending for bus access), a bus arbiter (deciding which processor will access the bus), and a memory unit (which the processors access for read and write operations). The top-level system description in SMV will appear as follows.

The processor modules each have a REQUEST signal that indicates a request for bus access. This request has to be conveyed to the arbiter, hence it appears as a parameter in the arbiter process. What this means is that, in every time unit (for the case of bus protocol a time unit is a clock cycle), the REQUEST lines of the processors are accessible to the arbiter; the arbiter reads these REQUESTs and makes a decision about which processor is granted bus access. This information is

```
MODULE main() {

    p1 : processor(a.GRANT1, s.RESP);
    p2 : processor(a.GRANT2, s.RESP);
     s : slave(a.GRANT1, a.GRANT2);
     a : arbiter(p1.REQUEST, p2.REQUEST);

    mutex: assert G( ~(a.GRANT1 & a.GRANT2) );
    nostarve1: assert G( p1.REQUEST -> F a.GRANT1 );
    nostarve2: assert G( p2.REQUEST -> F a.GRANT2 );
    using mutex prove nostarve1, nostarve2;
    assume mutex;
}


MODULE arbiter(REQUEST1, REQUEST2) {

GRANT1, GRANT2 : boolean;

    next(GRANT1) := case{
        REQUEST1 : {0,1};
        default: 0;
    }
    next(GRANT2) := case{
        REQUEST2 : {0,1};
        default: 0;
    }

}

...  // description of the other modules
```

Figure 2.46

Modeling of bus access mechanism in SMV.

available via the GRANT1 and GRANT2 signals of the arbiter, which are passed
to the corresponding processors (so that each processor knows whether it has been
granted bus access by the arbiter).

Now, let us study the transition relation of the arbiter in Figure 2.46. As mentioned
earlier, it is given in a per-signal fashion, describing how the grant request is given to
each processor. For GRANT1, the transition relation is very simple — it may or may
not grant bus access when the REQUEST1 signal (request from the corresponding
processor) is set. Note that the arbiter described in the preceding does not encode

any particular scheduling policy. This choice is often *deliberate* — the designer may model/validate a bus protocol but leave the bus arbitration policy unspecified. The main advantage gained is that validation results are not tied to any particular bus arbitration policy.

Thus, we see that by underspecifying certain parts of system behavior, we can achieve system validation in a more general way. There are, however, caveats in underspecifying any parts of the system behavior. The resultant system may be so underspecified that no meaningful validation can be carried out. In Figure 2.46 we see an example of such a situation. The bus arbitration policy within the arbiter is so underspecified that it can even grant bus access to both processors in the same clock cycle; the reader may try to convince himself/herself that this is indeed possible in the SMV description of Figure 2.46.

Interestingly, SMV provides an elegant feature to deal with such underspecified systems. The designer can specify certain desired properties of system behavior expressed in linear-time temporal logic, which need not be satisfied by all traces of the SMV system description. Thus in our example, even though mutual exclusion of bus access is not enforced by the described bus arbitration policy, we can specify it as a desirable property. This is done by the property `mutex` in Figure 2.46. It denotes the LTL property $G(\neg(\texttt{a.GRANT1} \wedge \texttt{a.GRANT2})$ — that is, along all paths globally, the `GRANT1` and `GRANT2` signals of the arbiter are never simultaneously set. This property is then assumed by the SMV checker while trying to prove other properties about the system description. Thus, in our example, the designer may be interested in verifying no-starvation properties about the bus protocol; the no-starvation property states that any particular processor requesting the bus will eventually be granted bus access (see the `nostarve1` and `nostarve2` properties in Figure 2.46). For this purpose, the designer can instruct the SMV checker to explore/examine only those protocol runs that satisfy mutual exclusion of bus access and then check whether these runs satisfy the no-starvation property being verified. Indeed, this is what appears in the SMV description in Figure 2.46 where the designer instructs the SMV checker to verify the LTL properties `nostarve1`, `nostarve2` by assuming the `mutex` property. This is an extremely useful feature for validating system descriptions where certain parts of the system behavior may not be specified (either deliberately or because those parts of the system description are not readily available). This feature of SMV has been successfully used for verification of real-life system protocols, an example being the verification of the AMBA Advanced High-Performance Bus (AHB) protocol deployed in ARM's System-on-Chip designs [75].

In terms of model checking, SMV has been widely used for verifying (parts of) various industrial hardware/protocol designs, such as the Futurebus protocol [14] and (parts of) the PowerPC microprocessor [6]. The tool employs sophisticated data structures for efficient storage of the state space while visiting it. In fact, the tool does not represent the transition system of the system being verified explicitly as a graph. Instead, the states and transitions are implicitly represented as logical formulae, and these are manipulated efficiently using sophisticated data structures. This implicit state-space search is often referred to as *symbolic* model checking in various books/articles in the area.

A full description of the data structures and algorithms inside the SMV checker is outside the scope of this book. The interested reader is referred to [18] and similar texts for a full treatment of this topic.

2.11 CASE STUDY: AIR-TRAFFIC CONTROLLER

We conclude the chapter by reverting back to our running example in this chapter — the air-traffic controller (ATC). We describe in detail some issues in modeling this example from the (simplified) informal requirements elaborated in Section 2.3.

We now present a snippet of Promela code for the ATC example. Recall that Promela is the modeling language of the SPIN validation tool we discussed in Section 2.9. One of the main activities in such a modeling is to convert the inter-process style requirements to intraprocess style Promela models. The English requirements focus on the sample interactions or protocols across the processes. On the other hand, the Promela models provide the description of each individual process.

Figures 2.47 and 2.48 visually capture part of the requirements of our air-traffic control example. The English requirements were given in Section 2.3. In Figure 2.47, we show that a client may send a `connect` request to the ATC; following by which the client receives new weather information from the ATC via the `get_new_wthr` message.

In Figure 2.48 we show that the client may succeed or fail in receiving the new weather information. If it succeeds, it proceeds to use the new weather information (possibly for computing the desired trajectory of the incoming aircraft). On the other

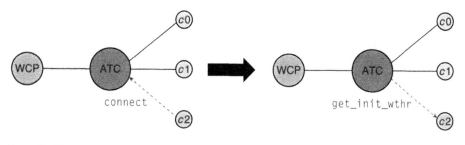

Figure 2.47

Client connection in the ATC example.

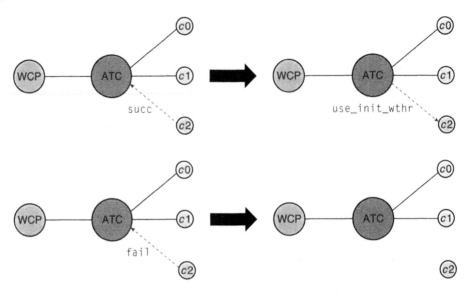

Figure 2.48

Initialization of a connected client in the ATC example.

hand, if the client fails to receive the new weather information, it will be disconnected from the ATC.

In the following we show the Promela modeling of a part of the client process. In particular, we show the Promela description corresponding to the system requirements captured by Figures 2.47 and 2.48. In our modeling, the client and ATC communicate via handshake. This is shown by defining a *communication channel* of capacity zero. In the following, the Client_ATC is this channel.

```
/* Messages exchanged between Client and ATC*/

mtype = {connect,close, ... };

chan Client_ATC = [0] of {mtype};

proctype client() {
    /* Non deterministic choice. Client can send connect request */
    /* or just stay idle.    */

    disconnected:
    do
        :: Client_ATC!connect -> break
        :: skip
    od;
```

```
Client_ATC?get_new_wthr; /* Receive new weather from CM */

/* Non-deterministic choice between success/failure
   in getting new weather */
if
   :: Client_ATC!yes     /* New wthr info recv ok */
   :: Client_ATC!no ->   /* New wthr info recv not ok */
       Client_ATC?close;
       goto disconnected   /* Close connection*/
fi;

Client_ATC?use_new_wthr;     /* Use the new weather info */
....
}
```

As we see in the foregoing, the client process nondeterministically connects, or does not connect. If it connects, it attempts to receive new weather information. We also model both the cases — where the client may succeed or fail in receiving the new weather information. If it succeeds, it proceeds to use the weather information. However, if it fails to connect, it goes back to the disconnected state. It is worthwhile to note that we are again modeling the control logic without the data transmitted across the processes. Thus, receiving the new weather information is abstractly denoted by a message of the name get_new_wthr — without actually representing the weather data. Furthermore, many details of actual implementations are abstracted away with the help of a nondeterministic choice. For example, the client receiving or not receiving the initial weather information is simply modeled via a nondeterministic choice — thereby capturing both the situations which may arise in a system implementation.

In the preceding, we present only a snippet of the Promela code, in particular for the client process. Modeling the other processes, namely the central controller (or ATC) and the weather control panel (WCP), is left to our readers as an exercise.

2.12 REFERENCES

There are many texts in model-driven software engineering and Unified Modeling Language. However, they do not focus on the validation aspects — the focus is only on the modeling. Moreover, there remain important differences between software modeling and system modeling. Software modeling focuses a lot more on the architecture — the classes, their relationship being expressed via a class diagram. Determining the associations between the classes lends the yet-to-be-written (object-oriented) software quite a bit of structure. In the case of system modeling, the system architecture is not the main focus. Instead, the behavior of the interacting processes in the system is modeled first (using state diagrams and/or sequence diagrams). Subsequently, during the later steps of embedded system design, the system architecture is determined so as to meet performance/energy/area/cost requirements. In those later stages, a process might be partitioned and allocated into several processing elements, or several processes could be allocated to the same processing element (a processing element could be a processor running software, or a piece of hardware). Thus, in summary, system modeling focuses much more on behavioral diagrams.

Among the behavioral diagrams, state diagrams have their origin in the seminal work on Statecharts by David Harel [34]. They extend finite state machines with hierarchy and concurrency. There exist several tools for developing/using Statecharts — notably Rhapsody [74] and Stateflow [88]. These tools support code generation from state diagrams.

Sequence Diagrams have their origins in the Message Sequence Charts [102] studied in the telecommunication domain. For a more formal treatment on this topic, the reader may refer to [73].

Model-based testing is a well-known system development activity. The starting point in model-based testing is the derivation of explicit behavioral models from informal system requirements. This forms a precise specification of the system's intended behaviors. A behavioral model is then searched for generating a set of test cases (a test suite), guided by a user-provided test purpose. A test purpose aids in selecting interesting model behaviors against which the user may want to test a system implementation. A survey of methods for model-based testing can be found in [8]. Rhapsody [74] allows for test generation from Statecharts. The UBET tool [92] allows for automatic test generation from high-level message sequence chart (HMSC) models.

Model checking is an automated method for *proving* temporal logic properties of finite-state machines. The idea of using temporal logic to describe properties of nonterminating reactive systems was first proposed by Pnueli [67]. Model checking is an algorithmic verification method that takes in a finite-state machine M, a temporal property φ, and checks whether M satisfies φ. The initial papers on model checking are [17, 72], and a text on this topic is [18]. An extension of state-transition graphs for real-time systems, called timed automaton, has been studied in [1], and model-checking tools for these formalisms have been developed. UPPAAL [56] is one such tool.

In terms of tools, there exist several mature model checkers today. The SPIN checker [38] is an explicit-state checker for asynchronous concurrent systems, often used for protocol verification. This tool has been used for validation system models synthesized from informal system requirements. The SMV checker [84, 85] has a modeling language suitable for synchronous systems and has been widely used for efficient hardware verification. There exist many different variations of

SMV (corresponding to variations in the search algorithms and the data structures used) such as CMU-SMV, Cadence SMV, and NuSMV. Model checkers for software verification include BLAST [7], MAGIC [16], and SLAM [12].

2.13 EXERCISES

Here we present a host of exercises, primarily based on the air-traffic control system we discussed earlier in the chapter (see Section 2.3.2).

2.1. Explain your understanding of platform modeling, and its differences from system behavior modeling. Are the system modeling approaches described in this chapter applicable to platform modeling — theoretically and pragmatically speaking?

2.2. Model the air-traffic control system's informal requirements given in Section 2.3.2 as a collection of finite-state machines (FSMs) — one for client processes, one for the communications manager, and one for the weather control panel.

2.3. Using the FSM model of the air-traffic control system as a guide, generate C/Java code for each of the three classes — client, weather control panel, and communications manager.

2.4. Model the air-traffic control system's informal requirements given in Section 2.3.2 as an HMSC. Clearly describe what fragments of the requirements correspond to which MSCs in the HMSC model.

2.5. Propose a methodology for generating candidate positive test specifications from an HMSC model of a system. What about negative test specifications?

2.6. Given the HMSC model of the air-traffic control system, synthesize a set of positive test specifications as per your test specification synthesis methodology (developed in the previous question).

2.7. For each test specification obtained in the previous question, manually generate a trace in the FSM model of the air-traffic control system (Exercise 2) that satisfies the test specification. How can you automate this test-generation process?

2.8. Try to convert the FSM or the HMSC model of the air-traffic control system into a Promela description in SPIN. Comment on the relative ease and difficulties of the two modeling exercises.

2.9. Using SPIN's simulation and/or model-checking feature, try to verify the absence of deadlocks in your constructed Promela model. If you had modeled the informal requirements correctly, this should produce a bug, that is, a deadlock situation in the design.

2.10. Modify the Promela description to remove the deadlock situation identified in Exercise 9. Try to trace back your fix to the FSM/HMSC model, and then try to trace it back further to the informal requirements. Comment on what links need to maintained across requirements, FSM/HMSC models, and the Promela code to enable such reverse translation of code fixes.

2.11. Try to model the ATC example in SMV. Compare and contrast the SMV/SPIN modeling styles. In particular, discuss whether you face any difficulties in modeling the ATC in SMV, owing to the absence of an explicit program counter in SMV's modeling language.

2.12. Consider the following program fragment. Can we use the model-checking technique covered in this chapter to show that x == 2 holds at the end of the program? Note that x is an integer variable.

```
int x;

x = 0;

x = x + 1; x = x + 1;
```

Communication Validation

In this chapter, we discuss the issue of correctly handling the communication between different components of an embedded system. During system design, there is increased emphasis on interface-based design, where the *core behavior* of a system component is separated from its *interface*. Unfortunately for us, the word "interface" is overloaded and is often used in the electrical engineering and computer science areas to capture very many different concepts. For this reason, it is important to precisely define what we mean by interface.

We define the interface of a system component as a behavioral entity. Thus, an interface is not necessarily just a syntactic entity providing mapping of an output from a component to an input of another component. Instead, we view an interface as a process with internal states — it contains a portion of the component's behavior. In particular, a component interface embodies the services provided/received by the component in question to/from other system components (or the external environment). We could think of an interface as a program with control flow of its own.

Thus, the interfaces of the embedded system components capture the part of the component behavior responsible for communication. In this chapter we are concerned with the problem of correct design, refinement, and validation of interfaces. We want to clarify here that the system components cannot communicate with each other without their interfaces. Although the interfaces enable communication, the designer may have flexibility about where to place them. In particular, there can be three different situations — (i) the individual components are endowed with interfaces that communicate with each other, (ii) there is a central protocol converter that enables communication, and (iii) the individual components have interfaces and there is also a central protocol converter. These three situations are shown schematically in Figure 3.1. We can view the component interfaces as well as the centralized protocol converter as processes with states, in general.

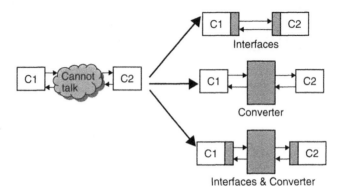

Figure 3 1

Converters and/or interfaces for enabling communication.

One may wonder why both component interfaces *and* a centralized converter may ever be necessary. It may seem that to make several incompatible components talk to each other, we can either design a centralized protocol converter or distribute the converter's logic into the individual components (which then become the interfaces). However, this view does not consider the reality of various bus-based system-on-chip designs where each component hooked to the bus is endowed with a bus interface. Furthermore, we need a bus controller that coordinates the communication between these component interfaces. Thus, the bus controller essentially acts as the centralized protocol converter.

To illustrate the difference between a component's core behavior and component interfaces, we consider a multiprocessor system-on-chip where several processors and memory units are hooked to a system bus. The processors act as the "masters" that request read/write services via bus access, whereas the memory units possibly act as "slaves" providing services. So, let us explain each of the terms we discussed in this setting.

- *Components*: Bus masters (processors), bus slaves (memory units).
- *Interfaces*: The bus interface for masters/slaves. These are the processes that participate in the bus protocol.
- *Centralized converter*: The bus controller or the arbiter is the centralized converter that snoops on the bus.

The overall communication mechanism is shown in Figure 3.2. Behavior of the processors connected to the bus can be subdivided into three different parts:

- *External environment*: The programs executing on a processor serve as its external environment. Execution of the programs generate memory read/ write requests. As a result of these read/write requests, the processor requests

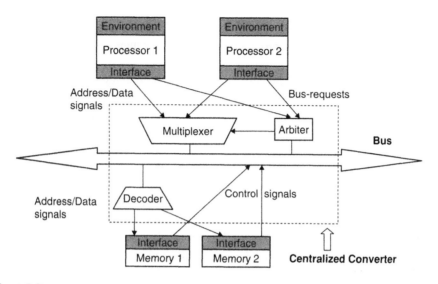

Figure 3.2

Converters and interfaces in bus-based communication.

bus access. When bus access is granted, the processor transmits address/data signals over the bus.

- *Core behavior*: This is the behavioral core of the processor with implementation of microarchitectural features such as pipelines and cache.
- *Bus interface*: This portion manages the communication of the processor with the bus. Its state remembers entities such as:
  - Pending requests of bus access from the processor, and
  - The current status of the processor in terms of bus access — idle/transmitting data and so on.

The processors request bus access, which is granted by a bus arbiter or bus controller. Based on the bus arbiter's output, a multiplexer could be triggered that then drives the appropriate address/data signals on the bus. Once these are sent, the address could be decoded so that the read/write request can be sent to the appropriate memory unit (bus slave). Thus, the bus arbiter acts a centralized converter or coordinator enabling the processors to communicate with the memory units. This is shown clearly in Figure 3.2. In particular, the figure shows that bus arbiter along with the multiplexer/decoder coordinate the communication between the bus interfaces of the processors (masters) and memory units (slaves).

Given the foregoing role of interface and converters in enabling communication across embedded system components, there is an issue about correct design of these interfaces and converters. However, more often than not, the system components are built out of predefined, readily available components such as Intellectual Property

(IP) cores. It is worthwhile to mention here that for well-known bus protocols such as PCI or AMBA, the IP core providers usually endow their components with bus wrappers.

Hence the designer's job includes communication debugging/validation apart from communication design. Usually the problem faced by the designer is as follows: given a set of components, possibly supplied by different vendors and having incompatible protocols, how to weave together an interconnect fabric that will allow them to communicate in *prespecified interaction patterns*. Thus, these "prespecified interaction patterns" give the desired protocol with which the predesigned components or IP cores should communicate.

Given such a desired interaction protocol and a set of components with incompatible native protocols, the designer thus needs to generate suitable component interfaces and/or a centralized converter. The interfaces and converter not only enable communication but also ensure that the communication conforms to the desired protocol. The issue of how much functionality with which to endow the component interfaces and how much functionality should be left to the centralized converter is a matter of design choice.

3.1 COMMON INCOMPATIBILITIES

Before proceeding further, we need to be clear about the representation of interfaces and converters. As already mentioned, we can view the component interfaces and the centralized converter as processes with states. However, this is a very general view and does not pinpoint the exact capabilities an embedded system designer may expect from the interfaces/converters. Hence, we present a series of illustrative examples here to capture the common protocol incompatibilities that may arise. For each of these incompatibilities we try to offer customized solutions, generating an interconnect fabric that can allow the incompatible components to communicate. In the next section, we will present a general method where the incompatible protocols are modeled as finite-state machines (FSMs) and a protocol converter can be automatically synthesized.

To show the common incompatibilities that arise, we need a notation for specifying the incompatible protocols. In this section, we adopt the sequence diagram notation for describing simple incompatible protocols. Recall that a sequence diagram represents an interaction pattern across processes; the processes appear as vertical lines, also called lifelines. So, to capture incompatible native protocols of n communicating components, we may use n different sequence diagrams, one from the viewpoint of each component. Each sequence diagram describes the native protocol of a component and the communication it expects from the other components.

Because these "expectations" are incompatible, the components cannot communicate. By designing suitable component interfaces and protocol converters, one can enable communication across these components.

In the following, we distinguish between *control* and *data signals*. The control signals enable data communication between the components; the actual data being transferred is captured in the data signals. Each component has a set of control/data signals it sends/receives; this set is called the *signal alphabet* of the component. Common incompatibilities across the components arise from differing signal alphabets and/or differing order of signals exchanged across components.

3.1.1 Sending/Receiving Signals in Different Order

In this situation, the components have the same signal alphabet. However, in the native protocols the signals may be exchanged in different order leading to incompatibility. In Figure 3.3, we see a simple example of this situation. There are two processes here — sender and receiver. The sender communicates the beginning of a data transfer with a *start* signal, and the receiver communicates the end of the transfer with a *stop* signal. The sender in this case can be a processor, and the receiver can be a memory unit, for example. The data transfer consists of communication of an *addr* and *data* signal. This could be the instruction of the sender (say, a processor) to the receiver (say, a memory unit) to perform a memory write; *addr* is the memory address to which the given *data* is to be written.

Figure 3.3a, b shows that the sender and receiver expect the *addr*, *data* signals in different order. This minor incompatibility of native protocols can be solved in many different ways:

- An interface is attached to either the sender or the receiver. If the interface is attached to the sender for example, it should store the *addr*, receive *data*, forward *data* to receiver, and then forward the *addr* to receiver. This requires the interface to have a register that can store the *addr* signal. This solution

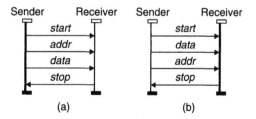

(a)   (b)

Figure 3.3

Different signal ordering: (a) sender's viewpoint, (b) receiver's viewpoint.

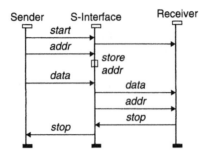

Figure 3.4

Using a sender interface to enable communication in Figure 3.3.

is shown schematically via a sequence diagram in Figure 3.4. The sender interface is shown via the lifeline marked *S-Interface*.

- We could also have a central converter that sits in between the sender and the receiver, rather than being attached to any of them as an interface. However, in terms of functionality, the difference between having a converter and having an interface for one of the processes is rather minimal.
- Finally, in the depiction of the protocols in Figure 3.3, the *addr* and *data* signals are sent one after another by the sender. Usually, this will happen when the *addr* and *data* signals share a resource — say, they are transmitted over the same bus but in different clock cycles. So, one way to get past the protocol incompatibility is to have separate address and data buses. The *addr* and *data* signals could be driven over separate buses in the same clock cycle. Of course, the receiver also needs to have separate address and data ports in this case.

3.1.2 Handling a Different Signal Alphabet

In this situation, the various interacting components communicate using different sets of signals. Usually, the sets of signals is not disjoint, but certain signals are sent/received by one component but not received/sent by others.

We show a simple example of such a protocol incompatibility in Figure 3.5. In this case, the sender generates the *request* signal, which is not expected by the receiver. Similarly, the receiver generates a *ready* signal, which is not expected by the sender. Both of these signals need to be consumed by the interfaces/converter to maintain protocol compatibility. On the other hand, the receiver expects the *stop* signal, which is not provided by the sender. Therefore, this signal needs to be generated by the interfaces/converter.

What are the solutions we can propose to resolve this protocol incompatibility? Basically, the extra logic we add should be able to generate/swallow signals that

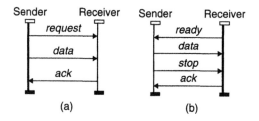

Figure 3.5

Differing signal alphabets: (a) sender's viewpoint, (b) receiver's viewpoint.

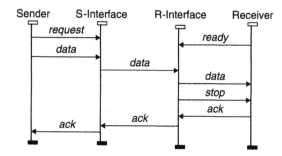

Figure 3.6

Using sender and receiver interfaces to remove incompatibilities in Figure 3.5.

appear in the signal alphabet of one component but not in another. The question is where we add the logic — as a central protocol converter or as two separate interfaces (one for the sender, one for the receiver).

Figure 3.6 illustrates a solution where both the sender and the receiver are endowed with separate interfaces. The sender interface swallows up the *request* signal from the sender, because it is not expected by the receiver. Likewise, the receiver interface swallows up the *ready* signal from the receiver, because it is not expected by the sender. The *stop* signal is expected by the receiver, but is not generated by the sender. Hence the receiver interface steps in to generate this signal at the "appropriate point" in the protocol. Finally, the *data* and *ack* signals appear in the signal alphabet of both the sender and the receiver; the interfaces only forward these signals.

Instead of having sender and receiver interfaces, we could also have a centralized converter that performs the functionality of both the interfaces. All control/data signals from the components flow to the converter. Similarly, all control/data signals to the components are generated by the converter.

In this example, the converter will be a process that performs the actions of both the sender and receiver interfaces. We cannot show the converter simply as a

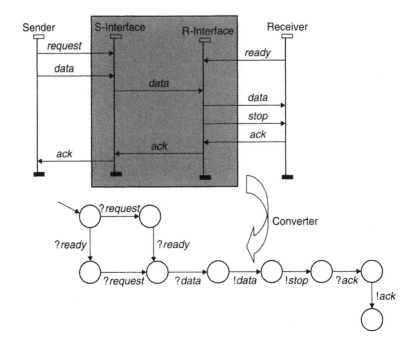

Figure 3.7

Using a centralized converter to remove incompatibilities in Figure 3.5.

vertical line in a message sequence chart (MSC), because a vertical line in an MSC represents a *sequence* of events. In this case, there might not be a strict ordering on the signals arriving/leaving the converter. For example, in Figure 3.7, the arrival of the *request* and *ready* signals to the converter are not strictly ordered. For this reason, we can present the centralized converter in a state machine format. The state machine captures the various possible interleavings of signal arrival/departure into/from the converter. In particular:

- Arrival of a signal into the converter is shown as a receive event, marked by the symbol *?*.
- Departure of a signal from the converter is shown as a send event, marked by the symbol *!*.

To remove the incompatibilities in Figure 3.5, we can use the finite-state machine shown in Figure 3.7 as a centralized protocol converter.

3.1.3 Mismatch in Data Format

This situation happens when the "type" of data sent by one component is different from the data type expected by the receiving component. Because we are discussing embedded system component communication at a fairly low level, the common *types* will of course be bits, bytes, and collections of bytes.

To see a simple example, consider two components: a sender and a receiver. The sender sends the data through a serial port, one bit per clock cycle. The receiver receives the data through an 8-bit parallel port — getting a byte at a time. To solve this data-width mismatch, we need a sender interface that will collect 8 bits at a time and transmit them to the receiver side. Thus, the interface should be endowed with at least 1 byte of storage capability.

Moreover, how the 8 bits are collected at the sender side also depends on the receiver's expectations about the byte it receives.

- If the receiver wants the last 8 bits sent out by the sender, the sender interface can simply contain a 8-bit *shift register*. In every clock cycle, the bit from the sender is shifted in and the oldest bit in the register is shifted out. The contents of the shift register can be propagated to the receiver side in every clock cycle.
- If the receiver expect to read the sender data one fresh byte at a time, we need a different arrangement. The sender interface then contains an 8-bit *buffer* that stores the latest 8 bits. Once 8 bits are collected, the contents are propagated to the receiver side. Thus, the receiver gets data from the sender in every 8 clock cycles in this case.

The two situations are illustrated in Figure 3.8.

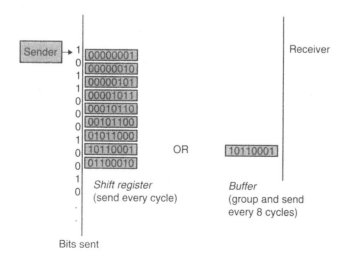

Figure 3.8

Sender sending bits, receiver expecting bytes.

Another common data type mismatch may result from the inability of embedded system components to synchronize while transferring several chunks (or packets) of data. A concrete realization of such a situation can again be shown with two components — a sender (possibly denoting a processor) and a receiver (possibly denoting a memory unit). The processor may send a sequence of read/write requests to the memory unit. When the memory unit is not ready to serve a particular request, this needs to be conveyed to the processor so that it does not send any more requests.

Suppose the processor is sending the address and data of a burst of write requests to the memory unit in consecutive cycles, that is:

- Cycle 1: *Addr1* sent — the first address in the burst
- Cycle 2: *Data1* sent — the data to be written to *Addr1*
- Cycle 3: *Addr2* sent — the second address in the burst
- Cycle 4: *Data2* sent — the data to be written to *Addr2*, and so on.

Suppose that when *Addr2* is sent, the memory unit conveys the information that it cannot service the write request in one clock cycle. So, in the next clock cycle also, the memory unit is expecting the address *Addr2* to be re-sent. On the other hand, if this is not conveyed to the sender (in this case, the processor), it will send *Data2*, which will be mistaken as an address by the receiver (the memory unit). As a result, the address-data correspondence maintained at the sender and receiver side is completely lost.

One solution to the problem is to have a centralized converter, as well as individual interfaces. The sender/receiver interfaces communicate only with the converter but not with each other. When the components are communicating over a bus, this forms a good depiction of the bus architecture (see Figure 3.9).

In particular, when the receiver is unable to service a request, it could assert, say, a WAIT signal that is conveyed to the sender interface via the converter. The sender interface then holds the current address/data in the next clock cycle instead of putting in a fresh address/data. This behavior is repeated by the sender interface until the WAIT signal is deasserted by the receiver.

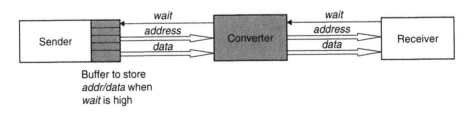

Figure 3.9

Maintaining address-data correspondence within a burst.

3.1.4 **Mismatch in Data Rates**

Our final example of a commonly arising protocol incompatibility refers to incompatible data rates between system components. Examples of this kind may arise in any stream processing application — any embedded system processing a stream of incoming events. This includes media-processing applications processing incoming audio/video streams (such as an MPEG encoder in a video phone) as well as healthcare monitoring applications processing incoming stream of medical data (such as blood pressure or heart rates).

An example setup involving a video encoder application in a video phone is shown in Figure 3.10. In this setup, the media processor (which is producing the encoded video stream) and the video decoder (which is playing the video at a specific rate) may have different data rates from the incoming video stream (captured via a camera). One common solution to smooth out such differences in data rates is to employ buffers at the interfaces of different system components. For example, to smoothe the difference between the sampling rate of the camera and the rate at which the MPEG encoder (running on the media processor) processes the data, we may employ an on-chip buffer. The buffer stores the portion of the incoming video stream that has been captured but has not yet been picked up for processing. Similarly, at the video decoding/playout end, a buffer may be placed as well.

The buffers in this case form the component interfaces that avoid overflow/underflow while processing/decoding streams. The storage requirement of the buffers (how big a buffer to place) may be decided by the designer based on several criteria:

- How much on-chip area is available for the buffers,
- The variability in the data rate for the stream produced by any one component (e.g., the variability in the processing time for the media processor), and
- The difference between the overall data rates for the various system components.

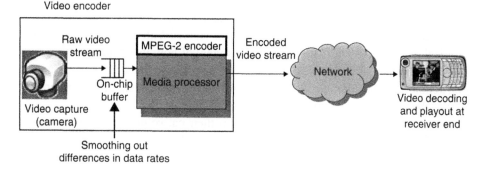

Figure 3.10

Buffers can smooth out differences in data rates.

3.2 CONVERTER SYNTHESIS

We now proceed to describe the task of generating a protocol converter given the representation of communicating incompatible protocols. As we will see, depending on the aggressiveness in converter synthesis, we can enable communication among more and more incompatible system components.

In the following, we assume a set of system components, each with their own native protocol. The concurrent composition of the native protocols "does not work," and hence we need a protocol converter to enable communication between these incompatible components. We discuss strategies to synthesize the converter. One important issue needs to be emphasized at this stage. We always generate a centralized converter that sits in the midst of all the components and enables their communication. However, often it is possible to distribute some of the functionality of this centralized converter into individual component interfaces. Toward the end of this chapter we also discuss certain heuristic strategies for doing so.

3.2.1 Representing Native Protocols and Converters

The native protocols of the system components can be described or represented in very many different ways. These range from informal English descriptions to more formal descriptions in the form of finite-state machines. We note here that the "native protocol" of a component refers to the portion of the component's behavior which is responsible for communication.

In order to talk about mechanisms to resolve protocol incompatibilities, we first need a mechanism for describing the native protocols of the components. The description should be general enough to capture various possible native protocols — not just those appearing in specific application domains.

Our description of native protocols will use labeled FSMs. Thus, a protocol is described using an FSM where each transition is labeled with action names. A native protocol of a component is the component's view of how its communication with other components should proceed. It captures the possible sequences of communication actions that the component goes through. These communication actions appear as the labels of the transitions in the protocol FSM.

Thus, given a set of n system components their native protocols are described as FSMs $M_1, \ldots, M_n$. Each FSM M_i is described as $M_i = (S_i, I_i, \Sigma_i, \rightarrow_i)$, where S_i is the set of states, $I_i \subseteq S_i$ is the set of initial states, Σ_i is the set of labels appearing on the transitions, and $\rightarrow_i \subseteq S_i \times \Sigma_i \times S_i$ is the transition relation. The question now is what the action labels in the set Σ_i look like. The action labels in Σ_i denote either *internal actions* (internal to component i) or *communication actions*.

Any communication action label in the set Σ_i is either of the form $i!\,j,m$ or of the form $i?\,j,m$ where

- ! denotes sending of a message, and ? denotes receipt of a message,
- $j \neq i$ is a component different from the ith component — thus $!j,m$ as an action label in the protocol for component i simply means the sending of message m by component i to component j, and
- m is a message name. We can assume a *universe of message names* $\mathcal{M}$ from which all names appearing in the individual native protocols are drawn.

Let us now illustrate the description of incompatible native protocols, first via a simple example. There are two components — a sender S and a receiver R. The native protocols of S and R are shown in Figure 3.11. Because there are only two components, the communication action labels do not need to explicitly contain a component name. This is because if the action labels in the native protocol of S contain a send/receive communication action, we know it is a communication to R (because R is the only other component). Similarly, if the action labels in the native protocol of R contain a send/receive communication action, we know it is a communication to S.

Why are the native protocols in Figure 3.11 incompatible? This can be explained at several levels of detail. Syntactically, we see that the signal alphabets of the two protocols are not the same. For example, the sender S sends the *req* signal, but the signal alphabet of the receiver R is {*ready, data, stop, ack*}, which does not contain the *req* signal. At a less syntactic level, we can say that the sender S sends the *req* signal, which the receiver R cannot receive. The solution to such incompatibility is to synthesize a converter that will receive the *req* signal. We now present

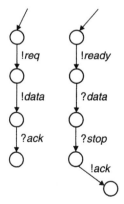

Figure 3.11

Incompatible native protocol FSMs.

the basic mechanism of converter synthesis. The converter will also be another labeled FSM.

3.2.2 Basic Ideas for Converter Synthesis

Let us see how the converter synthesis works with the example in Figure 3.11. All the communication actions from the sender S and the receiver R are now directed to the converter. The converter is a labeled FSM, which can then generate the matching communication actions if necessary.

We now elaborate the construction of the converter by traversing the FSMs of the incompatible protocol FSMs. The converter will be constructed in a manner similar to constructing product FSMs. While constructing the converter, we traverse the protocol FSMs and keep track of our "current state" in these protocol FSMs. In the figures, we do so by placing a black token in the "current state" of the protocol FSMs. Initially, the sender S and the receiver R in Figure 3.11 can send the *req* and *ready* signals. So, we let the converter execute the matching actions by receiving these signals. This is shown in Figure 3.12.

Once the converter executes a matching action, say, ?*req* (receiving the *req* signal from sender S), we need to ascertain what the enabled actions in the resultant state can be. This is shown in Figure 3.13. Based on the local states in the protocol FSMs (shown via black tokens in Figure 3.13), we can decide what actions the converter can execute. In particular, the converter will try to match communication actions, so that either of the protocol FSMs can progress. As shown in Figure 3.13, the enabled

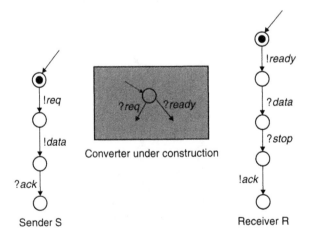

Figure 3.12

Converter FSM construction for Figure 3.11—Step 1.

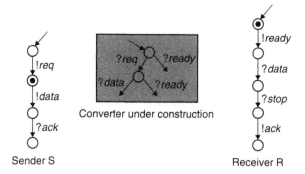

Figure 3.13

Converter FSM construction for Figure 3.11 — Step 2.

actions at the current local states of the two protocol FSMs are *!data* and *!ready* (meaning the send of *data* or the send of *ready*). Accordingly, the enabled actions of the converter are the matching communication actions *?data*, *?ready* (the receipt of *data*, *ready*).

Proceeding in this manner, we can construct the converter FSM shown in Figure 3.14. For clarity, we have marked the action labels of the converter to indicate whether they involve a communication with the sender S or the receiver R. Thus, the action label *R?ready* means the converter receiving the *ready* message from the receiver R. We have also summarized the input and output signals of the sender, receiver, and converter in Figure 3.14.

The mechanism for converter synthesis can now be described as follows. Given a set of incompatible protocol FSMs, we first find the communication action labels of these protocol FSMs. Let the protocol FSMs be $M_1, \ldots, M_n$ and their communication action labels be $\Sigma_1^{cm}, \ldots, \Sigma_n^{cm}$. For each of these sets of action labels, we can define the set of matching labels as follows:

$$\overline{\Sigma_i^{cm}} = \{converter?i,m \mid i!j,m \in \Sigma_i^{cm}\} \cup \{converter!i,m \mid i?j,m \in \Sigma_i^{cm}\} \qquad (3.1)$$

Thus, a send action $i!j,m$ from component i to component j is matched by a receive action from the converter denoted as *converter?i,m*. Similarly, a receive action $i?j,m$ involving receipt of message m by component i from component j is matched by the converter via the send action *converter!i,m*. To see why we need this concept of matching actions, consider the transfer of the *data* signal from the sender S to receiver R in Figure 3.14. This corresponds to two action labels in the protocol FSMs:

- *S!R, data* — the sending of *data* from S to R
- *R?S, data* — the receipt of *data* by R from S

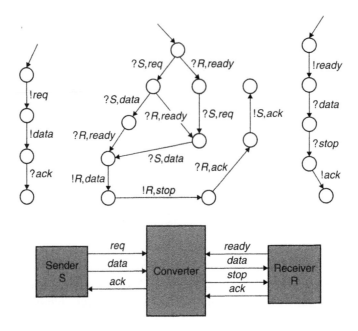

Figure 3.14

Converter FSM for Figure 3.11.

In Figure 3.14, the action *S!R, data* is simply shown as *!data* in the sender's FSM, because S and R are obvious from the context. Similarly, the action *R?S, data* is simply shown as *?data* in the receiver's FSM.

These are matched by two actions on the part of the converter:

- *converter?S, data* — the receipt of *data* by the converter from S, and
- *converter!R, data* — the sending of *data* by the converter to R.

In other words, the converter receives the *data* via the action *converter?S, data* when the *data* signal is sent by the sender. Thus, even though the sender S intends to send the *data* signal to the receiver R, it flows to the converter. The converter then forwards the *data* signal to its intended recipient process R via the action *converter!R, data*. In Figure 3.14, the action label *converter?S, data* is simply shown as *?S, data* as a notational shorthand; similarly, the action label *converter!R, data* is simply shown as *!R, data*.

The preceding explains the notion of "matching actions." Given protocol FSMs $M_1, \ldots, M_n$, corresponding to the communication action labels of each protocol FSM we can draw up a matching action by the converter. If the communication action labels of the protocol FSMs are $\Sigma_1^{cm}, \ldots, \Sigma_n^{cm}$, the corresponding matching action label sets $\overline{\Sigma_1^{cm}}, \ldots, \overline{\Sigma_n^{cm}}$ are as defined in Equation 3.1. In the same way, for each action label $\sigma \in \Sigma_i^{cm}$ we can define the matching action $\overline{\sigma}$ executed by the converter. Thus

$$\overline{\Sigma_i^{cm}} = \{\overline{\sigma} \mid \sigma \in \Sigma_i^{cm}\}$$

The converter is then given by an FSM whose action labels are drawn from the set $\overline{\Sigma_1^{cm}} \cup \ldots \cup \overline{\Sigma_n^{cm}}$.

We have now elaborated the action labels of the converter FSM. However, how do we construct the converter FSM itself? This can be done essentially via a product construction of the various protocol FSMs. In particular, let the incompatible protocol FSMs $M_1, \ldots, M_n$ be of the form

$$M_i = (S_i, I_i, \rightarrow_i, \Sigma_i)$$

where S_i is the set of states in the protocol FSM M_i, $I_i \subseteq S_i$ is the set of initial states, Σ_i is the set of action labels (including internal actions as well as communication actions), and $\rightarrow_i \subseteq S_i \times \Sigma_i \times S_i$ is the transition relation.

Then, the set of states of the converter FSM is given by $S_1 \times S_2 \ldots \times S_n$ while the set of initial states is given by $I_1 \times I_2 \ldots \times I_n$. We have already clarified what the set of action labels for the converter FSM looks like. So, the only thing we need to clarify is the transition relation or the set of transitions in the converter FSM. Consider a state of the converter FSM $(s_1, s_2, \ldots, s_n)$, that is, $s_1 \in S_1, s_2 \in S_2, \ldots, s_n \in S_n$. Then any transition from one of the local states can lead to a transition of the converter as follows.

- If $s_i \xrightarrow{\sigma}_i t_i$ is a transition in the protocol FSM M_i, we have

$$(s_1, \ldots, s_i, \ldots, s_n) \xrightarrow{\overline{\sigma}} (s_1, \ldots, t_i, \ldots, s_n)$$

  as a transition in the converter FSM (here $\overline{\sigma}$ is the matching action for action label σ as discussed in the preceding), provided:
  - For shared signals (which are sent from one component and received by another component), we do not allow the receipt of a message before it is sent.

To illustrate the converter FSM construction, we now refer back to our example in Figure 3.14. This example has an incompatible sender and receiver protocol FSM, and we are trying to construct a protocol converter as an FSM. In particular, we number the local states of the protocol FSMs, and we show the states of the converter FSM as compositions of the protocol FSM states. This appears in Figure 3.15.

We can discuss the functionality of the converter in another fashion. Suppose we split the space of communication signals into *shared signals*, *input signals*, and *output signals*. Shared signals are signals that are sent by one protocol FSM and received by another protocol FSM. These signals are received by the converter (from the sender of the signal) and forwarded by the converter (to the receiver of

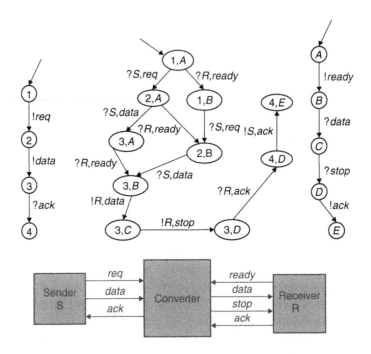

Figure 3.15

Converter FSM construction for Figure 3.11—the converter FSM as a product of the incompatible protocol FSMs.

the signal). Input signals are sent by one protocol FSM and received by none. These signals are simply gobbled up by the converter. Similarly, output signals are received by one protocol FSM and sent by none. These signals are generated by the converter.

For input and output signals, the converter's task is rather well defined — the converter needs to consume or produce these signals to smoothe out protocol incompatibilities. However, for shared signals, we have quite a bit of leeway in deciding how the converter should behave. In the preceding, we have put up only a simple common-sense restriction that the converter cannot send a shared signal to its receiver protocol until it receives it from the signal's sender protocol. This amounts to an asynchronous transfer of the shared signals (be it control or data signals) from the sender protocol to the receiver protocol.

However, there can be other restrictions leading to different implementations of the converter. For example, we might require that the transfer of the shared signals occur in a single step. This means that for any shared signal x, the converter receiving the signal x from the sender protocol and the converter forwarding x to the receiver protocol must happen in one step. In such a situation, the converter does not need to store the shared signals — this is particularly important for data signals (where the converter would have to store the data content otherwise). This also means that the sender protocol of a shared signal x cannot send the signal to the converter until and unless the receiver protocol for x is ready to receive the signal. Thus, effectively the sender protocol is blocked. Now if x is a data signal, while the sender protocol is blocked trying to send x, new data may arrive and overwrite the data content that was never sent (to the receiver protocol via the converter). Consequently, in such situations, apart from having a centralized converter, the protocols will also need individual interfaces. In particular, for any protocol FSM that sends shared data signal(s) (possibly to other protocol FSMs), the protocol interface can contain buffers to store data content that is ready to be sent but has not been sent (because the receiver is not ready).

In Figure 3.16, we show the converter FSM where any shared signals involve a synchronization between the sender and receiver of the signal. Consequently, the send and receive of these shared signals are not shown as separate actions. In particular, in the converter FSM certain transitions are marked with the name of a shared action label, such as the transition with action label *data* in Figure 3.16. Such a transition denotes the receiving and the forwarding of the *data* signal by

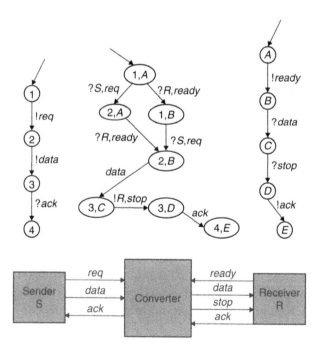

Figure 3.16

Converter FSM construction for Figure 3.11 — all shared signal transfer is done by synchronization.

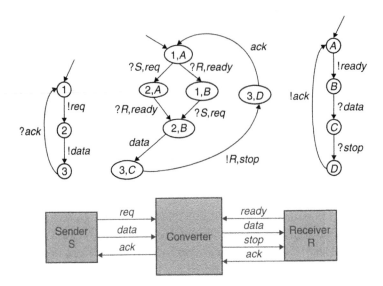

Figure 3.17

Converter FSM construction — all shared signal transfer is done by synchronization, and the protocols/converter capture infinite-length execution traces.

the converter (thereby resulting in a three-way synchronization between sender, converter, and receiver).

We also note that in the running example in this chapter, we have considered protocol FSMs that are acyclic. Consequently, the converter is also acyclic. This essentially corresponds to a "session" of the protocols, and the converter resolves protocol incompatibilities within that session. Clearly, we could have protocol FSMs that execute repeated "sessions," with the converter smoothing out incompatibilities in each session. In Figure 3.17, we show such an example — a minor modification of Figure 3.16 where the protocol FSMs and converter FSM repeatedly execute the same behavior.

When the protocol and the converter FSMs capture infinite-length execution traces (by having repeated "sessions" of interaction), a clean design of the converter would however avoid mixing up signals across different sessions. That is, the converter and the various protocol FSMs should preferably synchronize at the end of each session. In Figure 3.17 a "session" of data exchange refers to:

- The sender going through the states $1 \rightarrow 2 \rightarrow 3 \rightarrow 1$, and
- The receiver going through the states $A \rightarrow B \rightarrow C \rightarrow D \rightarrow A$.

In this example we did not add an explicit synchronization, because the last message exchange in a session (an *ack* message being sent from sender S to converter and forwarded from converter to receiver R) in any case involves a three-way synchronization between the two protocol FSMs and the converter FSM. Here we have made the receipt of *ack* by the converter (from the receiver R) and the forwarding of *ack* by the converter (to the sender S) into one single atomic action, marked simply as *ack* in the converter transition from state $(3, D)$ to state $(1, A)$. This ensures that actions across sessions are not mixed up.

3.2.3 Various Strategies for Protocol Conversion

So far, we have outlined one strategy for letting incompatible system components communicate. Our strategy is based on synthesizing a central converter such that all the system components talk only to the converter, and not to each other. This allows us to smooth out common communication incompatibilities such as:

- Component C is sending signal m to component C', but component C' never receives m, OR
- Component C is sending signal m to component C', but component C' is not ready to receive m in its current state.

In the first case, the converter can simply receive m from C and never transmit m. In the second case, the converter can receive m from C and then drive C' such that it comes to a state where it is ready to receive m (from the converter).

We first note that even this simple converter-generation strategy is a powerful one for solving protocol incompatibilities. In the past quarter-century, much research effort has been directed toward enabling communication among software components. Some of these approaches simply synthesize a converter that drives the components C and C' in such a way that whenever component C is sending a message m to component C', the component C' is ready to receive it. If it turns out that component C' can never receive message m, the converter will try to drive component C in such a way that it never sends message m in the first place.

Let us examine this approach with the help of an example. Let us again consider the example of Figure 3.11. Here we have two components — the sender and the receiver. The sender sends *req* to the receiver at the beginning, but the receiver can never receive *req* (i.e., *req* is outside the signal alphabet of the receiver). Similarly, the receiver sends a *ready* signal at the beginning, but the sender can never receive *ready*. Clearly, the converter cannot hope to drive the sender and receiver so that a message outside the signal alphabet of the sender (receiver) is never transmitted by the receiver (sender). With such a converter generation method, we cannot generate any converter to smooth out the protocol incompatibilities. However, using our approach we synthesized a converter FSM as shown in Figure 3.15. This was possible because when the sender (receiver) transmits a signal outside the signal alphabet of the receiver (sender) — we simply let the converter consume such a signal.

The foregoing discussion clarifies some of the power of the simple and elegant converter-generation mechanism we have discussed. However, it can be improved in many ways, namely:

- **Avoiding no-progress cycles:** Our simple converter generation method can produce converters that *livelock* the communicating components (whose protocol incompatibilities we are resolving).

  A livelock results from a no-progress cycle where the components communicate but no progress (in terms of data transmission) is achieved.

- **Speculative signal transmission to avoid deadlocks:** In the converter-generation policy we have presented, all signals sent/received by the system components flow to/from the converter. Consequently, if a signal x is sent by component C and received by component C':

  - The converter receives x from component C, and then
  - The converter sends x to component C'.

  However if x is a control signal, the converter could also send x to C' even before receiving it from C. We call this "speculative signal transmission." We will see how this feature can help avoid deadlocks in component communication.

  Note that the converter cannot transmit data signals speculatively, because the content of the data being transmitted cannot be speculated!

We now discuss some of these improvements.

3.2.4 Avoiding No-Progress Cycles

To see how no-progress cycles can be introduced by protocol converters, we consider the example in Figure 3.18. We have two processes, one of them a master (M) and the other a slave (S). The master process sends a *msg* and waits for an *ok*. Thus the master process could depict the behavior of a processing element that is trying to access memory units; the *msg* could signify the data being written to the memory units. The slave process, on the other hand, receives the *msg* and forwards the request via a *fwd* signal. In our processing element–memory unit analogy, the forwarding could denote the detection of the appropriate memory unit (possibly via address decoding) to service the request. Now, when an appropriate memory unit is detected, it may or may not service the request based on whether it is busy. This is denoted via the *yes/no* signals received by the slave. Once the slave receives a *yes* (*no*) signal from the environment, it sends an *ok* (*not_ok*) signal to the master. The state machines of the master, slave, and converter appear in Figure 3.18.

First of all, let us understand what the converter captures vis-à-vis the physical world. In the physical world, the master M and slave S function as an *open system*. In particular, the slave S communicates with the external environment while sending

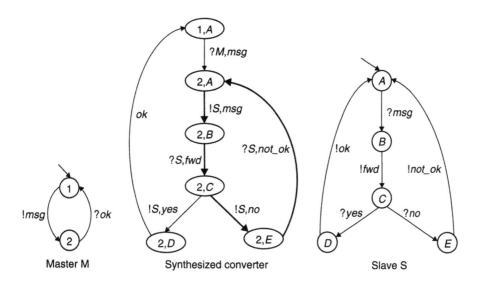

Figure 3.18

Converter FSM construction — synthesized converter can lead to no-progress cycles. The cycle marked in bold $(2,A) \rightarrow (2,B) \rightarrow (2,C) \rightarrow (2,E) \rightarrow (2,A)$ is a no-progress cycle.

the *fwd* signal; this action stands for forwarding the message *msg* received from the master M. Subsequently, the slave receives a *yes* or *no* answer from the environment. The converter synthesized in Figure 3.18 closes this open system. In other words, the master M, the slave S, and the synthesized converter are intended to work as a closed system. Consequently, the converter captures the functionality of the master/slave's external environment. The slave's *fwd* signal is received by the converter, and the converter makes a decision about whether to send a *yes/no* signal to the slave.

Referring to Figure 3.18, we see that the converter FSM has a cycle $(2,A) \rightarrow (2,B) \rightarrow (2,C) \rightarrow (2,E) \rightarrow (2,A)$ where the communication of *msg* from the master fails to evoke an *ok* response from the slave. Therefore, the converter and the slave could loop along this cycle forever, while the master is waiting for an *ok* response. This constitutes a no-progress cycle.

Conceptually, what the converter of Figure 3.18 achieves is not small. It receives the *msg* from the master and then evokes either an *ok* response or a *not_ok* response. Further, if it evokes a *not_ok* response the converter makes another attempt to make an *ok* response. This is what we would expect the converter to do, unless we explicitly instruct our converter generation method to avoid generating a *not_ok* response.

To avoid generating converters that can lead to no-progress cycles, we need to identify the "livelock states" — states that lead to themselves without making progress in data transmission. Of course, for defining these livelock states, the notion of "progress" in terms of data transmission needs to be clarified by the designer. Once the livelock states are identified, we identify the minimum set of transitions that can be removed so as to make any livelock state unreachable from itself. In other words, we modify the converter so that livelock states are simply not reached via no-progress cycles.

3.2.5 Speculative Transmission to Avoid Deadlocks

In Figure 3.19, we show an example involving two communicating components — a sender S and a receiver R. The signal alphabets of the two components are the same, {req,ok,data}. Thus, the incompatibility arises only from the order in which the components expect the signals to be sent/received. We have shown our normal converter construction using the product of the sender and receiver's protocol FSMs. All the signals exchanged here are shared signals — req, ok are shared control signals, whereas data is a shared data signal (involving data transmission). First of all, we can see from this example that shared signals exchanged may not always be achieved via synchronization. In the initial configuration, even though the sender S sends the

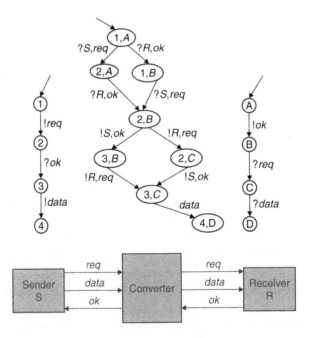

Figure 3.19

Converter FSM construction — speculative transmission is not allowed.

req signal, the receiver R is not ready to receive it. Therefore, the converter has to receive the *req* signal from the sender S (via the transition ?*S*, *req*) and then forward it to the receiver R later (via the transition !*R*, *req*).

Second, we notice that for shared control signals the protocol converter can be more aggressive and send the control signal speculatively to its intended recipient. In other words, the protocol converter need not wait for the signal to be sent by its sender; it can forward the signal even before receiving it! In Figure 3.20, we show a slight modification of Figure 3.19. The only difference here is that the sender (receiver) waits for the *ok* (*req*) signal before sending the *req* (*ok*) signal. Because both the components are waiting for a signal, this creates a problem. As per our converter generation strategy, the converter does not forward a shared signal before receiving it from its sender. However, none of the communicating components send anything in their initial states. Consequently, the converter will be blocked in its initial configuration waiting for a component to send some signal. The components also do not send any signals, and they are waiting to receive signals. This results in a deadlock scenario — something our converter generation strategy is unable to overcome. It is, however, worthwhile to note that the converter here is *not* introducing a deadlock. Clearly, there exists a circular wait situation in Figure 3.20 — the sender S is waiting for an *ok* from the receiver R, and the receiver R is waiting for an *req* from the sender S. This deadlock needs to be resolved for the components to communicate. However, our converter generation strategy is unable to do so.

To allow communication among the deadlocked components in Figure 3.20, the converter needs to break the circular wait. This is possible if the converter

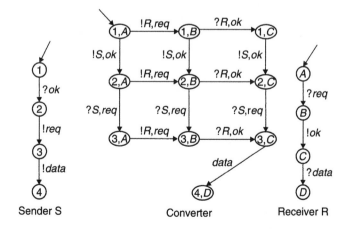

Figure 3.20

A situation where speculative transmission must be allowed to avoid deadlocks. A converter allowing such speculative transmission is also shown.

speculatively sends *ok* or *req* signal on behalf of the receiver or sender. Such a converter is also shown in Figure 3.20. As we can see, this converter is also obtained via a product FSM construction — we take the product of the protocol FSMs of the communicating components (in this case sender S and receiver R). However, the product FSM construction is less constrained than before — we also allow transitions where a signal is sent out by the converter before being received from another component. For example, in the converter of Figure 3.20, we allow the transition

$$(1,A) \overset{!S,ok}{\to} (2,A)$$

where $(1,A)$ is the initial configuration of the converter and it sends an *ok* signal to the sender S even before receiving it.

The preceding situation also points to us to certain *limits* in terms of converter synthesis. So far, we have seen a wide variety of incompatible communicating components where converters can be synthesized to enable their communication. This includes (a) components with differing signal alphabets, (b) components with the same signal alphabet but exchanging the signals in different order, and (c) components with same signal alphabet where all components wait to receive control signals (speculative transmission is required for breaking deadlocks). However, if all the components are initially waiting for the receipt of different data signals, we cannot synthesize any converter that will enable them to communicate. This will require the converter to speculatively transmit data signals. Because the sending of a data signal also involves sending the data content that comes along with it, this would require the converter to speculate on the data content — an impossible task. It is important for us to understand that the converters/interfaces only serve to smoothe the *protocol* incompatibilities across communicating system components. The converter/interface clearly cannot change/speculate the content of the *data* being communicated via the protocols between different system components. It is of course possible for the converter to do data formatting where it splits/merges data packets to suit the data format expected by another component. But the converter cannot change or guess the data itself!

A simple example requiring speculation of data content is shown in Figure 3.21 — *addr*, *rd_value* can be two different signals through which the address and value-read for some read request is being communicated. Because both of them involve some data content, a converter cannot speculatively transmit either of them. Consequently, the master and slave cannot communicate in this situation. Clearly, there is a bug in the master/slave communication protocol here — no reasonable master will expect the read value from a memory location even before passing the memory location's address to the slave. This bug is being manifested in the inherent incompatibility of the protocols, where we fail to synthesize a converter.

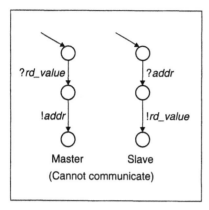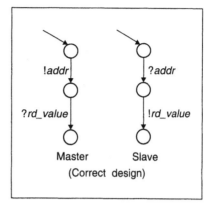

Figure 3.21

A situation where speculation of data content is required and hence protocol conversion is not possible. The correct design is also shown.

The correct design would require the master to pass the address and then expect the value read from the address. This correct design is also shown in Figure 3.21. The correct design of the master and slave would not even need any converter — the master and slave will simply synchronize on the *addr* signal (where the address is communicated to the slave by the master), and then they will synchronize on the *rd_value* signal (where the value read from the memory location is communicated to the master by the slave).

3.3 CHANGING A WORKING DESIGN

So far, we have discussed the issues in developing and validating the functionality of a working design — one in which system components are able to communicate.

However, as a design evolves, new features and functionality may be added. As a result, the native protocols of the individual components may also be changed (or rather, they may be enriched with new functionality). Once the native protocols of the system components change, designs that were "working" previously may again become unworkable. This means that enriching the behaviors of some of system components may mean that they are no longer able to communicate.

To elaborate the foregoing point, we need to first clarify what we mean by "enriching behavior." Our notion of behavior enrichment simply means more behaviors. Thus, if the behavior of a system component is captured by a state machine M and it is enriched to M', then the set of execution traces of M is included in the set of execution traces of M'. This means that all execution traces of M are execution traces of M', but not vice versa. As mentioned earlier, the execution traces of a state

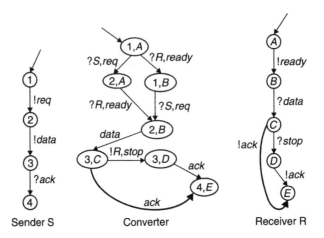

Figure 3.22

A change in one of the system component's behavior from Figure 3.16. The additional behaviors are marked in bold.

machine are obtained by unrolling the paths through the state machine starting from the initial state(s).

Let us take an example to illustrate our point. Consider the components shown in Figure 3.22, which is a modification of Figure 3.16. The only change is in the receiver, which can simply issue an acknowledgment *ack* after receiving the *data*. If we do not change the converter, it will simply wait for a *stop* signal from the receiver, which may never come. For this reason, we have changed the converter to allow for a synchronization on *ack* immediately after the transmission of *data*.

In this case, we have considered a simple example where only one transition is added to one system component, and this leads to a transition being added to the converter. In general, changes to system-component behavior may involve addition of states and transitions. However, the changes should be such that trace inclusion is preserved. That is, the traces of the old component are traces of the new component, but not vice versa. Subsequently we also add states/transitions to the converter's state machine. Again, the old and new converter will satisfy the trace inclusion property, that is, the traces of the old converter will be included in the set of traces of the new converter.

3.4 REFERENCES

Synthesizing protocol converters has been a topic of active research in the embedded systems community. Initially, the work was studied more for hardware, with the focus being on synthesizing glue logic between circuit blocks. The PhD thesis of Borriello [10] discusses this problem, with component interfaces being modeled as timing diagrams. Along similar lines, the work of [62] develops protocol interfaces from HDL descriptions.

In later works, developing converters to enable communication between system components has been studied in a generic setting. Here the components' communication behavior is modeled by generic formalisms such as finite-state machines. Hence such techniques may be applicable for enabling hardware-hardware and hardware-software as well as software-software communication. The work of [2] describes protocols as finite-state machines; the protocol converter is synthesized from the product of these finite-state machines. The works of [23, 64, 68] solve a related problem — determining whether several given components can be made to interact in a compatible way (without necessarily synthesizing a converter to resolve incompatibilities). Finally, the work of [78] studies the problem of resolving communication incompatibilities using a scenario-based description of the component behaviors.

> **Side Remark** *In terms of literature on enriching a working design by inserting behaviors (Chapter 3.3), the reader may want to refer to fundamental papers on behavioral inheritance. These papers study what it means for a finite-state machine to "inherit" the behaviors of another finite-state machine. The work of [35] may serve as a useful guidepost.*

3.5 EXERCISES

3.1. Suppose multiple processors are requesting bus access to read/write to several memory/peripheral modules. We want to model the communication between the different components in this system using the Unified Modeling Language (UML).

- What will be the classes in the system, and what will be the associations? Also, list some use cases from the point of view of a processor that is trying to access the bus. You may list the use cases in English or elaborate them using message sequence charts.
- Now, elaborate the design by filling in the state diagrams of each class you identified. Your design must satisfy the following criteria: (a) At most one processor must access the bus at any time; (b) if there are one or more processors requesting the bus, the bus should not be idle; and (c) any processor requesting the bus should eventually get access to the bus. Clearly state what parts of your statechart design are ensuring each of these three properties. If you make any assumptions for ensuring these properties, you should clearly state all your assumptions.

3.2. Figure 3.3, 3.5, and 3.8 show protocol incompatibilities that can be handled via component interfaces only (no centralized converter is necessary). Develop executable descriptions of these interfaces.

3.3. Figure 3.9 shows the difficulties that may arise from maintaining address-data correspondence in a burst while communicating over a bus. Elaborate on the converter design in Figure 3.9 — what are the storage capabilities of the converter and the sender interface? Also, can we have a solution that avoids a centralized converter and manages the address-data correspondence only via sender/receiver interfaces?

3.4. Section 3.2.2 presented the basic scheme for converter synthesis. As pointed out, the synthesized converter may contain no-progress cycles. Formalize the algorithm for the modified converter generation, that is, where the generated converter will avoid no-progress cycles. This can be done in two steps, by generating a converter and then removing transitions. Alternatively, the reader can try to generate the livelock free converter in one pass. Comment on the merits and drawbacks of the two approaches.

Performance Validation

Validation of embedded systems is invariably, and inextricably, linked to satisfying constraints on time. The correctness of embedded systems depends not only on the functionality being implemented, but also on the timeliness of the computation.

Most embedded control systems repeatedly acquire data from the environment (through radars/sensors), process the data, and output (via actuators). Thus, there is a response-time calculation involved — we want to find out the maximum response time in processing a data item. The response time of a data item is the total time to process it since its arrival. Thus, it includes (a) the waiting time when the data item waits for processing and (b) the actual processing time. If the processing element that processes a data item d also has other running tasks, these tasks may also delay the processing of d. Now, suppose a control system acquires data from the environment at the rate of n samples per second. Thus, if the maximum response time of any individual data item is less than $1/n$ seconds, we can infer that any data item is processed before the next data item arrives. Thus, there is no need to buffer or store data (in particular data that has been acquired but has not been processed).

Because data is coming in from the environment in an infinite stream, we may need to buffer or store the data if the processing time of a data item is too high. On the other hand, on-chip buffer space may be scarce, and hence it is not realistic to allow a large buffer of stored data items waiting to be processed. For this reason, we need to accurately estimate the response time in processing a data item.

An overall picture of the complexities in timing validation appears in Figure 4.1. Some of these issues arise in the system-level analysis. In particular, the system-level timing analysis deals with the overall system architecture rather than the software running on individual processing elements. Timing behavior due to

- Varying communication times over a bus or interconnection network on chip (as the case may be), and
- Scheduling of several tasks on a single processing element

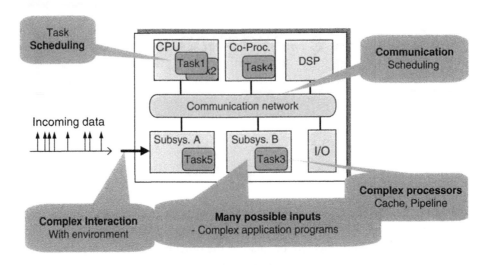

Figure 4.1

Issues in timing validation of complex embedded systems.

needs to be taken into account by the system-level timing analysis. The system-level scheduling should also consider the system's interaction with the external environment. A common case here is the input data (detected via sensors) coming in a periodic stream — say, one data item every 2 milliseconds.

The other factors come under the purview of software timing validation. In particular, classical results on system scheduling treat the tasks as abstract quantities whose computation time and deadlines are required for the system-level analysis. However, in reality, the tasks are programs written in standard programming languages (such as C) and executed on standard processors (with more and more complex processors being used in the embedded domain). Thus, timing validation of a piece of software is not a simple task — we need to develop methods to *guarantee* that a piece of software will terminate within a given deadline regardless of the program input. Moreover, our analysis cannot consider only the software — we also need to consider the microarchitecture of the underlying software to *tightly* estimate the maximum possible execution time of the program.

4.1 THE CONVENTIONAL ABSTRACTION OF TIME

Modeling timing constraints and developing validation methods for guaranteeing these timing constraints are essential in embedded system design. However, the programming languages and tools available for designing embedded systems are often drawn from what is on offer for general system design. In practice, we can expect most embedded system designers to write up the software in the C programming language, or even parts of it in assembly code! However, conventional mainstream programming languages such as C have steadfastly abstracted time. This has been observed and discussed at length recently by embedded systems researchers (e.g., see [49]).

Let us now examine the programming models of conventional imperative programming languages such as C. The individual operations (simple or compound statements) are not annotated with any timing constraints — the time within which these operations should be completed. Furthermore, conventionally it has been considered a virtue that the programmer will not be aware of the actual time that a program operation takes. Modern processors employ many many performance-enhancing optimizations such as pipeline, instruction and data cache, and branch prediction. These microarchitectural features makes the execution time of an operation variable. An instruction's execution time depends on:

- Whether it is hit or miss in the instruction cache,
- Whether its operands are hit/miss in the data cache (for load/store instructions),
- Whether it faces pipeline stalls due to data dependencies or resource contentions from other instructions,
- Whether it is correctly or wrongly predicted by the branch predictor (only for branch instructions), and so on.

Given such numerous sources of indeterminacy in the execution of a *single instruction*, we can only imagine the possible execution times of a coarser-grained operation — such as an operation in the source code level. Consequently, it is impossible to ascribe a single execution time to the operations at the C program level. Given this dilemma, we have come to accept the removal of time from our programming world. When we program, we do not worry about the time our program operations take. Timing is introduced as an afterthought, something to be worried about after the program(s) are written.

The need for timing analysis is particularly evident for embedded computing. Here, the computing component will typically require timely interactions with the enclosing physical world. However, analysis methods for real-time systems typically proceed at the system level — analyzing the time delay due to possible contention or preemption across *tasks*. So one question is, what is a task? Conventionally, real-time systems literature consider a task as *a computation that is executed by the CPU in a sequential fashion*. In other words, a task is a sequential program. To assign execution times to tasks, we need a mechanism to analyze the software of a task for finding its execution time. This goes beyond simulating/executing the task, because

- The program may have infinitely many inputs (say consider an image compression program which takes images as input), and

■ We are often trying to decide on what is a suitable platform to execute the task (i.e., task allocation is not predecided). Consequently, we cannot simulate/ execute the task on a *given* platform.

The difficulty in timing validation does not stem only from the issues in analyzing within a task. For communicating tasks executing in a multiprocessor environment (say, communication occurring over a bus), the communication patterns dictate the amount of contention over the bus. To illustrate this point, we show a schematic interaction in a bus-based electronic control unit network drawn from the automotive electronics domain. The communicating components include a wheel sensor, an antilock brake system (ABS), adaptive cruise control, and a brake control. We note that the traffic on the bus depends on the following:

■ The communication pattern, which may often be captured by a sequence diagram. From the visual order of Figure 4.2, we can see that message $m2$ is transmitted before message $m4$ — thus they do not contend with each other for bus access.

■ The timing of the events: For messages that are concurrent (i.e., not ordered as per the partial order prescribed by the communication pattern), whether they overlap and contend for bus access depends on their bus arrival times (which depends on prior computation/communication events). From Figure 4.2, we can see that messages $m2$ and $m3$ execute concurrently. Thus, depending on when they arrive at the bus, they can contend for bus access (or not).

To further elaborate the complexities arising in time estimation for bus-based communication, we show a schematic multiprocessor architecture in Figure 4.3. Here we have four processes P1, P2, P3, P4, each running on a *separate* processing element. We assume that the processing elements are connected to a bus, that is,

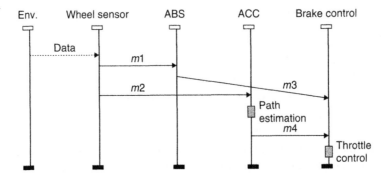

Figure 4.2

Schematic communication pattern among ECUs in automotive control.

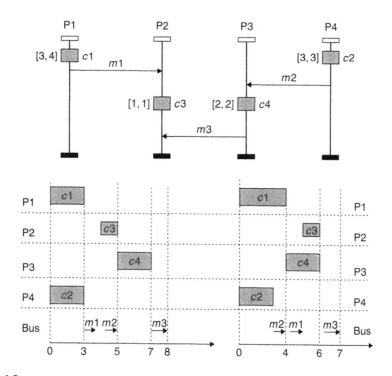

Figure 4.3

Anomalous timing behavior in bus-based communication.

any communication is bus-based communication. The sample bus interactions are shown in Figure 4.3 via a message sequence chart. It captures the computation within the processes as well as the communication across them (via bus). The bus is not explicitly shown as a process, but it is understood that any message transmission is over a bus and hence may need to wait if several processes are contending for bus access. We assume that the priority of the processes for bus access is P1, P2, P3, P4 — that is, P1 has the highest priority.

We now study the bus traffic arising from these computation and communication tasks. In particular, the bus traffic may vary depending on the exact execution time taken up by the computation tasks, because that may determine the timing of arrival of the messages. To concretely study this variation in bus traffic, we annotate each computation with execution times, given as an interval $[l, u]$ with l (u) denoting a lower (upper) bound on its execution time. Moreover, we make the execution time of all computations constant (i.e., $l = u$) except one; computation $c1$'s execution time is set to vary between 3 and 4 time units. We assume that each message transmission takes 1 time unit (i.e., only the time to transmit; this does not include the time to wait for bus access).

In Figure 4.3 we show the execution sequence corresponding to both the possibilities — $c1$ executing for 3 time units, and $c1$ executing for 4 time units. When $c1$ executes for 3 time units, the computations $c1$, $c2$ are executed in parallel in two different processing elements. At time $= 3$, both the processes P1 and P4 try to transmit messages $m1$ and $m2$ over the bus. However, bus access needs to be serialized, so P1 gets access first (based on its higher priority) and then P4. Once P1 transmits (to P2 over the bus), process P2 goes ahead and performs computation $c3$. Similarly, once P4 transmits (to process P3 over the bus), process P3 goes ahead and performs computation $c4$. Finally, P3 transmits message $m3$ over the bus. The total time taken is 8 time units.

However, if computation $c1$ takes more time (4 time units), the schedule of execution is different. In this case, while $c1$ is executing, process P4 executes computation $c2$ *and* transmits $m2$ over the bus. Thus, bus contention between P1 and P4 is avoided. The reduced bus contention allows computations $c3$ and $c4$ to finish earlier, following which the message $m3$ gets transmitted. The overall execution time is 7 time units! *Thus, when c1 takes less time, the overall execution time is increased, and when c1 takes more time, the overall execution time is reduced!*

The given example illustrates some of the subtleties in timing behavior of distributed embedded systems. Because computation may drive communication, increase in computation times may decrease resource contention (e.g., bus contention) for communication. The resultant decreased bus contention may result in an overall reduction in execution time of a distributed application running on a multiprocessor system-on-chip.

We call this phenomenon anomalous timing behavior or *timing anomaly* [58, 59]. We will need to grapple with such anomalous behavior for performance validation of embedded systems. This simple example illustrates some of the difficulties in performance validation, which we now proceed to address. Our discussion on performance analysis is chiefly presented over the next three sections. In Section 4.2, we discuss execution time estimation of a single program. In the embedded systems literature, these works are often referred under worst-case execution time (WCET) analysis. In Section 4.3, we broaden the scope of our timing analysis to capture intertask interference or interference from the environment. Then, in Section 4.4, we discuss some system-level communication methods. In the later parts of this chapter (Section 4.5), we discuss system-level solutions for building embedded systems with predictable performance. Here we do not try to estimate execution times; instead we adapt small changes in the system development to make its execution times more predictable. We conclude the chapter with a discussion of emerging application domains where some of our performance-based analysis/design methods can be used (Section 4.6).

4.2 PREDICTING EXECUTION TIME OF A PROGRAM

We now concentrate on the issue of predicting or conservatively estimating the execution time of a program. Clearly, we are only talking of terminating programs — it would make no sense to estimate the execution time of a nonterminating program. In other words, all loops and recursion depths in our programs have to be bounded. In fact, our analysis will take these bounds as input and estimate the execution time of a program.

What does it mean to conservatively estimate the execution time of a program? It means that one tries to find an upper bound or a lower bound on the execution time of a program. We will typically be interested in finding an *upper bound* on the execution time of a program. We call it the *worst-case execution time* or WCET. Similarly, a *lower bound* on the execution time of the program will be referred to as the *best-case execution time* or BCET.

Why do we need estimation of WCET (and BCET)? Clearly, we could find the maximum execution time of a program by running it against all possible inputs, measuring the execution time, and taking the maximum. The first difficulty in doing so is the large number of inputs that we need to try out. In fact, there can be infinitely many inputs — consider an image compression program that takes an image as input. Clearly we cannot try out all possible images in the world on this program and measure the execution time! The second difficulty in finding the WCET by measurement is that the execution time of a program for even a given input depends on the processor on which the software is run. Usually, in embedded system design, we are given the application and we are trying to design the platform (in this case a processor) that is suitable for running the application. We do not have access to all the possible processor choices for us to try and run our program, because this may be expensive.

The preceding explains why a simple solution like measuring a program's execution time against selected inputs does not allow us to safely estimate WCET. For same or similar reasons, we also cannot use architectural simulation (e.g., using tools such as SimpleScalar [5]) for estimating WCET of a program. This takes us beyond simulation/execution-based approaches — we need a *static analysis* of the program. In other words, we do not gain information about the program's execution time by executing it for selected inputs. Instead, we analyze the program's code and give an overestimate of the program's maximum execution time by considering all possible execution paths in the program.

Figure 4.4 shows the relationship between the estimated WCET and the actual WCET. Because we do not know the actual WCET of a program, we estimate to find an upper bound, which we call the estimated WCET. Furthermore, we can also find a lower bound on the actual WCET by running the program against selected inputs. To illustrate the point, consider a program P with only one integer input variable v,

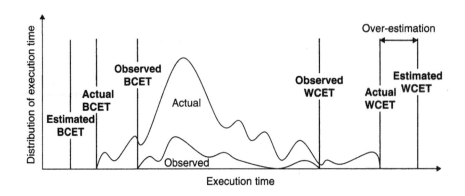

Figure 4.4

Estimated, actual, and observed WCET/BCET.

which takes in values in the range $1...100$. Let $T_P(i)$ be the execution time of program P with input $v = i$. Then, we have

$$Actual\ WCET = max_{1 \leq i \leq 100}\ T_P(i)$$

Now, suppose we run the program P against some "selected" inputs, say, $i \in \{1, 50, 100\}$, and measure the execution times. We call the maximum of these observed execution times the *observed WCET*. Thus, if we run the program against inputs $i \in \{1, 50, 100\}$, we have

$$Observed\ WCET = max_{i \in \{1,50,100\}}\ T_P(i)$$

Clearly, because the observed WCET is the maximum execution time among a subset of possible inputs, we always have

$$Observed\ WCET \leq Actual\ WCET$$

Our estimated WCET is obtained by analyzing the program code. The estimated WCET is not obtained by running the program against any input. To clarify the concept of "static analysis" to readers who may be new to the topic, I quote the following from the Wikipedia entry for static analysis.[1]

> Static code analysis is the analysis of computer software that is performed without actually executing programs built from that software (analysis performed on executing programs is known as dynamic analysis). In most cases the analysis is performed on some version of the source code and in the other cases some form of the object code. The term is usually applied to the analysis performed by an automated tool, with human analysis being called program understanding or program comprehension.

---

[1] See http://en.wikipedia.org/wiki/Static_code_analysis.

Our static analysis method for estimating execution time may be performed on the object code (actually the assembly code that can be obtained via disassembly of the object code). By construction, our static analysis will produce a safe overestimate — that is, it will produce an estimate that is greater than the actual WCET, but never lesser. Furthermore, we will try to design the static analysis in such a way that the estimate is also tight — that is, it is as close to the actual WCET as possible. In summary, we have

$$Observed\ WCET \leq Actual\ WCET \leq Estimated\ WCET$$

Figure 4.4 shows this relationship between the three quantities. In a similar fashion, we can say the following about BCET:

$$Observed\ BCET \geq Actual\ BCET \geq Estimated\ BCET$$

Usually, we will be more interested in the WCET. The motivation for the WCET estimate comes from various domains, but the most conventional usage has been in schedulability analysis of hard real-time systems. Let us look at the popular rate-monotonic schedulability analysis. It takes as input periodic task sets $\{T_1, \ldots, T_n\}$ where for each task T_i in the task set, the computation time, period, and deadline are given. For safe decisions to be made by schedulability analysis, the computation time taken as input should be an upper bound on the task's execution time. Thus, for each task (which is actually a program), the WCET estimate will be obtained offline (by static analysis) and provided to schedulability analysis as input.

4.2.1 WCET Calculation

So far, we have motivated the importance of estimating the WCET. However, we have not discussed how the estimation will proceed, and what are the main steps in the time estimation.

The obvious and common-sense fashion to proceed with the estimation is to break up the given program into fragments. The WCET estimate of each fragment is then composed to give the overall WCET estimate of the program. So, the questions we face are:

- How to systematically cut up a program into fragments,
- How to estimate WCET of the program fragments (it should consider all "contexts" in which the fragment may be executed), and
- How to compose the WCET estimates of the program fragments to get the program's WCET.

We postpone the discussion on finding the WCET of program fragments to a later stage. This will take us into the full details of time estimation, considering the underlying hardware microarchitecture on which the program is executing. Instead, at this point, we only concentrate on how to subdivide a program into pieces and how to compose the WCET estimates of the pieces (to get the WCET estimate of the whole program). Conventionally, this step is called the *WCET calculation*.

How do we cut up a program systematically into pieces? This truly depends on the program representation we use. Conventionally, (at least) two kinds of program representation have been considered/used in programming languages and compiler literature. These are control flow graphs and syntax tree. The syntax tree is a tree structure where each node of the tree corresponds to a programming language construct — the common constructs being if, while, assignment, procedure call, and so forth. Depending on the construct represented by a node u, it has $n_u \geq 0$ children. Thus, if a node u represents an if-then-else statement, it will have three children corresponding to the guard, the code for the "then" part and the code for the "else" part. Figure 4.5 shows the syntax tree for an example code fragment. We can see that it captures the hierarchical structure implicit in the compound control constructs of a program. If we use the syntax tree representation for WCET estimation, it is clear how the program will be cut up into pieces. Basically, the estimation method will try to assign WCET estimates to each node of the syntax tree (starting from the leaves). We elaborate how this is done through an approach called the *timing schema* [81].

For the syntax tree representation, the WCET estimation proceeds by a bottom-up pass of the syntax tree. Essentially, for every programming language construct

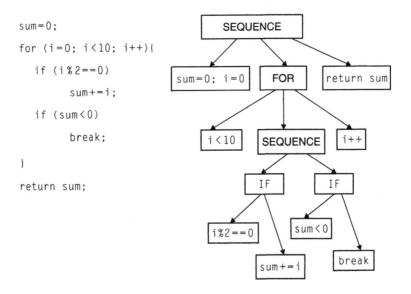

Figure 4.5

A program and its associated syntax tree.

(if, while, assignment etc), a rule is given which dictates how to estimate the WCET of a statement with that construct. Some of the prominent rules for sequential composition, if-statement and while-statement are as follows:

- Time(S1; S2)
  = Time(S1) + Time(S2)
- Time(if B {S1} else {S2})
  = Time(B) + max(Time(S1), Time(S2))
- Time(while B {S})
  = $(n + 1)*$Time(B) + $n*$Time(S)

where n is the loop bound (maximum number of loop iterations). The loop bound needs to be estimated by a separate analysis; it may also be given by the programmer. Clearly, the timing schema rules always try to consider the most time-consuming execution of a statement. In particular, for the if-then-else statement it considers the option that takes more time. For the while-loop, it considers maximum possible number of iterations of the loop.

In the preceding, we have not given the rules for estimating the WCET of an assignment or of a condition evaluation or of control transfer statements such as break/continue/procedure-call/procedure-return. We can do this by considering the schematic assembly code to which these statements are compiled. Indeed, instead of defining the timing schema rules at the source-code level (for if/while statements), we could define it for different instructions at the assembly-code level. The advantage of such an approach is that we can then take into account the effect of compiler optimizations. However, here, for simplicity of exposition, we define the timing schema rules at the source-code level. Also, for simplicity, let us assume for now that every assignment, condition, and control transfer statement is constant and takes one time unit. As we will see later, this assumption is not true owing to timing effects of microarchitectural features such as cache.

Using the rule for the while-loop, we can derive a rule corresponding to for-loop as follows:

- Time(for(Init; B; Inc){ S})
  = Time(Init) + $(n + 1)*$Time(B) + $n*$(Time(S) + Time(Inc))

In the foregoing, Init is the initialization condition of the for-loop, B is the guard of the for-loop, and Inc is the counterincrement code for the for-loop; S constitutes the body of the for-loop; and n is the loop bound (which is estimated separately). Similarly, we can slightly modify the rule for the if-then-else statement to get a timing schema rule for the if-then statement.

- Time(if B {S}) = Time(B) + Time(S)

Now, let us estimate the WCET of the program fragment given in Figure 4.5. For convenience we refer to the first if-statement `if (i % 2 == 0)...` as `if1` and the second if-statement `if (sum < 0)...` as `if2`. We also call the for-loop in the code-fragment as `for1`.

In the following, for simplicity, we assign one time unit to each conditional and assignment. Thus, the assumption is that the time taken to execute an assignment statement or a branch condition is 1 time unit. In reality, this is *not true*. The time taken to execute a statement depends on the context in which it is executed. As we will see in our subsequent discussions on microarchitectural modeling (Section 4.2.2), the time taken to execute an instruction depends on the microarchitectural state in which the instruction is executed.

- Time(`if1`)
  = Time(`if (sum < 0) break`)
  = Time(`sum < 0`) + Time(`break`)
  = 1 + 1 = 2 time units.
- Time(`if2`)
  = Time(`if (i % 2 == 0) sum+=i`)
  = Time(`i % 2 == 0`) + Time(`sum+=i`)
  = 1 + 1 = 2 time units.
- Time(`for1`)
  = Time(`i=0`) + 11*Time(`i < 10`) + 10*(Time(`if1;if2`) + Time(`i++`))
  = 1 + 11*1 + 10(Time(`if1`) + Time(`if2`) + 1)
  = 1 + 11 + 10 * (2 + 2 + 1)
  = 12 + 10 * 5 = 12 + 50 = 62 time units.
- Time(Program of Figure 4.5)
  = Time(`sum=0`) + Time(`for1`) + Time(`return sum`)
  = 1 + 62 + 1 = 64 time units.

Now, let us understand what contributes to the foregoing WCET estimate. The number of loop iterations in Figure 4.5 is 10, and this is used by the WCET estimation. In each iteration, it considers the most time-consuming execution of both the if-statements. However, the first if-statement's then-part is executed only when the variable `i` is even (refer to Figure 4.5). When `i` ranges from 0 to 10, we know that `i` cannot be even in every loop iteration. Similarly, since the variable `sum` starts with a value 0 and always increases, we know that `sum < 0` is never possible. In other words, the then-part of the second if-statement (refer to Figure 4.5) is never executed. However, the timing schema approach does not take into account such information, leading to overestimation of WCET. At this point, we introduce the notion of an *infeasible path*.

Definition 11 (Infeasible Program Path) *An infeasible path in a program P is a sequence of program statements that does not appear in the execution trace corresponding to any input of P.*

Revisiting Figure 4.5, we see that the statement `break` itself constitutes an infeasible path because the condition `sum < 0` guarding this statement is never true. The general problem of detecting all infeasible paths in a program is intractable. As far as WCET estimation is concerned, we need to separate two issues:

- Automated detection of infeasible paths, and
- Even if the infeasible path information is available, taking it into account during the WCET estimation.

Because detecting all infeasible paths is undecidable, any automated infeasible path detection method is sound but incomplete. In other words, any path detected as infeasible is indeed infeasible, but not all infeasible paths may be detected by an automated method. The second issue involves integrating infeasible path information with our WCET calculation procedure. This is difficult to do in the timing schema approach, because this approach assigns the costs to a program fragment without considering the control flow with which the program fragment was arrived at. Let us demonstrate this with examples. As a trivial example, we again refer to Figure 4.5. We said earlier that the statement `break` itself constitutes an infeasible path because it is never executed. How will we take this information into account in our timing schema approach? Well, this appears to be easy! We can simply assign Time(`break`) as zero — that is, the time to execute the `break` statement is zero. Let us now consider a slightly more difficult (and more realistic) situation. Suppose we have an infeasible path

```
stmt1; ... ; stmt2
```

where `stmt1`, `stmt2` are statements. Thus, `stmt1`, `stmt2` may appear in execution traces, but they cannot appear together. Because the timing schema approach assigns the costs of `stmt1` and `stmt2` separately, it cannot consider this information in the WCET calculation. We will now see how this problem can be alleviated in WCET calculation methods based on a different program representation — the control-flow graph.

Apart from the syntax tree, another popular program representation that is most commonly used in compilers is the *control-flow graph* (abbreviated CFG). The control-flow graph is a directed graph whose nodes denote *basic blocks* and edges denote control transfer across basic blocks. Now, what is a basic block?

Definition 12 (Basic Block) *A basic block is a maximal code fragment executed without branching of control flow.*

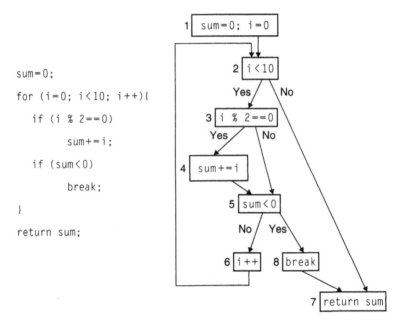

```
sum=0;

for (i=0; i<10; i++){

    if (i % 2==0)

        sum+=i;

    if (sum<0)

        break;

}

return sum;
```

Figure 4.6

A program and its associated control-flow graph (CFG).

Figure 4.6 shows an example program and its associated control-flow graph. We have chosen the same program as the one used to explain syntax trees in Figure 4.5. For convenience, the basic blocks are numbered in Figure 4.6. For each basic block ending in a branch, there are two outgoing edges; we mark these two outgoing edges with "yes"/"no." When a branch is true, the outgoing edge marked with "yes" is taken. Similarly, when a branch is false, the outgoing edge marked with "no" is taken.

Superficially, both the program representations seem to capture the program structure, but there are key differences. Suppose the break statement in the example program of Figures 4.5 and 4.6 is replaced with a vacuous statement sum = sum. Note that this change does not impact the hierarchical structure of the program in any way. Thus, the syntax tree structure is not affected at all; only the node where break appeared now contains the statement sum = sum. However, since the control flow potentially changes (i.e., if sum < 0 is ever encountered we no longer break out of the loop), the edges of the control-flow graph must change. The changed control-flow graph appears in Figure 4.7. It is worth noting that this simple change in the program actually did not change the semantics of the program, because sum < 0 is never true during the execution of the program. However, still we had to change the control-flow graph, because it captures all *possible* execution paths, some of which may never be encountered for any input.

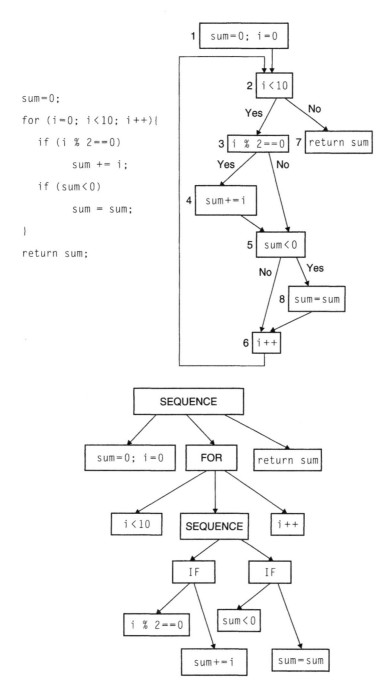

Figure 4.7

Change in the control-flow graph and syntax tree corresponding to a small change in the program (compare the program and control-flow graph with Figure 4.6).

If the control-flow graph (CFG) is used as program representation, WCET estimation will involve finding the WCET of the basic blocks — the nodes of the CFG.
These estimates will then be composed according to the edges in the CFG to calculate
the WCET estimate of the whole program. Indeed, this is how most state-of-the-art
WCET tools proceed. To compose the WCET estimates of the basic blocks, these
tools use a linear equation-solving method called integer linear programming. We
discuss this method through an example later in this section.

We now show WCET calculation on the control-flow graph representation. As
we will see, this approach allows us to effectively integrate many kinds of infeasible
path information. Recall that a control-flow graph is a directed graph whose nodes are
basic blocks and whose edges denote control transfer. The basic blocks are maximal
fragments of code executed without encountering branching of control flow. To show
the details of WCET calculation, we work out the example of Figure 4.6. This is the
same example program as Figure 4.5.

The basic idea is to reduce WCET estimation to an optimization. Clearly, in
estimating WCET we are trying to find a path through the program that will maximize
the execution time. The idea here is to maximize the execution time without having
to enumerate the execution traces of the program. For this reason, the approach is
also known as implicit path enumeration (IPET). Moreover, since the technology
employed is linear constraint solving over integer domain variables, it is also called
as integer linear programming or ILP.

Now, how does the ILP approach proceed? It first defines certain *variables* corresponding to the execution counts of the nodes and edges in the control-flow graph.
Let us refer to our example in Figure 4.6. For convenience, we have numbered the
nodes of the control-flow graph 1...8. For every node i in the control flow graph, we
introduce a variable N_i denoting the number of times node i is executed. Once again,
we assume for simplicity that every assignment/condition/control transfer takes 1
time unit. With this simplifying assumption, the time for one execution of a node
can be obtained as follows:

- c_1 = time to execute node 1 once
  = time to execute (`sum = 0; i = 0`) = 2 time units.
- c_2 = time to execute node 2 once
  = time to evaluate (`i < 10`) = 1 time unit.
- c_3 = time to execute node 3 once
  = time to evaluate (`i % 2 == 0`) = 1 time unit.
- c_4 = time to evaluate node 4 once
  = time to execute (`sum += i`) = 1 time unit.
- c_5 = time to execute node 5 once
  = time to evaluate (`sum < 0`) = 1 time unit.

- c_6 = time to execute node 6 once
  = time to execute (`i++`) = 1 time unit.
- c_7 = time to execute node 7 once
  = time to execute (`return sum`) = 1 time unit.
- c_8 = time to execute node 8 once
  = time to execute (`break`) = 1 time unit.

Clearly, in deriving the foregoing values, we have used the simplifying assumption that each assignment/condition/control transfer takes one time unit. As mentioned earlier, this assumption is not true. So, in general we need to have accurate estimation methods that (a) work on the assembly code, and (b) consider the timing effects of the underlying microarchitectural features (such as cache). However, the key point is that these accurate estimation methods will work on a basic block to produce the values of c_i for each basic block i. The constants c_i are pieced together by the integer linear programming method described here.

Given the constants c_i (the time to execute basic block i once) and variables N_i (number of executions of basic block i) we can define the execution time of a program as

$$Time = \sum_i c_i * N_i$$

For our example program of Figure 4.6, taking the simplifying assumption that each assignment/condition/control-transfer takes one time unit, we have

$$Time = c_1 * N_1 + c_2 * N_2 + c_3 * N_3 + c_4 * N_4$$
$$+ c_5 * N_5 + c_6 * N_6 + c_7 * N_7 + c_8 * N_8$$
$$= 2N_1 + N_2 + N_3 + N_4 + N_5 + N_6 + N_7 + N_8$$

In other words, irrespective of whether we employ the simplifying assumption of each assignment/condition/control transfer taking one time unit, the program's execution time is a linear function of the N_i variables. To find the WCET estimate we need to maximize this function, subject to constraints on the N_i variables. If the constraints on the N_i variables are also linear equality/inequality constraints, maximization of the objective function amounts to a linear programming problem. Furthermore, since the N_i variables denote execution count of a basic block, they are integer variables (and not real numbers). Hence our problem is one of integer linear programming. For solving ILP problems, we can use linear programming solvers (such as the freely available lp_solve) as long as the solution produced gives integer values to all the variables. Alternatively, one can use more efficient commercial solvers such as the CPLEX ILP solver [19].

How do we define the constraints on the execution count variables N_i? We can say the execution count of a basic block is equal to the number of times control flows into the block — the inflow. Similarly, the execution count of a basic block is equal to the number of times control flows out of the block — the outflow. Let us now define variables corresponding to the edges of the control-flow graph as well. For every edge $i \rightarrow j$ in the control-flow graph, we introduce a variable $E_{i \rightarrow j}$ denoting the number of times control flows from node i to node j (i.e., the number of times the edge $i \rightarrow j$ is executed). Then, we can define the following constraint for the execution count of basic block i:

$$\sum_{j \ s.t. \ j \rightarrow i} E_{j \rightarrow i} = N_i = \sum_{j \ s.t. \ i \rightarrow j} E_{i \rightarrow j}$$

The inflow into basic block i is the sum of the execution counts of the edges coming into basic block i. Similarly, the outflow from basic block i is the sum of the execution counts of the edges going out of basic block i. For our example program of Figure 4.6, this produces an ILP problem of the following form:

Maximize	$2N_1 + N_2 + N_3 + N_4 + N_5 + N_6 + N_7 + N_8$
	$1 = N_1 = E_{1 \rightarrow 2}$
	$E_{6 \rightarrow 2} + E_{1 \rightarrow 2} = N_2 = E_{2 \rightarrow 3} + E_{2 \rightarrow 7}$
	$E_{2 \rightarrow 3} = N_3 = E_{3 \rightarrow 4} + E_{3 \rightarrow 5}$
	$E_{3 \rightarrow 4} = N_4 = E_{4 \rightarrow 5}$
Flow constraints	$E_{3 \rightarrow 5} + E_{4 \rightarrow 5} = N_5 = E_{5 \rightarrow 6} + E_{5 \rightarrow 8}$
	$E_{5 \rightarrow 6} = N_6 = E_{6 \rightarrow 2}$
	$E_{8 \rightarrow 7} + E_{2 \rightarrow 7} = N_7 = 1$
	$E_{5 \rightarrow 8} = N_8 = E_{8 \rightarrow 7}$

The preceding constraints bound N_1 and N_7 (execution counts of basic blocks 1 and 7) but do not sufficiently bound the execution counts of the other basic blocks. Trying to maximize our objective function will drive it to infinity. This is because a crucial constraint is missing — the loop bound(s). In this case, because Figure 4.6 contains only one loop, there is one loop-bound constraint. We have

$$E_{6 \rightarrow 2} \leq 10$$

This loop-bound constraint can be estimated separately or user-provided. For our example program, deriving this loop-bound information is trivial; most automated analyses will suffice. Of course, in general the loop-bound inferencing problem is also undecidable. So, any WCET estimation tool contains a feature where the user is asked to input certain loop bounds. Even if the user has to provide all the loop bounds, the tool still has the arduous task of mapping these loop-bound constraints (at the source-code level) to the assembly-code level — because the WCET estimation is often performed on the control-flow graph at the assembly code level.

Using the loop-bound information, the constraint system for our example program gets simplified to the following:

Maximize	$Time = 2N_1 + N_2 + N_3 + N_4 + N_5 + N_6 + N_7 + N_8$
	$E_{6 \to 2} \leq 10$
	$1 = N_1 = E_{1 \to 2}$
	$E_{6 \to 2} + E_{1 \to 2} = N_2 = N_3 + E_{2 \to 7} \leq 11$
	$N_3 = N_5 \leq 10$
Constraints	
	$N_4 \leq 10 \; N_5 = N_6 + E_{5 \to 8} \leq 11$
	$N_6 = E_{6 \to 2} \leq 10$
	$N_8 + E_{2 \to 7} = N_7 = 1$
	$N_8 \leq 1$

A possible solution to the above system of equalities and inequalities is

- $N_1 = 1, N_2 = 11, N_3 = 10, N_4 = 10, N_5 = 10, N_6 = 10, N_7 = 1, N_8 = 0$
- $Time = 2N_1 + N_2 + N_3 + N_4 + N_5 + N_6 + N_7 + N_8 = 54$ time units

Clearly, we can see that the ILP-based approach leads to a tighter estimate. One reason here is that the syntax tree data structure does not properly capture control transfer because of the break statement. Thus, the timing schema considers the situation where the break statement is executed at every loop iteration — which is impossible, because it causes the control to flow out of the loop.

Exercise: The reader is encouraged to work out the WCET estimate of the program in Figure 4.7 using both the approaches — timing schema and ILP. In this case, the two estimates should be the same.

Infeasible Path Exploitation

The timing schema and the ILP approach for WCET calculation differ primarily in their ability to exploit infeasible path information. We now illustrate this with an example. Again, consider the program in Figures 4.5 and 4.6. Clearly, the guard (i % 2 == 0) of the first if-statement cannot be true in consecutive loop iterations. Because the loop bound is 10, this means that the then-part of the if-statement cannot be executed more than $10/2 = 5$ times. In the ILP approach this can easily be expressed as the linear constraint

$$N_4 \leq 5$$

leading to a tighter WCET estimate. However, in the timing schema approach we simply estimate the maximum execution time of a fragment of code without considering the control-flow context. So, it is not straightforward to integrate this information.

Indeed, the ILP approach's ability to integrate infeasible path information has made it the chosen method for WCET calculation in all state-of-the-art tools. As an example, consider the control-flow graph schematic denoting two if-then-else statements within a loop shown in Figure 4.8. In this program fragment, if $i > 0$ evaluates to true, the branch $j < 0$ cannot evaluate to true. Hence, the sequence of basic blocks $2 \rightarrow 3 \rightarrow 5 \rightarrow 6$ denotes an infeasible program path. This information can be encoded in the ILP formulation of the WCET analysis problem in several different ways. Again, recall that the ILP variable N_i denotes the execution count of basic block i and the ILP variable $E_{i \rightarrow j}$ denotes the execution count of the edge $i \rightarrow j$ between basic blocks i and j. So, we may encode the information that blocks 3 and 6 are never executed in the same loop iteration as

$$N_3 + N_6 \leq LB$$

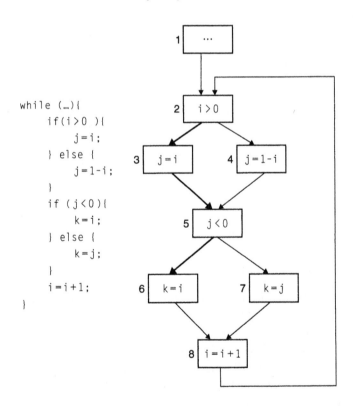

Figure 4.8

A control-flow graph fragment for illustrating infeasible paths; an infeasible path is marked in bold.

where LB is a constant denoting the loop bound (for the loop in Figure 4.8). We can also encode this infeasible path information in a different way. Note that $2 \rightarrow 3 \rightarrow 5 \rightarrow 6$ is an infeasible path because whenever the branch in block 2 evaluates along the outgoing edge $2 \rightarrow 3$, the branch in block 5 evaluates along the outgoing edge $5 \rightarrow 7$. Therefore we have

$$E_{2 \rightarrow 3} = E_{5 \rightarrow 7}$$

The interested reader is referred to [25, 69] for a more detailed treatment of infeasible path information exploitation in WCET analysis.

Infeasible Path Detection

Integrating an infeasible path pattern into the WCET estimation is possible only if the infeasible path patterns are known. As mentioned earlier, the general problem of infeasible path detection is undecidable. However, we can develop automated methods for infeasible path detection that are sound (any path found as infeasible is indeed so) and incomplete (not all infeasible paths may be found). There exist several infeasible path detection approaches based on data flow analysis, constraint solving, or heuristic methods. [40, 83] should give the interested reader some idea about state-of-the-art techniques.

4.2.2 Modeling of Microarchitecture

The overall WCET of a program is obtained by maximizing the function

$$Time = \sum_i c_i * N_i$$

where i ranges over the basic blocks in the program's control-flow graph. In the foregoing function, c_i is a constant denoting the maximum execution time of basic block i, and N_i is a variable denoting the number of times basic block i is executed. We have already seen how equalities and inequalities on N_i can determine the maximum value of $Time$. However, this assumes the availability of the constants c_i — the maximum execution time of a basic block. We now discuss how to tightly estimate c_i.

Can the constant c_i be found by executing/simulating basic block i in isolation? Unfortunately, the answer is no. Executing a fragment of code in isolation does not identify the "context" in that it is executed. Let us now see what sort of "context" we need to take into account. A basic block is a straight-line fragment of code that gets compiled to a sequence of instructions (with at most one branch instruction). If the execution time of each instruction is fixed, the execution time of a basic block will be fixed.

Herein lies the problem — the execution time of an instruction depends on the microarchitectural state in which the instruction is executed. Of course, this depends on the processor on which the program is being executed. If the program is executed on a simple microcontroller, the execution time of any given instruction can be constant (i.e., independent of the microcontroller state). However, most processors employ popular performance-enhancing features such as pipeline, cache, and branch prediction. Even in the embedded domain, it is common for processors to have at least cache and in-order pipelined execution.

In the presence of any meaningful processor microarchitecture, the execution time of an instruction is no longer constant. Let us consider the impact of cache on the execution time of an instruction. A cache is a small on-chip memory that remembers recently accessed code and/or data, over and above the main memory. Often, separate caches are maintained for code and data. Any instruction/data is first searched in the corresponding cache, and only then is the main memory accessed. The main purpose of having a cache is, of course, faster program execution. Most processors at least have an instruction cache, because it is very common for programs to execute the same instructions repeatedly; consider the statements in a program loop that are iterated several times.

Now, imagine an ADD instruction that is executed twice — the first time it misses in the cache, and the second time it hits in the cache (because it is already there). We consider in-order execution: That is, the instructions in a program are fetched, decoded, executed, and committed according to their order in the program. Note that whether the execution is pipelined or not (i.e., whether there can be any overlap in the execution time of two instructions) is irrelevant here — we only show the execution times of two instances of the same instruction. Assuming a 10-cycle cache miss penalty (which is very modest; typically the time to go to main memory is much higher), following is the breakup for the two executions.

	Execution with miss	Execution with hit
Fetch	1+10 cycles	1 cycle
Decode	1 cycle	1 cycle
Execute (in ALU)	1 cycle	1 cycle
Commit	1 cycle	1 cycle
Total	14 cycles	4 cycles

The table shows the importance of modeling the timing effects of cache for WCET estimation. Indeed, modeling the timing effects of processor microarchitecture is crucial for tightly estimating the WCET of basic blocks. Because the basic-block WCETs are fed as constants to an ILP problem solving the WCET of a program, modeling the timing effects of microarchitecture becomes very important for tightly estimating a program's WCET. In this book, we primarily discuss the modeling of cache. The main reason for covering cache modeling is twofold: (a) It gives us a sense of the issues in microarchitectural modeling, and (b) the issues in cache modeling are relatively simpler compared to modeling of other features such as out-of-order pipelines. The interested reader is referred to the survey article [61] for a more detailed treatment on microarchitecture modeling, such as modeling of pipelines and branch prediction.

Cache Modeling via Integer Linear Programming

We assume here a direct-mapped instruction cache. What this means is that the cache is divided into a finite number of cache lines, such as 64 cache lines with 64 bytes each for a 4KB cache. Any given memory address is thus mapped to exactly one line in the cache. The modeling discussed here is based on the work of [55].

A basic block B_i is partitioned into n_i memory blocks, denoted as

$$B_{i.1}, B_{i.2}, \ldots, B_{i.n_i}$$

A memory block is a sequence of instructions in a basic block that belongs to the same instruction cache line. In Figure 4.9, we show the control-flow graph schematic for an if-then-else statement within a loop. The memory blocks within each basic block are also shown. All basic blocks in our Figure 4.9 contain only one memory block, excepting basic block 4, which has two memory blocks. In principle, it is also

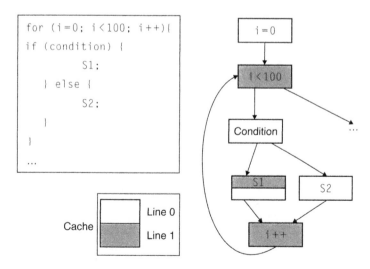

Figure 4.9

Control-flow graph fragment, and the *I*-blocks showing which (parts) of which basic block correspond to which cache line. A simple direct-mapped cache with only two cache lines is assumed.

possible for memory blocks to span across basic blocks — but, for simplicity, we do not show this situation in our example.

Let $CM_{i,j}$ be the total cache misses for memory block $B_{i,j}$ and cmp be the constant denoting the cache-miss penalty. Then, the total execution time is

$$Time = \sum_i (c_i \times N_i + \sum_{j=1}^{n_i} cmp \times CM_{i,j}) \qquad (4.1)$$

The index i ranges over the basic blocks in the program's control-flow graph. As before, the constant c_i is the WCET of basic block i, and the variable N_i denotes the execution count of basic block i. Note how the ILP objective function has been modified with the additional $CM_{i,j}$ variables. We now need to find constraints on these new variables.

For each cache line c, we construct a *cache-conflict graph (CCG)* G_c. The nodes of G_c are the l-blocks mapped to c. An l-block is a line block corresponding to a chunk of memory mapped to a cache line. An edge $B_{i,j} \rightarrow B_{u,v}$ exists in G_c if and only if there exists a path in the CFG s.t. control flows from $B_{i,j}$ to $B_{u,v}$ without going through any other l-block mapped to c. In other words, there is an edge between

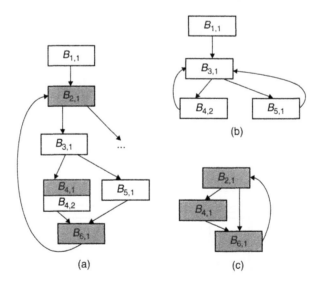

Figure 4.10

(a) Control-flow graph fragment from Figure 4.9. (b) Cache-conflict graph for cache line 0, assuming direct-mapped cache with only two cache lines. (c) Cache-conflict graph for cache line 1. The memory blocks for cache line 0 are white and those for cache line 1 are shaded.

l-blocks $B_{i,j}$ to $B_{u,v}$ if $B_{i,j}$ can be present in the cache when control reaches $B_{u,v}$. The cache-conflict graphs for the two cache lines in Figure 4.9 are shown in Figure 4.10.

Let $R_{i,j \rightarrow u,v}$ be the execution count of the edge between memory blocks $B_{i,j}$ and $B_{u,v}$ in a cache-conflict graph. Now, the execution count of memory block $B_{i,j}$ equals the execution count of basic block B_i. Also, at each node of the CCG, the inflow equals the outflow and both equal the execution count of the node. Therefore,

$$N_i = \sum_{u,v} R_{i,j \rightarrow u,v} = \sum_{u,v} R_{u,v \rightarrow i,j} \tag{4.2}$$

The cache-miss count $CM_{i,j}$ equals the inflow from *conflicting* memory blocks in the CCG (whether two memory blocks are conflicting or nonconflicting is statically determined by portions of their instruction addresses, which are used as tags in cache lines). Thus, we have

$$CM_{i,j} = \sum_{\substack{u,v \\ B_{u,v} \ conflicts \ B_{i,j}}} R_{u,v \rightarrow i,j} \tag{4.3}$$

This concludes the overall discussion on cache modeling via ILP. Basically, we have modified the ILP problem for program-level WCET analysis to integrate the cache modeling. The overall technology for WCET estimation is still ILP solving. The objective function is now

$$Time = \sum_i (c_i \times N_i + \sum_{j=1}^{n_i} cmp \times CM_{i,j})$$

The variables N_i denote the execution counts of basic blocks. The constraints on these variables are as before, derived from the flow equations in the control-flow graph, the loop bounds, and the user-provided additional constraints (typically capturing infeasible path information). The new variables $CM_{i,j}$ denote the cache-miss counts of individual memory blocks lying inside basic blocks. The constraints on these variables are obtained via the cache-conflict graph construction elaborated in the preceding. All of these constraints together form a jumbo ILP problem that then needs to be submitted to an ILP solver (such as CPLEX) for WCET estimation. We should, however, mention that scalability is a concern with ILP solvers; hence, microarchitectural modeling via ILP suffers from such scalability issues as well. In the following, we discuss an alternative way of modeling cache's timing behavior via abstract interpretation.

Cache Modeling via Abstract Interpretation

In the ILP-based approach, we modified the objective function from

$$Time = \sum_i (c_i \times N_i)$$

to

$$Time = \sum_i (c_i \times N_i + \sum_{j=1}^{n_i} cmp \times CM_{i,j})$$

when we integrated cache modeling. Consequently, we also defined constraints to bound the new $CM_{i,j}$ variables. We now discuss an approach where integration of cache modeling does not require any new ILP variables. Thus, by performing cache modeling over and above the program flow analysis, we do not increase the size of the ILP problem. Indeed, we solve the same ILP problem as the one resulting only from program flow analysis — our objective function will be

$$Time = \sum_i (c_i \times N_i)$$

However, the WCET estimation of the basic blocks, that is, the estimation of the constants c_i, is done differently.

Recall that a basic block is divided into memory blocks, where a memory block is a sequence of instructions that fit into the same cache line of the instruction cache. Given any memory block m, suppose we try to find all the possible cache contents with which m will be reached during program execution. If in all these possible cache contents, block m is already in the cache, the access of m is guaranteed to be a *cache hit*. The abstract interpretation approach finds such guaranteed cache hits and computes the WCET estimates of the basic blocks tightly (instead of pessimistically considering all possible cache accesses as misses).

Now, how do we analyze the program to find the guaranteed cache hits? This requires us to find all the possible cache contents with which a program point can be reached. However, clearly we do not want an exhaustive program execution on different inputs to find what are the cache contents with which a given program point is reached. Herein lies the trick — abstract interpretation can *approximate* the set of cache states with which a particular program point is reached. So, if the set of cache states with which a program point loc in program P is reached is given as $S_P(loc)$, abstract interpretation will try to compute the set

$$\bigcap_{s \in S_P(loc)} s$$

If, indeed, one could compute this set, we could say that the intersection contains all those memory blocks that *must* be in the cache whenever program point loc is reached. The trouble, of course, is that we do not precisely know the set $S_P(loc)$ and we cannot compute the aforementioned intersection. For this purpose, abstract interpretation will compute

$$\bigcap_{s \in S'_P(loc)} s$$

where $S'_P(loc) \supseteq S_P(loc)$ is an overapproximation of the actual set of cache states with which program point *loc* is reached. If by examining the intersection of states in $S'_P(loc)$ our analysis can infer that a certain memory block in program point *loc* will be a cache hit, clearly the same inference would have been obtained by examining $S_P(loc)$. This is the main power of abstract interpretation — by approximating important metrics (in this case cache states) at program points, it allows for sound inferencing of program behavior.

We now describe the abstract interpretation (AI)-based cache modeling more formally. We start with a general discussion on abstract interpretation and then clarify the technical details of the cache modeling.

Abstract interpretation [15] is a theory for formally constructing conservative approximations of the semantics of a programming language. A concrete application of abstract interpretation is in static program analysis, where a program's computations are performed using *abstract values* in place of concrete values. Abstract interpretation is used in WCET analysis to approximate the "collecting semantics" at a program point. The collecting semantics gives the set of all program states (cache, pipeline etc.) for a given program point. In general, the collecting semantics is not computable. In abstract interpretation, the goal is to produce an abstract semantics that is less precise but effectively computable. The computation of the abstract semantics involves solving a system of recursive equations/constraints. Given a program, we can associate a variable $[\![p]\!]$ to denote the abstract semantics at program point p. Clearly, $[\![p]\!]$ will depend on the abstract semantics of program points preceding p. Because programs have loops, this will lead to a system of recursive constraints. The system of recursive constraints can be iteratively solved via fixed-point computation. Termination of the fixed-point computation is guaranteed only if (a) the iterative estimates of $[\![p]\!]$ grow monotonically, and (b) the domain of abstract values (which is used to define the abstract program semantics) is free from infinite ascending chains.[2] The latter is ensured if the semantic functions in the abstract domain, which show the effect of the programming language constructs in the abstract domain and are used to iteratively estimate $[\![p]\!]$, are monotonic.

Once the fixed-point computation terminates, for every program point p, we obtain a stable estimate for $[\![p]\!]$ — the abstract semantics at p. This is an overapproximation of all the concrete states with which p could be reached in program executions. Thus, for cache behavior modeling, $[\![p]\!]$ could be used to denote an overapproximation of the set of concrete cache states with which program point p could be reached in program executions. This abstract semantics is then used to conservatively derive the WCET bounds for the individual basic blocks. Finally, the WCET estimates of basic blocks are combined with ILP-based path analysis to estimate the WCET of the entire program.

---

[2] Hence the estimates cannot grow forever.

To illustrate AI-based cache modeling, we will assume a fully associative cache with a set of cache lines $L = \{l_1, \ldots, l_n\}$ and least recently used (LRU) replacement policy. Because the cache is fully associative, a memory block, once brought into the cache, can be placed anywhere within it. Also, the LRU replacement policy implies that when a memory block needs to be evicted from the cache (because a new memory block needs to be brought in), the least recently used block is evicted from the cache. Let $\{s_1, \ldots, s_m\}$ denote the set of memory blocks. The absence of any memory block in a cache line is indicated by a new element I; thus $S = \{s_1, \ldots, s_m\} \cup \{I\}$.

Let us first define the concrete semantics.

Definition 13 *A* **concrete cache state** *is a function* $c : L \to S$.

If $c(l_x) = s$ for a concrete cache state c, then there are $x - 1$ elements $(c(l_1), \ldots, c(l_{x-1}))$ that are more recently used than s. In other words, x is the relative age of s. C_c denotes the set of all concrete cache states.

Definition 14 *A* **cache update function** $\mathcal{U} : C_c \times S \to C_c$ *describes the new cache state for a given cache state and a referenced memory block.*

Let $s = c(l_x)$ be the referenced memory block. The cache update function shifts the memory blocks $c(l_1), \ldots, c(l_{x-1})$, which have been more recently used than s, by one position to the next cache line. If s was not in the cache, then all the memory blocks are shifted by one position and the least recently used memory block is evicted from the cache state (if the cache was full). Finally, the update function puts the referenced memory block s in the first position l_1.

The abstract semantics defines the abstract cache states, the abstract cache update function, and the join function.

Definition 15 *An* **abstract cache state** $\hat{c} : L \to 2^S$ *maps cache lines to sets of memory blocks.*

Let $\hat{C}$ denote the set of all abstract cache states. The abstract cache update function $\hat{U} : \hat{C} \times S \mapsto \hat{C}$ is a straightforward extension of the function U (which works on concrete cache states) to abstract cache states.

Furthermore, at control-flow merge points, join functions are used to combine the abstract cache states. That is, join functions approximate the collecting semantics depending on program analysis.

Definition 16 *A* **join function** $\hat{\mathcal{J}} : \hat{C} \times \hat{C} \mapsto \hat{C}$ *combines two abstract cache states.*

Because L is finite and S is finite, clearly the domain of abstract cache states is finite, and hence free from any infinite ascending chains. Furthermore, the update and join functions $\hat{U}, \hat{J}$ are monotonic. This ensures termination of a fixed-point computation based analysis over the aforementioned abstract domain. We now mention two such analysis methods.

The program analysis mainly consists of *must analysis* and *may analysis*. The must analysis determines the set of memory blocks that are always in the cache at a given program point. The may analysis determines the memory blocks that may be in the cache at a given program point. The may analysis can be used to determine the memory blocks that are guaranteed to be absent in the cache at a given program point.

The must analysis uses abstract cache states with *upper bounds* on the ages of the memory blocks in the concrete cache states. That is, if $s \in \hat{c}(l_x)$, then s is guaranteed to be in the cache for at least the next $n - x$ memory references (n is the number of cache lines). Therefore, the join function of two abstract cache states $\hat{c}_1, \hat{c}_2$ puts a memory block s in the new cache state if and only if s is present in both $\hat{c}_1$ and $\hat{c}_2$. The new age of s is the maximal of its ages in $\hat{c}_1, \hat{c}_2$. Figure 4.11 shows an example of the join function for must and may analysis.

The may analysis uses abstract cache states with *lower bounds* on the ages of the memory blocks. Therefore, the join function of two abstract cache states $\hat{c}_1, \hat{c}_2$ puts a memory block s in the new cache state if s is present in either $\hat{c}_1$ or $\hat{c}_2$ or both. The new age of s is the minimal of its ages in $\hat{c}_1, \hat{c}_2$.

At a program point, if a memory block s is present in the abstract cache state after must analysis, then a memory reference to s will result in cache hit (*always hit*). Similarly, if a memory block s is absent in the abstract cache state after may analysis, then a memory reference to s will result in cache miss (*always miss*).

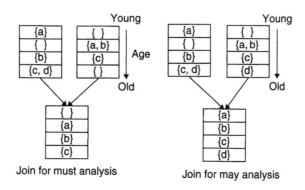

Join for must analysis   Join for may analysis

Figure 4.11

Join for must and may analysis.

The other memory references cannot be classified as hit or miss. To improve the accuracy, a further "persistence analysis" can identify memory blocks for which the first reference may result in either hit or miss; but the remaining references will be hits. These categorization of memory references is used to define the WCET for each basic block as a constant. Once the WCETs of basic blocks are found, these estimates are combined to get the WCET of the whole program using integer linear programming as before.

A thorough discussion on abstract interpretation–based WCET analysis can be found in [96]. Details about the abstract interpretation–based cache modeling can be obtained from [90].

Remarks about the Two Approaches

In studying the two approaches toward microarchitecture modeling, we see that the ILP-only approach combines path analysis and microarchitecture modeling into one single ILP problem. On the other hand, in the abstract interpretation–based approach, only the path analysis is done by integer linear programming; the microarchitecture modeling is done separately (via abstract interpretation) for estimating the WCET of basic blocks. It is worthwhile to note that most state-of-the-art WCET analysis tools current employ such a *separated* approach, where only the program path analysis is accomplished by integer linear programming.

WCET Analysis Tools

Finally, we wish to inform the readers of the availability of several mature WCET analysis tools, such as aiT [30] and Chronos [53]. A summary of existing WCET analysis tools is presented in the survey article [61].

4.3 INTERFERENCE WITHIN A PROCESSING ELEMENT

Worst-case execution time (WCET) analysis is useful for estimating the execution time of a program fragment, assuming uninterrupted execution. In reality, programs do not execute uninterrupted. During the execution of embedded software, we have to consider at least two kinds of interference:

- Interference from peripheral devices, typically via interrupts, and
- Interference from other programs executing on the same processor.

Clearly, in a multiprocessor system-on-chip, there can be interference from programs executing on other processing elements. This is because the processing elements are connected via a bus on which all interprocessor communication takes place. We discuss such communication time analysis in the next section under "system-level performance analysis."

4.3.1 Interrupts from Environment

It is common for embedded software (particularly driver software) to communicate with peripheral devices. There are two alternative strategies that the software can use to manage such communication. The software can busy-wait in a loop and poll for signals from the peripheral device. This is an extremely time-expensive method of managing peripheral communication. Alternatively, the peripherals can asynchronously generate "interrupts" that are serviced by special-purpose code called interrupt handlers. An interrupt handler may be thought of as a procedure that is invoked when an interrupt arrives. Thus, there is no explicit procedure call to these handlers, but they are invoked by the system on the arrival of the interrupt. It is important to note that interrupts do not get serviced immediately on arrival. The processor needs to save important state information before transferring control to the appropriate interrupt handler. One of the issues in performance validation of embedded software is whether all interrupts are handled within a "deadline."

For example, consider an automotive controller software where the pressing of the brake pedal by the driver generates an interrupt. To determine whether the braking action indeed takes effect within a given time t, we need to estimate

- The time between the arrival of the interrupt and the servicing via the interrupt handler, and
- The WCET of the interrupt handler that actually does the necessary computations for the braking action to take effect.

The difficulty in analyzing the time interference owing to interrupts is that interrupts can arrive asynchronously at any program point. Consequently, from any control location in the program, one would have to assume a potential nonlocal transfer of control to the interrupt handler(s). This makes it difficult to estimate the maximum time between the arrival of the interrupt and the servicing of the interrupt (because we have to consider all possible locations in which a program can be when an interrupt arrives).

Usually, interrupts are controlled by an interrupt mask register (IMR). The IMR contains a bitvector where each bit states whether a particular interrupt is currently enabled/disabled. A disabled interrupt is, of course, not serviced. To find the maximum time to service an interrupt, one can construct an extended control-flow graph, where apart from the control location we also model the contents of the IMR. In this extended graph, given a control location l and an interrupt i that is enabled as per the current contents of the IMR, we can compute the weighted longest path from control location l to the start of the interrupt handler for interrupt i. This will give the maximum time to service an interrupt i, if one arrives while the program is at control location l. The same task has to be repeated for all other control locations. Thus, the maximum time to service a given interrupt can be formulated as a multisource-weighted longest-path calculation problem.

Brylow and Palsberg [11] report methods for finding the maximum time to service an interrupt via modeling an extended control-flow graph. Their approach is to model both the control location and the interrupt mask register, as mentioned earlier. Moreover, they show that an analysis of the extended control-flow graph may reveal interesting insights, such as interrupt servicing not being guaranteed within any bounded time at certain control locations in the program. This may happen, for example, if in a control location l several interrupts are enabled and one of them has higher priority than the others. Thus, if in a location l, two interrupts i_1, i_2 are enabled and i_1 has higher priority than i_2, we cannot guarantee that repeated arrival of i_1 interrupts will not starve out the servicing of i_2, unless something is known about the interrupt sources. The analysis of [11] allows the user to input such information, and this is taken into account while computing the maximum time to service an interrupt.

Figure 4.12 shows an example user annotation that can be taken into account in timing analysis. The figure shows a fragment of the extended control-flow graph where each node denotes a control location (i.e., program counter value) and IMR value. In this extended graph, there could be an unbounded loop involving communication of the embedded software with a peripheral device. However, in reality the loop may be bounded because of the user's knowledge about the peripheral.

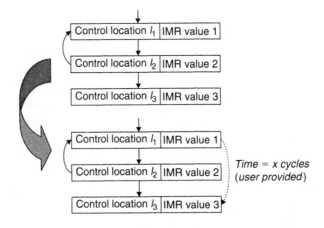

Figure 4.12

Taking into account user annotations for timing analysis of interrupt-driven software.

This may bound the maximum amount of time spent in the loop (as denoted by the dashed edge in Figure 4.12).

4.3.2 Contention and Preemption

In Section 4.2, we discussed WCET analysis methods that estimate the uninterrupted execution time of a program. However, in reality, a program is subject to interruptions owing to several reasons such as:

- Asynchronously coming interrupts from peripheral devices (i.e., the "environment" of the program),
- Resource contention with other programs running on the same processing element, and
- Resource contention due to other programs running on other processing elements.

Estimating the time required to process an interrupt allows us to capture the time involved in a program's interaction with the environment. However, several programs could be executing on the same processing element, sharing hardware data structures such as the processor cache. This may create interference in a program's execution time — which we seek to estimate here. Of course, programs running on different processing elements could also interfere with each other's execution time, because they share communication resources such as the system bus. We will discuss communication timing analysis in Section 4.4.

Resource contention within a processor by many programs is conventionally studied under the name of *schedulability analysis*. The primary resource here is the CPU on which the various programs are run. In the last section, we presented the methods for worst-case execution time analysis, which estimate the uninterrupted execution time of a program on a processor. Clearly, these estimates do not consider a multitasking environment where several programs share a CPU. In general, we consider programs $P_1, \ldots, P_n$ executing on a processor where for each program P_i there is a period p_i. In other words, every p_i time units, an instance of program P_i is released. In this situation, for any instance of program P_i, suppose we monitor the time when it is released to the time when it is completed. In schedulability literature, this time is referred to as the *response time*. The response time can be attributed to the following:

- *Waiting time:* Once an instance (say, the jth instance) of a program P_i is ready, it may not start immediately. The CPU may be occupied by other programs when the jth instance of P_i is ready.
- *Own Execution time:* The execution time of program P_i is part of the response time of the jth instance of program P_i. WCET estimates can potentially be used here.

- *Execution time of preempting programs:* While the *j*th instance of program P_i is running, it may be preempted because of the arrival of instances of other programs (which may be deemed to be higher priority than P_i as per the scheduling policy of the CPU). Because of such preemption, (parts of) the execution time of certain higher priority processes will also be part of the response time for P_i.

In Figure 4.13, we show a sample preemptive execution of three periodically invoked programs. For each of the programs P_i, we provide the arrival time a_i, execution time (say, the WCET estimate) c_i, and the period p_i. Thus, a_i is the time at which the first instance of program P_i arrives, c_i is the WCET estimate of one execution of P_i, and p_i is the time interval between the arrival of two instances of P_i.

Now let us observe the response time of the first instance of program P_2 in Figure 4.13. It arrives at time = 0 and immediately starts executing, because there are no other competing programs. Thus, there is no waiting time. After executing for one time unit, the first instance of program P_1 also arrives. At this point, there are two program instances contending for the CPU — the first instance of program P_1, and the first instance of program P_2. Which one should be allowed to run first? This is decided by the *scheduling policy* of the CPU. There is a vast literature on scheduling algorithms (e.g., see the book [13]) that decide which program to allocate the CPU when several programs are contending for the CPU. Thus, a scheduling algorithm can be seen as a prioritization mechanism — from among several contending program instances, it decides which program instance will run first on the CPU. To prioritize program instances, we need to prioritize the programs that are periodically invoked.

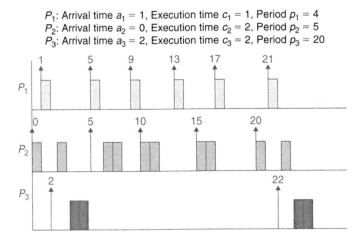

P_1: Arrival time $a_1 = 1$, Execution time $c_1 = 1$, Period $p_1 = 4$
P_2: Arrival time $a_2 = 0$, Execution time $c_2 = 2$, Period $p_2 = 5$
P_3: Arrival time $a_3 = 2$, Execution time $c_3 = 2$, Period $p_3 = 20$

Figure 4.13

Preemptive execution of periodically invoked programs.

Thus, in Figure 4.13, we will need to assign priorities to P_1, P_2, P_3. A common scheme is to assign priorities to programs based on periods — the smaller the period, the higher the priority. The intuition here is that any instance of a program P_i should complete prior to the arrival of the next instance of P_i. Thus, the period of a program P_i also serves as a deadline for its instances. The scheduling algorithm that prioritizes program instances based on the periods of the corresponding programs is commonly known as *rate monotonic scheduling (RMS)* [52]. Thus, in the example of Figure 4.13, the periods of P_1, P_2, P_3 are 4, 5, and 20, respectively — P_1 has the highest priority, followed by P_2, and then by P_3. In fact, Figure 4.13 shows the rate monotonic scheduling of the three periodically invoked programs P_1, P_2, P_3.

In RMS, the Worst-case Response Time (WCRT) of a program instance can be formulated as follows. Let the programs $P_1, P_2, \ldots, P_n$ be invoked periodically with periods $p_1 \leq p_2 \leq \ldots \leq p_n$. Thus P_1 has the lowest period (and highest priority) and P_n has the largest period (and lowest priority). The WCRT of any instance of program P_i is given by the following recursive equation:

$$w_i = c_i + \sum_{j=1}^{i-1} c_j * \lceil \frac{w_i}{p_j} \rceil \qquad (4.4)$$

Here c_i is the execution time of any instance of P_i (the WCET estimate) and p_j is the period of program P_j. The above equation (proposed by Lehoczky et al. in [60]) can be explained as follows. The WCRT of an instance of program P_i includes (a) the execution time of P_i and (b) execution times of higher-priority programs. Because in RMS the priorities of programs are given by their periods and we assume that the programs are ordered according to their periods (with the program with the lowest period appearing first), the higher-priority programs for an instance of program P_i are $P_1, P_2, \ldots, P_{i-1}$. This explains the summation on the right-hand side of the equation. Moreover, for each higher-priority program P_j we conservatively add up

(Execution time of P_j) $*$ (# of times P_j can preempt one instance of P_i)

The execution time of program P_j is c_j. The number of times the program P_j can preempt one instance of program P_i is given by $\lceil \frac{w_i}{p_j} \rceil$ where w_i is the WCRT of program P_i and p_j is the period of program P_j.

Equation 4.4 is solved iteratively via a fixed-point computation. For every program P_i, the WCRT w_i is initialized to c_i, and then Equation 4.4 is iteratively applied until the w_i values become stable. These stable values form the WCRT estimates of the programs. It can be shown that this iterative fixed-point computation is guaranteed to terminate (see [13, 87] for details). If the WCRT of each program is less than its deadline (in RMS often the deadline = period), then RMS deems the set of programs as *schedulable*.

RMS is only one possible scheduling policy. The various scheduling policies studied in literature differ from each other in the following issues.

- *Task Model:*
  - Whether the programs executing are invoked periodically (at regular intervals), sporadically (at irregular intervals with a minimum time interval between two consecutive instances of a program), or completely aperiodically (no guarantees about the time between two instances of a program so each program instance can be treated as a separate program).
  - Whether a program instance can be preempted by another program instance; or whether a program instance, once scheduled on the CPU, runs to completion.
- *Priorities:*
  - *Static/Dynamic:* Whether the priorities of all program instances are tied to the corresponding program. If yes, the priority scheme is static (priorities known at compile time); otherwise it is dynamic (priorities computed during run time).
  - *Prioritization:* Based on certain characteristics of the programs or program instances, the priorities are computed. The RMS algorithm assigns the priorities to be inversely proportional to the period.

Given the various choices of task model and the priority scheme, the wide array of existing scheduling algorithms is not surprising. For a set of independent periodic programs (i.e., no data dependencies across the programs), if the priorities are fixed statically, it can be shown that RMS is an optimal scheduling scheme. In other words, if a set of periodic programs is deemed to be not schedulable (i.e., not meeting deadlines) under RMS, it cannot be scheduled using any other scheduling policy using static priorities. RMS is a widely used scheduling algorithm that has been implemented inside many real-life system, including various real-time operating systems. It can also be extended to sets of programs where there exist dependencies across programs.

RMS uses static priorities — that is, the priority of the program instances are derived from the priorities of the programs. It is not possible to vary the priorities at run time — that is, different instances of the same program cannot have different priorities. If we allow this flexibility we have a dynamic priority scheme, where the priorities of the currently contending program instances (contending for the CPU) are updated at run time. Naturally, there arise pragmatic issues in implementing dynamic priority schemes — how frequently the priorities need to updated and how efficiently they can be updated.

Earliest deadline first (EDF) is one of the best-known dynamic priority scheduling algorithms. It prioritizes the contending program instances based on their deadlines. The program instance that is closest to its deadline is allowed to run. Naturally, when

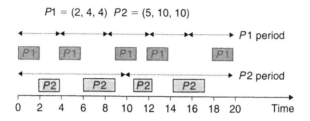

Figure 4.14

Preemptive execution of periodically invoked programs — EDF scheduling.

a new program instance arrives, an interrupt needs to be generated. This results in a reevaluation of the priorities of the contending program instances, based on which one is closest to its deadline.

Figure 4.14 shows the EDF scheduling of two periodically invoked programs. The programs are $P1 = (2, 4, 4)$ and $P2 = (5, 10, 10)$, where for $P1$ the computation time is 2 and the period/deadline is 4. Similarly, for $P2$ the computation time is 5 and the period/deadline is 10. Suppose an instance each of $P1$ and $P2$ is ready to execute initially at time $= 0$. $P1$ is allowed to execute because it is closest to its deadline. After $P1$ stops, $P2$ executes from time $= 2$ to time $= 4$. However, when a new instance of $P1$ arrives at time $= 4$, the program instance of $P2$ is preempted. This is because the time to next deadline of $P2$ is $10 - 4 = 6$, whereas the time to next deadline of $P1$ is 4. However, at time $= 8$, when another instance of $P1$ arrives, program $P2$ continues executing. This is because now the the time to next deadline of $P2$ is $10 - 8 = 2$, whereas the time to next deadline of $P1$ is 4.

For a detailed understanding of scheduling algorithms and their usage, the reader is referred to [13].

4.3.3 Sharing a Processor Cache

So far, we have seen two possible ways in which uninterrupted execution of a program on a processor may be prevented:

- Interrupts from the external environment, and
- Preemption by other programs executing on the same processor.

Both of these make it difficult to estimate the finish time of a program once it starts, because the finish time is not merely the execution time of the program.

In reality, there are (at least) two other factors affecting the finish time of a program:

- The impact of several programs running on a processor sharing resources (such as the processor cache), and

■ Communication between programs running on different processors (possibly connected via a bus).

We now discuss the first of these two — the impact of shared resources, in particular a shared processor cache.

When a program P_1 is running, by default it is eligible to use the entire processor cache. Now, P_1 might be preempted by the arrival of a higher-priority process P_2 that runs to completion. Clearly, when P_2 executes it will also be eligible to use the processor cache. Suppose P_2 finishes execution, and P_1 resumes. Clearly, some of the contents of P_1 that were cached earlier would have been replaced by contents of P_2. This will lead to additional cache misses when P_1 resumes. How to take into account these additional cache misses in the performance estimation/validation of programs P_1, P_2? There could be several solutions to this problem.

■ *Conservative estimate:* The easiest solution might be to conservatively assume that the entire cache needs to be refilled when a preempted program resumes execution. This might cause a gross overestimation in execution time.
■ *Cache partitioning:* Alternatively, we can partition the cache among the several programs running on a processor. A program now uses only the portion of the cache allocated to its partition. The trouble with this approach is that it leads to an inefficient use of the cache. Consequently, the actual *performance* of the programs may suffer quite a lot, even though we can now obtain tight estimates of this degraded performance.
■ *Cache analysis:* We can analyze the cache behavior of the different application programs running on a processor, and tightly estimate their cache behavior interference. This approach does not require us to partition the cache among the applications. At the same time, we do not need to assume that all cache lines are affected by preemption. We now illustrate this approach. Overall, we devise a method to summarize the cache behavior of a program. By comparing the cache behavior summary of two programs executing on the same processor, we can find their relative interference in execution times due to the shared cache.

Cache Behavior Summarization

We now formally describe our static analysis method for computing cache behavior summary for a given application program. To model cache behavior, we first need the notion of a *cache state*. For simplicity of notation, let us assume a direct-mapped cache; the analysis can be straightforwardly extended for set-associative caches. For a direct-mapped cache with n blocks, a cache state cs is simply a mapping $\{1, \ldots, n\} \to M \cup \{\bot\}$, where M is the set of code memory blocks being mapped to cache, and $\bot$ indicates the situation where a cache block is empty.

We use $cs[i]$ to denote the content of the ith cache block in cache state cs. Also, for convenience, we describe the analysis for *instruction cache*. The method can be straightforwardly used, with little conceptual change, for summarizing data cache behavior of an application.

In order to statically summarize the overall cache behavior, we associate program points or control locations in the program with *sets of cache states*. We develop and use two quantities: reaching cache states (RCS) and live cache states (LCS).

Definition 17 (Reaching Cache States) *Given a program point p of a program Prog, the set of reaching cache states RCS(p) is defined as the set of cache states with which p can be reached (via any incoming path to p in Prog).*

Definition 18 (Live Cache States) *Given a program point p of a program Prog, the set of live cache states LCS(p) is the set of possible first references to cache blocks via any outgoing path from p in Prog.*

Given a program point p in program *Prog*, the quantities $LCS(p)/RCS(p)$ are computed by exploring the paths to/from p in the control-flow graph of *Prog*. This is done efficiently (without path enumeration) by (a) associating each program point with an LCS/RCS, (b) defining the RCS of a program point using the RCS of its predecessors, and (c) defining the LCS of a program point using the LCS of its successors. Because a program contains loops, the foregoing will produce a set of recursive equations on LCS/RCS that needs to be solved iteratively. Assuming an empty cache at the beginning of the program, we can iteratively solve the recursive equations for LCS and RCS separately. This is done until the LCS and RCS estimates at each program point are stable — that is, until the iterative computation reaches a fixed point.

The resultant RCS estimate for the exit point of the program is denoted as $RCS(Prog)$; these are the possible cache states at the end of the program. Similarly, the LCS estimate at the entry point of the program is denoted as $LCS(Prog)$; these are the possible first references to cache blocks during the program's execution. Given a program *Prog*, the quantities $RCS(Prog)$ and $LCS(Prog)$ form the *summary of the cache behavior* for *Prog*. For details of the iterative computation of LCS and RCS, the reader is referred to [63]. We now show how the LCS/RCS quantities, once computed, can be used for estimating cache interference across programs.

Utilizing Cache Summaries

We can utilize the cache behavior summary for different purposes. In a preemptive multitasking system where several programs (with deadlines) are running on the same processor, we can use the cache summaries to tightly estimate the additional

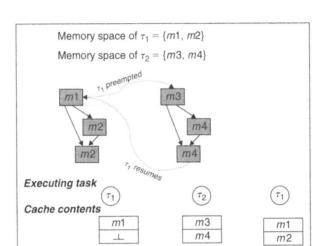

Memory space of $\tau_1 = \{m1, m2\}$

Memory space of $\tau_2 = \{m3, m4\}$

Figure 4.15

Cache-related preemption delay calculation — example 1.

cache misses owing to preemption. In the absence of the cache summaries, we would have to assume that every cache line's contents should be changed because of preemption.

Figure 4.15 illustrates this usage. For simplicity, we have depicted a direct-mapped cache with two cache lines. The $\perp$ symbol denotes an empty cache line. Here, task (or program) τ_1 executes initially but is preempted by a higher priority task τ_2, which then runs to completion. When τ_1 resumes execution, both the cache lines are replaced by contents of τ_2. However, there is only one additional cache miss encountered by τ_1, because only the first cache line contained a useful memory block required in τ_1's resumed execution. As a result, the cache effects of preemption on τ_1's execution time is the time for resolving one cache miss. Note that irrespective of the path executed in τ_1 (there are two paths in this program), we encounter one additional cache miss when τ_1 resumes.

In Figure 4.16 we show a slightly different situation. Suppose τ_1 is preempted while it is executing the first iteration of the loop. Again, assume that τ_2 preempts τ_1 and then runs to completion. How many additional cache misses are encountered when τ_1 resumes? This, of course, depends on the cache contents at the preemption point of τ_1. The cache content at the preemption point, again, depends on which path is taken in τ_1 prior it being preempted by τ_2. Thus, to find the additional cache misses owing to preemption we need:

- The possible cache contents of the preempted program at the different possible preemption points (this is given by the reaching cache states or RCS at the different control locations of the preempted program),

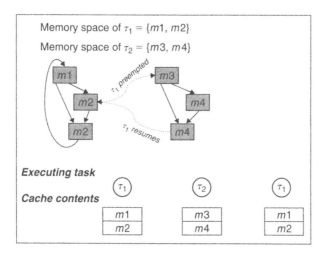

Memory space of $\tau_1 = \{m1, m2\}$

Memory space of $\tau_2 = \{m3, m4\}$

Figure 4.16

Cache-related preemption delay calculation — example 2.

- The possible cache contents at the end of the preempting program (again, this is given by the RCS at the termination point of the preempting program), and
- The possible first use of cache lines by the preempted program once it resumes (this is given by the live cache states or LCS of the different control locations of the preempted program).

The foregoing gives an idea about how the cache behavior summaries can be used to find the maximum cache interference across programs. The interested reader is referred to [42, 48, 63] for the details of the method, and its integration to system-level schedulability analysis.

4.4 SYSTEM-LEVEL COMMUNICATION ANALYSIS

So far, we have discussed how the finish time of a program P can be impacted by (a) interrupts from external environment and (b) execution of other programs on the same processor. Other programs executing on the same processor can affect the finish time of P either directly (by preempting the execution of P) or indirectly (via shared resources such as processor cache).

In a multiprocessor system-on-chip (SoC) platform, we have multiple processing elements on the same chip. How the communication across the processing elements is supported is a question. There are several possibilities — a bus, on-chip interconnects, and communication via FIFO buffers. Here we discuss some of the intricacies in estimating the times for bus communication.

Having several processing elements hooked up via a common bus is the most common communication topology. The difficulties in analyzing the timing properties of bus-based communication can be illustrated via the following example. Consider the following schematic code executing on a processing element *PE*.

```
if (b > 0){
    ... // costly computation, computing a variable x
} else{
    ... // light computation, computing a variable x
}
send x  // sending to a different processor via bus ...
```

Clearly, the value of variable *b* impacts the subsequent computation of *x*, and hence the time at which the processing element *PE* tries to send *x* over the bus. If the send of *x* conflicts with another processing element *PE'* attempting bus access, the send of *x* may be delayed. This will affect the future computation on *PE*, and hence the future bus traffic. Thus, since computation and communication go hand-in-hand, timing analysis to find the worst-case communication behavior will involve unrolling the sequence of computation and communication for all possible bus schedules (i.e., all possible serializations generated by the bus arbiter for all possible bus traffic). Naturally, this is not practically feasible.

We also cannot simplify our communication timing analysis by assuming the worst-case execution time of each computation fragment in each program. This is because the worst-case execution time of the computation fragments need not produce the worst-case contention for bus access (i.e., the maximum bus traffic). In the preceding schematic code fragment, the costly computation for variable *x* in processing element *PE* can conceivably avoid bus access contention with another processing element *PE'* (depending when the bus access request from *PE'* arrives), whereas the light computation for *x* can contend with a bus access request from *PE'*. This was earlier elaborated in Figure 4.3, reproduced here as Figure 4.17 for the reader's convenience. The computations $c1, c2, c3, c4$ are program fragments not involving any send/receive; the send/recieve events are shown explicitly via arrows. Because the computation $c1, c2, c3, c4$ may involve conditional branches, their execution time may be variable. In particular we show in Figure 4.17 that the execution time of $c1$ may vary between 3 and 4 time units. Further, it is shown that if $c1$ executes for 3 time units, the overall execution time is more than if $c1$ executes for 4 time units. In the literature on timing analysis, such phenomena are often referred to as "timing anomaly." It makes the estimation of worst-case communication behavior particularly difficult.

Let us consider a set of programs $P_1, \ldots, P_n$ executing on processing elements $PE_1, \ldots, PE_m$ ($m \leq n$) hooked on a bus. Furthermore, each program P_i may be visualized as a *task graph*—a directed acyclic graph of "tasks." The nodes of the

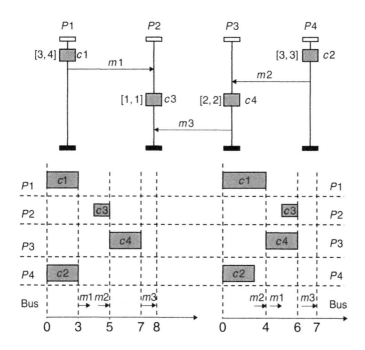

Figure 4.17

Anomalous timing behavior in bus-based communication — Figure 4.3 reproduced for convenience.

graph are program fragments, and the edges denote precedence and (possibly) data communication. Thus, a program P_i is seen as a directed acyclic graph (V_i, E_i) where V_i denotes a set of "task" or program fragments and E_i denotes the edges between the program fragments. Let $(u \rightarrow v)$ be an edge from E_i where $u, v \in V_i$; this means v cannot start before u completes and the output data of u (if any) is passed as input to v. We can also assume a mapping of the tasks to the processing elements, given as

$$\left(\bigcup_{1 \le i \le n} V_i \right) \rightarrow \{PE_1, \ldots, PE_m\}$$

Because the tasks are mapped to processing elements, we can have two tasks u, v from program P_i where $u \rightarrow v$ in the task graph of P_i and u, v are mapped to different processing elements. Because the end of u and the start of v involve data communication, the end of u will generate a request for bus access.

Clearly, for estimating or validating timing properties of bus-based communication, we cannot afford to enumerate all possible bus schedules. So, what are the options? There are several techniques in this regard, which differ in the accuracy and guarantees resulting from their estimates. Primarily, the methods can be divided into two categories:

- *Dynamic analysis:* Here a sample bus trace is collected, and the trace is used to extract various information (such as information about precedences among events). Thus, from the trace (which denotes a total order of computation and communication events), we first extract a partial order (captured via a directed acyclic graph). The timing analysis then explores this acyclic graph to find the communication times. Note that this approach is *different* from simulating a trace for performance numbers. A sample technique in this category can be found in [57].
- *Static analysis:* These methods work directly on the programs whose communication time we are analyzing. No trace is collected. Furthermore, the time estimates obtained are *guaranteed upper bounds*. Sample techniques in this category can be found in [44, 101].

We now describe the key ingredients of a static analysis approach — the ones outlined in [44, 101]. Let us discuss the inherent difficulties in finding the end-to-end delay of applications running on different processing elements and communicating via bus in a multiprocessor SoC. Apart from the usual contention among different tasks mapped to the same processing element, we need to consider the following factors:

- *Bus contention:* Execution of a program may be delayed because it is waiting to communicate over the bus, but the bus is currently being accessed by another application.
- *Data dependencies:* Execution of a task in a program may have to wait for other tasks to complete. This is conventionally taken into account in uniprocessor scheduling methods as well.
- *Conditional execution:* The execution of a task in an application may depend on some condition that is set either by other applications (via communication) or by the external environment.

As observed earlier, the combination of these factors leads to the timing anomaly phenomenon — where the overall worst-case delay cannot be obtained by assuming the worst-case execution time of the individual tasks. To get past this problem, we can represent the start and finish times for each task as an interval. Thus, the start time of a task i is represented as an interval $[s_{i1}, s_{i2}]$, where s_{i1} (s_{i2}) is the earliest (latest) time in which task i can start. The end-to-end delay of the applications is then the maximum of the latest finish times of all the tasks. The estimation of the end-to-end delay now involves an iterative estimation of the intervals for the start and finish times. The estimation starts by assuming very relaxed intervals for the start and finish times of tasks, and gradually tightening them. The estimation stops when we reach a fixed point, that is, the interval estimates of the start/finish times no longer change.

4.5 DESIGNING SYSTEMS WITH PREDICTABLE TIMING

So far, we have invested our energies in discussing methods for timing analysis and validation. Such analysis proceeds at different levels — software analysis for WCET, analysis of multiple tasks within a processor, and system-level analysis across processors (for a multiprocessor system-on-chip platform). However, as systems get increasingly complex, enriching the analysis to estimate timing behavior becomes harder. An alternative strategy is to design systems with timing validation in mind. In other words, time-unpredictable system features are replaced in favor of features whose timing behavior is easy to estimate and predict. In the following, we discuss two important design innovations that allow more predictable timing behavior. The first of these is *scratchpad memory*, which alleviates the timing unpredictability of a processor cache. The second one is time-triggered communication over a bus, which alleviates the unpredictability in bus communication times owing to varying bus traffic.

4.5.1 Scratchpad Memories

Let us examine the major source(s) of timing unpredictability during the execution of a program on a processor. In particular, we examine the difficulties in assigning the execution time of an instruction to be a constant. The variation in the execution time of an instruction of course comes from the performance-enhancing microarchitectural features of the underlying processor, such as pipeline, cache, and branch prediction.

The processor cache is an important source of timing unpredictability. One of the reasons for this is the high penalty incurred as a result of a cache miss. So, even if we consider only instruction cache, a difference of a hit/miss during the fetch of an instruction from the code memory causes a huge variation in the instructions execution time. To concretize our discussion, let us consider a standard five-stage pipeline with stages: Instruction Fetch (IF), Instruction Decode (ID), Execute (EX), Write Back (WB), and Commit (CM). Now let us see the impact of instruction/data cache on the execution time of these individual stages.

IF	Instr. cache hit = 1 cycle, Instr. cache miss = 50 cycles
ID	1 cycle
EX	Data cache hit = 1 cycle, Data cache miss = 50 or 100 cycles
WB	1 cycle
CM	1 cycle

In the IF stage, depending whether the fetched instruction is a hit or miss in the instruction cache, the time taken is 1 clock cycle or 50 clock cycle (assuming a cache-miss penalty, that is, the time for retrieving the corresponding memory block, to be 50 clock cycles). In the EX stage, the operands of an instruction are needed, and typically an instruction has up to two operands. If the operands are not available in the data cache, this results in a cache miss, and they have to be fetched from the data memory. If both the operands do not appear in the cache and the memory has only one port (allowing one memory block to be accessed at a time), this will result in a delay of two cache-miss penalties (100 clock cycles). If only one operand misses in the cache, or both operands miss but can be retrieved from the data memory in parallel, this incurs a delay of one cache-miss penalty (50 clock cycles).

In the preceding, we have shown, in terms of concrete numbers, the wide variation in the execution time of an instruction owing to processor cache. The processor cache constitutes an additional layer in the memory hierarchy that causes unpredictability of execution time, but greatly reduces the average execution time of a program. Conventionally, researchers in computer systems have been concerned about the overall average-case performance of a program, leading to the widespread popularity of caches in processor design. However, for designing predictable embedded systems, the wide variation in execution times caused by caches is a huge concern. A naive solution would be to completely remove the caches. However, this is not feasible because it will greatly undermine the performance of the application program being executed. In this context, researchers have proposed the use of compiler-controlled memories or scratchpad memories (e.g., see [65]).

We now explain the concept of a scratchpad memory in stages. We start with the concept of a cache and gradually develop the notion of scratchpad memory. For simplicity, we consider a direct-mapped cache. A direct-mapped cache is a mapping from the address space to the cache lines. The content of each cache line changes dynamically during execution, and the programmer has no direct control over the cache contents. Instead of letting the cache contents change dynamically, we can fix the cache contents statically. This brings us to the concept of *cache locking*. In a statically locked cache, the content of each cache line is fixed statically prior to program execution (typically by static analysis to find the maximally accessed memory blocks along various execution paths). However, in a locked cache there is still some restriction (based on the cache line mapping) on what we can lock in the cache. In Figure 4.18 we show a simple example where a memory space with eight memory blocks is mapped to a direct-mapped cache with two lines. Clearly, memory blocks 1,3,5,7 map to the first cache line and blocks 2,4,6,8 map to the second cache line. If we statically lock the cache (based on an analysis of which memory blocks are most accessed across various execution paths), we must lock one of the memory blocks 1,3,5,7 (2,4,6,8) into the first (second) cache line. However, the scratchpad memory has no such restrictions based on cache line mapping (see Figure 4.18). We find the frequently accessed memory blocks, and these are allocated to the scratchpad memory based on the total available space.

In the presence of a scratchpad memory, we can assume the address space to be viewed as shown in Figure 4.19. What we show in the figure could denote either the instruction or the data address space, meaning both code and data scratchpad are possible. A portion of the address space is mapped to scratchpad memory, meaning content of addresses in this range will be retrieved from the on-chip scratchpad memory. Content of the other addresses is retrieved from the main memory. The important point here is that, given a memory address, the time for accessing its contents is fixed. Note that this is not the case in the presence of a conventional cache memory — the time to retrieve the content for a given address may vary depending on whether the address leads to a hit/miss in the cache. Clearly, scratchpad memory

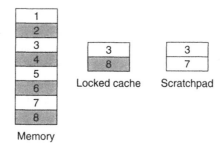

Figure 4.18

Differences between cache-locking and scratchpad memory.

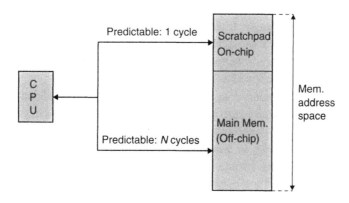

Figure 4.19

Mapping of address space to scratchpad memory.

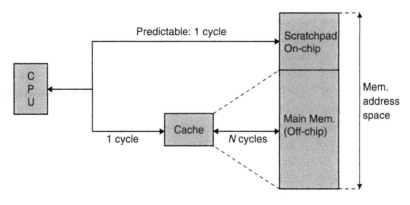

Figure 4.20

Memory architecture combining scratchpad and cache memory — [65].

may also be combined with cache. In this situation, the address space can be viewed as in Figure 4.20. In this situation, a portion of the address space is mapped to scratchpad memory. Content of addresses in this range is directly retrieved from the scratchpad memory. For other addresses, first the cache is looked up; if the address is absent in the cache, its contents are retrieved from the main memory.

We now discuss various scratchpad memory allocation strategies. Let us consider the simplest architectural setup — the presence of a scratchpad memory, but no cache (Figure 4.19). Further, the scratchpad memory is *statically* allocated — it is loaded with chosen memory blocks prior to program execution, and this set of memory blocks is never changed during program execution. The aim of the scratchpad allocation is to reduce the "execution time" of the application program. In this context, we are faced with the issue of whether the scratchpad allocation should aim to reduce the average-case execution time of an application, or the worst-case execution (say for real-time applications). In the following, we discuss profile-based scratchpad allocation strategies that reduce the average-case execution time. For worst-case execution time (WCET)-driven scratchpad allocation methods, the interested reader is referred to [82].

To concretize our discussion, let us consider scratchpad allocation for data memory. Suppose the candidate program variables to be allocated to scratchpad are $v_1, \ldots, v_n$. The list of candidate program variables is constructed with obvious restrictions — for example, an array is treated as one variable, meaning either all elements in the array are allocated to the scratchpad or no element is allocated. Depending on the *type* of a variable v_i, we know how much scratchpad area will be taken up if v_i is allocated to scratchpad; let this quantity be $area_i$. Finally, we assume that a profile of the program is available — say, an execution path, or a count of how many times each basic block is executed. From this execution profile, we can find the number of times variable v_i is accessed — let this number be n_i. We can now estimate the gain accrued (in terms of execution time) if a variable v_i is allocated to the scratchpad. This gain is, in fact, a constant, given as

$$gain_i = n_i * (N - 1)$$

where N is the number of cycles required to access any location from the main memory. Thus, the gain in execution time due to each access of v_i is $N - 1$ (as compared to the situation where v_i is allocated to scratchpad — accessing a memory location from scratchpad takes only 1 clock cycle). Because v_i is accessed n_i times in the profile, the overall gain in execution time by allocating variable v_i to scratchpad is $n_i * (N - 1)$.

By assuming an execution profile of the program, the gain accrued by allocating a given variable can be treated as an integer constant. The problem of deciding the scratchpad allocation can now be solved via the well-known knapsack problem. In the knapsack problem we have n items that we are trying to put in a knapsack. The knapsack can carry a total weight of C. For each item i, the weight of the item w_i is a given positive integer constant. Each item also comes with a "value" val_i — a positive integer constant. The knapsack problem tries to choose items such that (a) the value of the included items is maximized, and (b) the weight constraint of the knapsack is respected. In other words,

$$\text{maximize} \sum_{1 \le i \le n} choice_i * val_i \text{ subject to} \sum_{1 \le i \le n} choice_i * w_i \le C$$

where $choice_i$ is 0 or 1 (it is 1 if item i is included in the knapsack and 0 otherwise).

The scratchpad memory allocation problem can be formulated as a knapsack problem as follows. The knapsack to be filled is the scratchpad memory. The items to be placed in the knapsack are the program variables $v_1, \ldots, v_n$. The weight of the knapsack C is the total scratchpad capacity, and the weight w_i of each variable v_i is the area occupied by variable v_i. The value val_i of variable v_i is the gain in execution time accrued by allocating v_i to the scratchpad. Thus

$$val_i = gain_i = n_i * (N - 1)$$

where n_i is the number of times variable v_i is accessed in the execution profile and N is the number of cycles required to access any location from the main memory (we assume only 1 cycle is needed to access a variable from the scratchpad). Thus, for reducing average case execution time of a program, we can solve the well-known knapsack problem to derive the scratchpad memory allocation.

If we want to drive our scratchpad allocation to reduce the WCET of a program, a knapsack formulation is no longer applicable. This is because the gain $gain_i$ accrued in allocating a variable v_i to the scratchpad is no longer a constant — because there is no execution profile we can use for finding the number of times v_i is accessed. The interested reader may refer to [82] for discussion on WCET-based scratchpad memory allocation.

4.5.2 Time-Triggered Communication

One of the major sources of timing unpredictability in a distributed embedded system is the communication time. It is common for various subsystems or processing elements to be connected via a system bus. The exact time taken by a communication depends on the bus traffic, and this in turn determines the timing of the future computation/communication steps. We have seen earlier that developing analysis methods to bound communication times are extremely difficult. This is because we need to take into account the dependencies between the computation/communication steps, as well as the contention across them (for resources such as the system bus).

Conventionally, we consider event-triggered communication where communication is initiated by the occurrence of specific "events." For example, when a processing element encounters a LOAD instruction and the corresponding data is not present locally, a communication over the bus is initiated to retrieve the data. The time taken by such a communication request is unpredictable, because it depends on how many other nodes are trying to transfer data over the bus at that time. For safety-critical distributed embedded systems (which are common in application domains such as automotive electronics), this is unacceptable. The time-triggered communication protocols fill this gap.

The time-triggered communication architecture [45] is based on a global time being established across communicating nodes. This is an important abstraction, which needs to be implemented in reality by synchronizing the local clocks of the communicating nodes. The time-triggered architecture holds a discrete view of time, where the timeline is cut up into discrete time steps. As long as these time steps are less than the precision of clock synchronization, we can argue that any two timings within a time step refer to the same discrete time. Hence, all events that happen within the same time step can be considered to happen at the same time. In fact, in a time-triggered architecture, the time steps are marked as "activity time step" or "inactivity time step." Any activity time step is usually followed by several inactivity time steps.

Once a global timeline is established across processing elements in a distributed embedded system, a time-triggered architecture ensures predictability of timing behavior as follows. Assume that the communicating processing elements are connected via a bus. The bus access during the activity time steps is statically predetermined. Here, the communication takes place in a round-robin fashion.

In each round, each processing element gets a chance to send one message. This communication mechanism is popularly known as time-division multiple access or TDMA. Clearly, for such a communication mechanism to work, a global timeline needs to exist across processing elements, as mentioned earlier.

In recent years, several automotive manufacturers (such as BMW, Volkswagen, and General Motors) have formed a consortium to develop an automotive network communications protocol standard called Flexray [27]. The Flexray protocol is designed to be time-triggered in nature and follows variants of the TDMA communication scheme discussed in the preceding. The Flexray protocol assumes a simple architecture — several electronic control units (ECUs) connected to a bus. Each ECU is endowed with a communication controller. Several tasks may be allocated to an ECU, and the tasks running on an ECU can be assigned priorities.

The Flexray protocol is an adaptation of the TDMA communication scheme. The protocol proceeds by repeating "bus cycles." Each cycle has a complex structure and is divided into static and dynamic segments. The static segment is divided into *equal-length* slots, and each slot is preassigned to a specific ECU. The dynamic segment is divided into variable-length slots, and again each slot is assigned to a specific ECU. However, the lengths of these slots are adjusted based on the communication requirements of the ECUs. This is usually done by dividing the whole dynamic segment into fixed-length mini-slots, and then adjusting the number of mini-slots corresponding to a given slot. In Figure 4.21, we show one single bus cycle for a

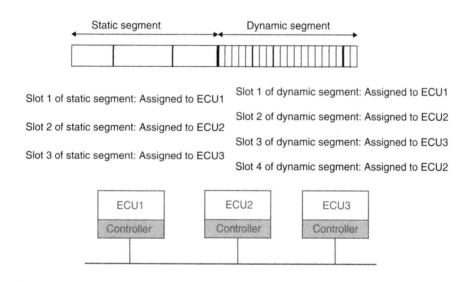

Figure 4.21

A bus cycle in a Flexray bus with three ECUs.

bus with three ECUs. The static segment is divided into equal-length slots — one for each ECU. In the dynamic segment, one ECU may be allocated several slots (e.g., ECU2 in Figure 4.21). Moreover, the number of mini-slots in a slot varies from one slot to another (e.g., slot 4 has only two mini-slots) and also from one bus cycle to another. The Flexray protocol thus provides almost entirely predictable communication timings. Timing unpredictability, however, comes from the fact that a message to be transmitted by an ECU may be postponed to the next bus cycle, if the number of mini-slots left in the current bus cycle is not enough to transmit the message.

4.6 EMERGING APPLICATIONS

In this chapter, we have primarily discussed issues in embedded systems performance analysis, estimation, and validation. These methods are of use both in soft real-time embedded systems (such as media processing) and in hard real-time embedded systems (such as automotive electronics). Apart from these well-studied application domains, newer emerging domains may see the use of performance validation methods. In particular, the performance validation methods mentioned in this chapter can be used or adapted for successful deployment of wireless sensor networks (or networks of sensor nodes). Often such sensor networks are deployed for mission-critical defense applications (e.g., spying on enemy territory), and must satisfy tight timing and power budgets. For such applications, the worst-case execution time analysis methods (and their adaptation for analyzing energy [43]) can be useful.

Wireless body-area sensor networks (or BANs) and related *wearable computing* technologies have also lately become very popular [26, 47, 66]. Growth in this area has been largely fueled by the recent technological advancements in embedded processors, availability of lightweight and small-factor sensor nodes, and advances in wireless networking. As a result, BAN-based health monitoring is increasingly becoming a viable alternative to traditional wired biomonitoring techniques, which require a patient to be hospitalized and hooked up to large monitoring equipment. However, most biomonitoring applications require continuous processing of large volumes of data streams arriving through multiple sensors. As a result, both computation time and power consumption turn out to be serious constraints while designing sensor network–based computing platforms for high-end biomonitoring applications [51]. Both the software and system-level performance validation methods discussed in this chapter are useful in this regard.

As newer application domains continue to develop, there is increased possibility of employing performance analysis methods in novel settings.

4.7 REFERENCES

The abstraction of time in modern-day programming languages has been articulated and elucidated in position papers by Edward Lee [49]. Issues in designing concurrent systems with predictable execution timings have been discussed in [50]. With regard to works on static timing analysis of embedded software, a comprehensive survey of worst-case execution time analysis methods and tools appears in [61]. Another recent survey with focus on specific WCET analysis tools appear in [95].

Among the works on timing analysis of interrupt-driven programs, the work of [11] deserves mention. For system-level timing analysis, the works on worst-case response time analysis are worth mentioning. The works of Lehoczky et al. [60] are among the first in this direction. Extension of worst-case response time analysis in the presence of shared resources such as a processor cache has been discussed in [42, 48, 63].

System-level communication analysis is still a developing area, and currently there are lot of research efforts with this goal. Formal communication analysis of multiprocessor Digital Signal Processors (DSPs) has been studied in [91]. This work uses a formal event model for capturing the arrival/service of event streams in stream-processing applications. The work of [44] presents a formal performance analysis framework for distributed real-time systems. The framework can be applied for estimating communication times in a setup where several processing elements are communicating via a shared bus. The work of [79] studies formal performance analysis of Multi-processor system-on-chips (MpSoCs) with detailed modeling of the processor-memory traffic.

System-level support for predictable software execution timings also has been studied in the embedded systems community. These works typically attack one of the two major unpredictabilities — unpredictable execution times due to the memory subsystem, and those due to bus communication. For the former, works on compiler-controlled memories or scratchpad memories are worth mentioning [65, 82]. For the latter, works on time-triggered architectures and protocols [45, 46] form an important guidepost.

4.8 EXERCISES

4.1. Consider the following program fragment that computes in z the product of x and y. Thus, x and y serve as inputs to the program fragment, and z serves as the output of the program fragment. Both the inputs are positive integers, given as unsigned 8-bit numbers (when represented in binary). Using the timing schema WCET analysis method, derive the maximum execution time of the program fragment. You may assume that each assignment/return/condition-evaluation takes 1 time unit.

```
z = 0;
while (x !=0){
        if (x %2 != 0){ z = z +y; }
        y = 2 * y; x = x/2;
}
return z;
```

4.2. Formulate the maximum execution time estimation of the program fragment in Question 1 using integer linear programming (ILP). Clearly show the objective function and all constraints. Your ILP problem should perform only program path analysis and not microarchitectural modeling. The estimate produced by your ILP problem should be as tight as possible. Also, comment on how the estimate from your ILP problem will compare with the estimate you produced using timing schema.

4.3. Consider the following program fragment:

```
sum = 0; i = 1;
while (i < 101){  if ( i % 2 == 0) sum += i ;    i++; }
return sum;
```

Try to find as many infeasible paths as possible in the control-flow graph of the program. Try to encode them as ILP constraints if possible (and if not possible, give proper explanations).

4.4. Deadline monotonic scheduling (DMS) is a fixed-priority preemptive scheduling algorithm that is similar to rate monotonic scheduling (RMS). In this case, priorities assigned to tasks are inversely proportional to the length of the deadline. Thus the task with the shortest deadline is assigned the highest priority, and the longest-deadline task is assigned the lowest priority. For a set of tasks, is it possible that RMS does not meet all the deadlines, but DMS can meet all the deadlines? If your answer is no, then you should give a formal proof of your claim. If your answer is yes, you should give an example.

4.5. Suppose several periodic processes are running on a processor (with a cache) that employs a preemptive scheduling policy. Thus, the processes share the processor cache. Now, when a process is preempted by another process, the preempting process pollutes the processor cache, which can affect the execution time of the preempted process once it resumes execution. In this chapter, when we presented preemptive scheduling policies such as rate monotonic scheduling (RMS), we always assumed a zero context-switch overhead. However, in reality, it is not so, and the shared cache is one reason contributing to a nonzero context-switch overhead. How can we make our discussion on preemptive scheduling fit the reality of nonzero context-switch overheads due to cache effects? There is no unique solution to this question, so you are encouraged to propose several solutions and compare their relative merits/demerits.

4.6. Consider three processors $P1$, $P2$, and $P3$. Processor $P1$ has only a data cache and no scratchpad memory. Processor $P2$ has only scratchpad memory (for data variables) but no data cache. Finally, processor $P3$ has both scratchpad memory and a data cache. Now, consider three applications $A1$, $A2$, and $A3$. Of these, $A1$ is a brake controller program (running in your car) that runs under strict performance constraints. $A2$ is an application that repeatedly traverses a large array; this program has no performance constraints. $A3$ is a video decoder application where the decoding should be done in a time bound almost always (although it is permissible for it to miss the time bound once in a while). You have to decide which processor on which to run each of $A1$, $A2$, and $A3$. You may assume that multiple copies of the same processor configuration are available (i.e., you can even decide to run two applications on $P1$, say). Explain how your decision is made.

4.7. Suppose we have two processors connected via a bus. The data dependencies between programs $P1 \ldots P5$ appear as edges in Figure 4.22. The computation and bus communication times are shown along the nodes and edges of Figure 4.22. Communication within a processor, of course, costs zero time. Suggest a partitioning of programs $P1 \ldots P5$ to the two processors, so that the overall execution time is minimized.

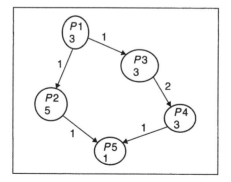

Figure 4.22

Diagram for Question 4.7.

Functionality Validation

5

So far, we have discussed various aspects of validation, namely, (a) system modeling from informal requirements and validating the model, (b) validating the communication across system components, and (c) validating timing properties of embedded software. In this chapter, we discuss the functionality validation of embedded software. Some of the techniques we discuss here are generic to software validation and can be integrated with any software development life cycle. However, some of the methods are specifically useful for classes of software. For example, the software model checking method is particularly useful for control-intensive (and less data operation–dominated) programs that are common in controllers or device drivers.

In discussing software validation methods, we need to clarify what we precisely mean by "validation" here. A loose definition of validation will be checking whether the software behaves as expected. However, such a definition also implies that the "expectation" from the software is properly documented. So, the first question we face is how to document or describe the "expected" behavior of embedded software. There are several ways to answer this question, and indeed the answer to the question depends on what kind of validation methods we are resorting to. If our validation method is software testing, the description of expected behavior consists of the expected program output for selected test cases. If our validation method is software model checking, the description of expected program behavior will consist of the temporal properties being verified.

Having clarified the issue of expected behavior, we ought to differentiate software validation from model validation. After all, our discussion on model validation (Chapter 2) covered how to check properties of the models via model checking. In principle, one could validate the model and generate the implementation software from the models, automatically or semiautomatically. However, in practice, this is rarely done. The modeling mostly serves the purpose of design documentation and comprehension. The modeling activity gives the system designer a methodical way of eliciting the requirements and putting them together in the form of an initial design. Validating the model clarifies the designer's understanding of what the system ought to be. On the other hand, software validation is a much more downstream activity where the actual implementation to be deployed is validated.

Depending on whether the software being validated is constructed from a design model (or not), the flow of software validation can be different. Figure 5.1 shows the overall software validation flow in the case where the software is written with a design model as a guide. Here we could first employ static checking on the design model to ensure that it satisfies certain important properties. Subsequently, we write code using the design model as a guidepost (certain parts of the code could even be automatically generated). This code can be subjected to dynamic checking such as testing/debugging for specific program inputs.

Figure 5.2 shows the overall software validation flow, where the software is written directly by the programmer. In this case, the software is hand-written and not generated automatically or semiautomatically from a design model. This is often the situation in industrial practice where the design model, even if one exists, is primarily used for the purposes of documentation. We note that in this case, the code is potentially subjected to three kinds of validation:

- Dynamic checking,
- Static checking, and
- Static analysis.

Dynamic checking corresponds to software debugging via software testing — we run test cases, check whether the observed behavior is the same as the expected behavior, and if not, analyze the execution trace(s) for possible reasons. Static checking corresponds to checking predefined properties against a given program — a prime example of static checking methods being model checking (Section 2.8). Recall that model checking verifies a temporal property (a property about the sequence of events in system execution) against a finite-state model of the implementation. In this case, because we wrote the software without any model, the model needs to be extracted from the software, as shown in Figure 5.2. The final kind of validation illustrated in Figure 5.2 is static analysis. Unlike static checking, here we do not have a property to verify — instead we attempt to infer program properties by analyzing it. Typically, we may use static analysis to infer *invariants about specific program locations*; for example, whenever control flow reaches line 70, the variable v must be 0. These properties can then be exploited in static checking methods such as model checking. In other words, the role of the static analysis methods here is primarily to help methods such as model checking.

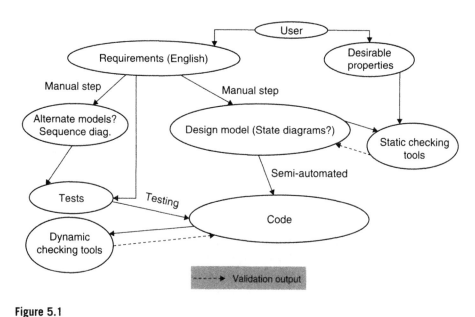

Figure 5.1

Validation in model-driven software engineering.

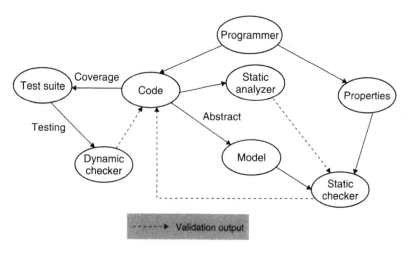

Figure 5.2

Software engineering without a model: possible validation mechanisms.

In the rest of this chapter, we elaborate on static and dynamic checking methods with illustrative examples. In the later part of the chapter, we present some hybrid methods that combine static and dynamic checking.

5.1 DYNAMIC OR TRACE-BASED CHECKING

Dynamic checking of software corresponds to checking its behavior for specific test cases. Dynamic checking goes by many other (similar-sounding) names such as run-time monitoring, dynamic analysis, or software debugging. The basic idea in these methods is to run the program against specific tests and compare the observed program behavior against expected program behavior. The tests may have been generated during model validation (Section 2.7), or they could be generated from the program itself through some coverage criterion (such as covering all statements in the program).

If the observed program behavior is different from the expected behavior, the corresponding test case is considered as failed, and the execution trace for the test case is examined automatically/manually to find the cause of failure. It is important to note here that the "observed" and "expected" behavior may not necessarily be given by output variable values. For example, the observed behavior of a program for a given test case may be that the program crashes, and the expected behavior may be the absence of a crash.

Economic importance

Let us illustrate the economic issues that drive interest in software testing and debugging. A report on the "Economic Impacts of Inadequate Infrastructure for Software Testing" published in 2002 by the Research Triangle Institute and the National Institute of Standards and Technology (USA) estimates that the annual cost incurred as a result of an inadequate software testing infrastructure all over the United States amounts to $59.5 billion — 0.6% of the $10 trillion U.S. GDP.

Industrial studies on quality control of software have indicated high defect densities. Ebnau in an ACM Crosstalk article[1] reports case studies where on an average 13 major errors per 1000 lines of code were reported. These errors are observed via slow code inspection (at 195 lines per hour) by humans. So, in reality, we can expect many more major errors. Nevertheless, conservatively let us fix the defect density at 13 major errors per 1000 lines of code. Now consider a software project with 5 million lines of code (the Windows Vista operating system is 50 million lines of code, so 5 million lines of code is by no means an astronomical figure). Even assuming a linear scaling up of defect counts, this amounts to at least $(13 \times 5000,000/1000) = 65,000$ major errors. Even if we assume that the average time saved to fix one error using

---

[1] See http://www.stsc.hill.af.mil/crosstalk/1994/06/xt94d06e.asp.

an automated debugging tool as opposed to manual debugging is 1 hour (this is a very modest estimate; often, fixing a bug takes a day or two), the time saved is 65,000 man-hours = 65,000/44 = 1477 work weeks = 1477/50 = 30 man-years. Clearly, this is a huge amount of time that a company can save, leading to more productive usage of its manpower and saving of precious dollar value. Assuming an employee salary of $ 40,000 per year, the foregoing translates to $ 1.2 million savings in employee salary simply by using better debugging tools. A much bigger savings, moreover, comes from customer satisfaction. By using automated debugging tools, a software development team can find more bugs than via manual debugging, leading to increased customer confidence and enhanced reputation of the company's products. Finally, manual approaches are error-prone, and the chances of leaving bugs can have catastrophic effects in safety-critical systems.

Related Terminology

To clarify the terminology related to dynamic checking methods, let us start with the "folklore" definition of software bug in Wikipedia:

> A software bug (or just "bug") is an error, flaw, mistake, "undocumented feature," failure, or fault in a computer program that prevents it from behaving as intended (e.g., producing an incorrect result). Most bugs arise from mistakes and errors made by people in either a program's source code or its design, and a few are caused by compilers producing incorrect code. A program that contains a large number of bugs, and/or bugs that seriously interfere with its functionality, is said to be buggy. Reports detailing bugs in a program are commonly known as bug reports, fault reports, problem reports, trouble reports, change requests, and so forth.

The conventional notion of a software bug is an error in the program that gets introduced during the software construction. It is worthwhile to note that the manifestation of a bug may be very different from the bug itself. Thus, the main task in software debugging is to trace back to the software bug from the manifestation of it. A good bug report will be able to take in a manifestation of a bug and locate the bug. In case this sounds unclear, let us consider the following program fragment marked with line numbers, written in Java style:

```
1. void setRunningVersion(boolean runningVersion)
2.     if( runningVersion ) {
3.           savedValue = value;
       }
       else{
4.           savedValue = "";
       }
```

```
5      this.runningVersion = runningVersion;
6.     System.out.println(savedValue);
}
```

Suppose this program is "buggy," the bug being that the variable savedValue is set to a wrong value in line 4. However, the manifestation of the bug is different — the variable savedValue is printed in line 6, and that is where the bug is indeed *manifested*. So, naturally there is a "distance" between where the software error is, and where it is observed (possibly via an output or a program crash). As another example, consider the following program fragment, written in C style:

```
1. a = 1;
2. b = a;
3. c = b;
4. if (c){
       v = 10;}
5. else { v = 20;}
6. println("%d", v);
```

Suppose the bug is in line 1, where variable a is set to a wrong value. Let us see how this bug will be manifested. The wrong value of variable a will be propagated to variable b — thereby "infecting" variable b. This wrong value will then be passed from variable b to variable c. Based on the wrong value passed to variable c, a branch or a decision will be made in line 4 and, in this case, the decision for the branch evaluation is wrong as a result. Because of the wrong branch evaluation, the variable v is set wrong, and this wrong value is printed in line 6 — the manifestation of the "bug" in line 1! So, as we can see, the bug in a program is usually quite different from its manifestation during program execution.

Now, what should a debugging method do? Of course, while testing the software, that is, running it against selected test cases, the programmer can see only the manifestation of the bug and not the bug itself! The task of a debugging method is to start from the manifestation the bug, and trace back to the bug itself. So, in the preceding C program fragment, the *observable error* will be an unexpected value of variable v being printed. From here, the debugging method has to reason that (i) variable v was set in lines 4 or 5, (ii) the setting of variable v depends on a branch that is evaluated based on the value of c, (iii) the value of c depends on the value of b, and (iv) the value of b depends on the value of a. Thus, the reasoning here uncovers a chain of *dependencies* starting from the observable error (line 6), in order to locate the *error cause* (in line 1). We now discuss the dynamic slicing method, which traverses an execution trace to uncover the program dependency chains of an observable error. The lines of program captured in these program dependency chains are highlighted in a bug report, which is also called the "slice." The programmer can then inspect the bug report to locate the probable error causes.

Manual versus Automated

Before describing the dynamic slicing method in details, let us ponder a bit and explain its difference from conventional software debugging tools such as the gdb for C, jdb for Java, or VBwatch for Visual Basic. All of these tools essentially track the program execution for a given input. The programmer can set "breakpoints," guiding the tool to freeze the program execution at specific control locations, and then observe values of specific variables at these locations. However, note that the entire debugging process is still *manual*. The programmer has to instruct the debugging tool about where to stop (i.e., where to set the breakpoint), and then manually observe selected variables at these breakpoints. The tool is only keeping track of the program execution, but not analyzing the program execution in any way! Thus, existing debugging tools do not employ any *analysis* of the execution trace — they only record or profile the execution trace and display the trace information. The real issue at hand is *not* the visualization of the trace information — many of the existing debuggers have detailed graphical user interfaces (GUIs) for this purpose. Figure 5.3 shows a snapshot of a conventional debugger — actually the well-known gdb debugger for C. It collects and lets the user visualize relevant information about the program execution — the figure shows the user inquiring about the value of a program variable h at a specific control location of the program. What is missing is an analysis of the execution trace to explain a possibly unexpected value of the variable h — this has to be done manually by the user. The dynamic slicing method provides such an analysis.

5.1.1 Dynamic Slicing

Dynamic slicing is a generic method for program debugging and comprehension. The method takes in the following: (a) a program P, (b) an input I of the program P, and (c) a description of the error observed during the execution of P for input I. The output of the method is a fragment of P that is likely to be responsible for the observed error. Thus, the output of the method is essentially a "bug report" of sorts, an explanation of the cause of the observed error.

To discuss the method, we first need to understand how the observed error is described. Usually, the observed error is presented as a pair (l, v), where l is a line in the program P being debugged and v is a program variable. This usually means that the programmer is unhappy about the value of v observed in line l of a given program for a given input. That is, when a given program P is executed with a given input I, the user is unhappy about the value of v observed in line l of the program and would like to seek an explanation for it. The explanation will be provided by dynamic slicing, which acts as a debugging method. One issue needs to clarified in this regard. A line l may be executed several times during the execution of program

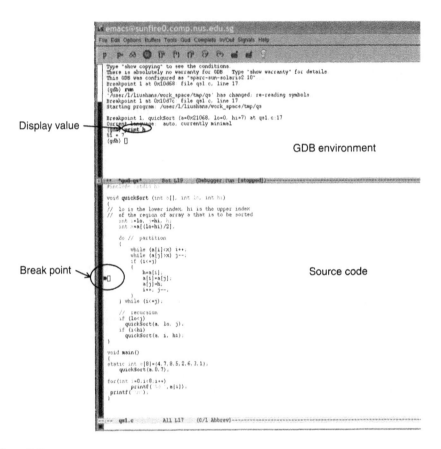

Figure 5.3

Snapshot of a conventional debugger (gdb for C).

P with input I. Therefore, when the programmer seeks an explanation of the value of v in line l, he or she could be interested in the value of v in the last execution of l, or the value of v in some specific execution of l, or the value of v in all executions of l. Note that whichever executions of l we are interested in, it makes little difference to the dynamic slicing method itself; it only makes a difference to the initialization of the dynamic slicing method.

Having explained the notion of observed error, we need to discuss the notion of dynamic slice and what it stands for. The dynamic slice stands for a detailed explanation of the observed error. In other words, the dynamic slice can be thought of as a "bug report," and the task of dynamic slicing as "debugging" — finding the source of a bug that is observed elsewhere. How is the bug report constructed? Let us say we are performing dynamic slicing of a program P with input I, where the slicing criterion is the value of variable v in the last occurrence of line l. Slicing can now proceed in one of two ways:

- Via a backwards traversal of the execution trace of program P for input I; the traversal starts from the last occurrence of line l in the execution trace.
- Via a forward execution of the program P for input I.

The first possibility involves storing the execution trace in some form and hence leads to space overheads. However, the computation in this case is goal-directed (i.e., redundancy free), because we compute the slice of only the slicing criterion we are interested in — the value of variable v in the last occurrence of l. In the second option, we do not encounter any space overheads owing to storing of the program execution trace. We do, however, have to compute and store many slices during the execution. For each executed statement, we compute and store the slices of the variables used in the statement; these slices are used for computing slices of the subsequent variable usages. Thus, even though the program execution trace does not need to be stored, there is a time and space overhead in computing many dynamic slices (many of which are unrelated to the actual slicing criterion the programmer is interested in). In other words, the dynamic slice computation is not goal-directed in this situation.

Whether a dynamic slice is computed by forward or backward traversal of program execution, it is computing chains of data and control dependencies. To explain these concepts, let us first consider a simple program fragment, written in C-style (see Figure 5.4). The program constructs the sum of all even numbers from 1 to N and the product of all odd numbers from 1 to N, where N is a given integer. We will use this example program to define the necessary concepts — (static and dynamic) control dependencies, (static and dynamic) data dependencies, dynamic dependence graphs, and dynamic program slices.

```
1    scanf("%d", &N);
2    i = 1;
3    sum = 0;
4    prod = 1;
5    while (i < N)}{
6        if (i % 2 == 0){
7                sum = sum + i;}
8        else { prod = prod * i;}
9         i = i + 1; }
10   printf("%d%d", sum, prod);
```

Figure 5.4

An example program to explain the concepts behind dynamic slicing.

Consider an execution of the program for $N = 3$. The execution trace is as follows:

$\langle$ 1,2,3,4,   // *initialization*
5,6,8,9,   // *first iteration, i = 1*
5,6,7,9,   // *second iteration, i = 2*
5,10$\rangle$ // *i = 3, end of execution*

Suppose the programmer wants an explanation of the value of sum printed in line 10; thus the slicing criterion is (10, sum). We seek an automated method that can find the fragment of the program which influences the value of sum at line 10; this fragment will be treated as the *explanation* of the value of sum in line 10. In constructing the explanation, we try to answer the following questions:

- *Dynamic data dependence:* Which variable assignment was propagated to the value of sum printed in line 10?
- *Dynamic control dependence:* What is the nearest conditional branch statement that enables line 10 to be executed, in the execution trace under consideration?

These questions can be answered by a backwards traversal of the execution trace starting from line 10, the slicing criterion. In particular, the value of sum in line 10 contains the value set in the last execution of line 7. As far as dynamic control dependencies go, we observe that the execution of line 10 is unconditional, it does not depend on any conditional branch statement evaluating in a certain direction. In case the reader is reasoning that line 10 got executed only because the while-loop (line 5) terminated and hence line 5 and line 10 are control dependent, here is the way to think about this matter. Any program execution from line 5 to the end of the program will pass through line 10. Hence line 5 does *not* enable line 10 to be executed.

The dynamic control and data dependencies in an execution trace are typically summarized in a dynamic dependency graph. Because one statement may be executed several time in an execution trace, we distinguish between the different occurrences of the same statement — each occurrence is a separate *statement instance*. The nodes of a dynamic dependency graph are the statement instances, and the edges are dynamic dependencies (both data and control dependencies). Part of the dynamic dependency graph for the example program of Figure 5.4 with input $N = 3$ is given in Figure 5.5; dashed edges denote control dependencies, and solid edges denote data dependencies. We show only the part of the dynamic dependency graph that is relevant to our slicing criterion — the value of sum in line 10 of the program.

Each node in the dynamic dependency graph in Figure 5.5 is of the form i^j denoting the jth occurrence of line i in the execution trace of the program in Figure 5.4 with input $N = 3$. Let us now explain the dependencies shown in Figure 5.5. Statement instance 10^1 is dynamically data dependent on 7^1, because the definition of sum in

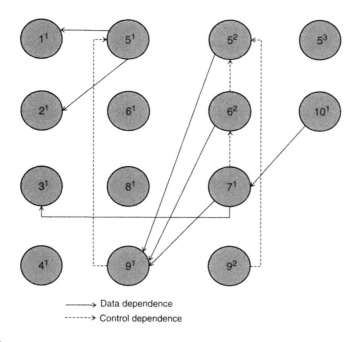

Data dependence
Control dependence

Figure 5.5

Portion of dynamic dependency graph that is relevant to the slicing criterion — the variable sum in line 10 of Figure 5.4. We consider an input $N = 3$.

7^1 is used in 10^1. Also, statement instance 7^1 is dynamically control dependent on statement instance 6^2; 6^2 is the nearest enclosing branch statement instance s.t. the evaluation of the corresponding branch, which allows 7^1 to be executed. Figure 5.5 shows only a fragment of the dynamic dependency graph — the fragment that is reachable from our slicing criterion, the value of sum in line 10. The slice consists of the following statement instances from which statement instances

$$10^1, 7^1, 6^2, 5^2, 9^1, 3^1, 5^1, 2^1, 1^1$$

that is, instances of the following statements:

$$\{1, 2, 3, 5, 6, 7, 9, 10\}$$

Lines 4 and 8, which manipulate the variable prod, are not in the slice.

Method

We now formally describe the dynamic slicing method for software debugging. Traditionally, dynamic slicing is performed w.r.t. a slicing criterion (H, l, v), where H represents an execution trace of the program being debugged, l represents a control location in the program, and v is a program variable. A dynamic slice contains all statement instances (or statements) that have affected the value of variable v referenced at l in the trace H. A dynamic slicing algorithm can proceed by forward or backward exploration of an execution trace. Here we summarize a backwards slicing algorithm that is goal-directed (w.r.t. the slicing criterion), but requires efficient storage/traversal of the trace. During the trace traversal that starts from the statement in the slicing criterion, a dynamic slicing algorithm maintains the following quantities: (a) the dynamic slice φ, (b) a set of variables δ whose dynamic data dependencies need to be explained, and (c) a set of statement instances γ whose dynamic control dependencies need to be explained. Initially, we set the following: (a) $\varphi = \gamma = $ last instance[2] of location l in trace H, and (b) $\delta = \{v\}$.

For each statement instance *stmt* encountered during the backward traversal, the algorithm performs the following two checks. The algorithm terminates when we reach the beginning of the trace.

- *Check dynamic data dependencies.* Let v_{def}^{stmt} be the variable defined by *stmt*. If $v_{def}^{stmt} \in \delta$, it means that we have found the definition of v_{def}^{stmt} which the slicing algorithm was looking for. So, v_{def}^{stmt} is removed from δ, and variables used by *stmt* are inserted into δ. In addition, *stmt* is inserted into φ and γ.
- *Check dynamic control dependencies.* If any statement instance in γ is dynamically control dependent on *stmt*, all statement instances which are dynamically control dependent on *stmt* are removed from γ. Variables used by *stmt* are inserted into δ, and *stmt* is inserted into φ and γ.

When the dynamic slicing algorithm terminates, the resultant dynamic slice, (i.e., the set φ) is reported back to the programmer for inspection.

Figure 5.6 describes how slicing can be made to fit in with software testing and debugging. Usually a program is tested against inputs from a test suite. If the program outputs are as "expected," the tests are said to pass. For a failed test (i.e., where the output is "unexpected"), the programmer needs to find the cause of unexpected program behavior. This brings us to debugging, and dynamic slicing is one debugging method. The slicing criterion comes from the failed test case itself; the slicing criterion is (I, l, v), where I is the input for the failed test case, l is the line number where the "unexpected" output is observed, and v is the output variable whose observed value is "unexpected." For dynamic slicing, the program is run against the same input (the one leading to a failed test case) in an instrumented fashion — that is, (part of) the execution trace is collected. The execution trace is analyzed via dynamic slicing as mentioned in the preceding. The constructed dynamic slice acts as the bug report. The programmer can use it for program comprehension and

---

[2] We could also consider any other instance, or even all instances.

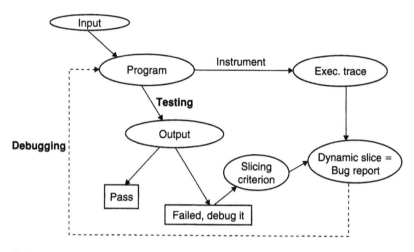

Figure 5.6

Software testing and debugging with slicing as the debugging method.

debugging, thereby locating the source of error. Needless to say, only the computation of the slice is automatic. Comprehension and debugging of programs using the slice is a fully manual activity.

Time and Space Complexity

Note that dynamic slicing is an algorithmic framework, and it can be adapted for different programming languages. The complexity of dynamic slicing algorithm for modern programming languages such as Java is as follows:

- Worst-case space complexity is linear in the length of the execution trace, and
- Worst-case time complexity is quadratic in the length of the execution trace.

The quadratic time complexity is owing to the dependence computation, which involves checking pairs of operations in the trace. We note that state-of-the-art slicing tools (such as the JSlice tool for Java [97, 98]) employ online compression of the execution trace — where the execution trace is compacted as it is collected, achieving compaction ratios (memory taken up by original trace versus memory taken up by compact trace) of 10 to 1000 [100].

Dealing with Large Slices

The reader may be concerned that the dynamic slice of real-life programs may be too large for human comprehension. Here we would like to point out that dynamic slicing is a core method of program understanding, debugging, and validation. There exist very many different improvements to the dynamic slicing method to reduce the slice size, such as not computing the full slice (e.g., certain programmers may inspect only the chains of data dependencies). A most recently proposed method called hierarchical dynamic slicing [99] addresses this problem as follows. It builds a dynamic slicing method where the human programmer is gradually exposed to a slice in a hierarchical fashion, rather than having to inspect a very large slice after it is computed. The key idea is simple — we systematically interleave the slice computation and comprehension steps. Conventional works on slicing have concentrated only on the computation of the slice, comprehension of the slice being left as a post-mortem activity. In hierarchical dynamic slicing, the two activities are integrated in a synergistic fashion as follows:

- Computation of the slice is guided (to a limited extent) by the human programmer so that very few control/data dependencies in a large slice need to be explored and inspected.
- The programmer's comprehension of the slice is greatly enhanced by the nature of our slice computation, which proceeds hierarchically. Thus, for programs with long dependence chains, this allows the programmer to gradually zoom in to selected dynamic dependencies.

To understand the potential benefits one can gain from the method, let us examine the factors that make the comprehension of dynamic slices difficult.

- Many programs have long dependence chains spanning across loops and function boundaries. These dependence chains are captured in the slice. However, the slice being a (flat) set of statements, much of the program structure (loops/functions) is lost. This makes the slice hard to comprehend.
- Programs often also have a great deal of inherent parallelism. So, a slice may capture many different dependence chains.

Let us now discuss how hierarchical computation/exploration of slices can help programmers to comprehend large slices containing these two features: (a) long dependence chains, and (b) many different dependence chains. Figure 5.7a shows an example program with a long dependence chain. Consider an execution trace of the program ...3, 4, 5, 6 — where lines 3,4,5,6 of Figure 5.7a are executed. Slicing this execution trace w.r.t. the criterion ($line6, y$) (i.e., the value of y at line 6) yields a slice that contains lines 3, 4, 5, 6 as well as lines *inside* the body of the functions $f1, f2, f3$. In other words, because the slice is a (flat) set of statements, the program structure is lost in the slice. This structure is explicitly manifested in Figure 5.7b, where we show the dependence chain in a *hierarchical fashion*. In other words, the dependencies inside the functions $f1, f2, f3$ are not shown. Here, a hierarchical exploration of the dependence chains will clearly be less burdensome to the

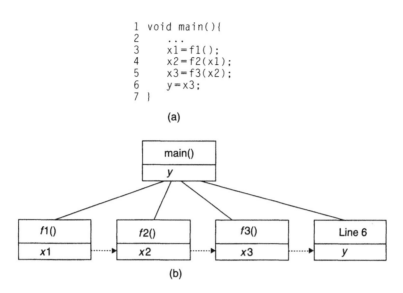

```
1 void main(){
2     ...
3     x1=f1();
4     x2=f2(x1);
5     x3=f3(x2);
6     y=x3;
7 }
```

(a)

(b)

Figure 5.7

(a) A program with a long dynamic dependence chain. (b) The corresponding phases. Dashed arrows represent dynamic dependencies that a programmer needs to follow for debugging.

programmer. Thus, in Figure 5.7b, by inspecting the dependencies hierarchically, the programmer may find it necessary to inspect the dependencies inside a specific function (say, $f2$). As a result, we can avoid inspecting the dependence chain(s) inside the other functions (in this case $f1, f3$).

Now, let us consider programs with many different dependence chains. Figure 5.8a shows a schematic program with several dependence chains, and hence substantial inherent parallelism. If the slicing criterion involves the value of y in line 6, we need to consider the dependencies between y and $x3$ and those between y and $x2$, as well as y and $x1$. These three dependencies are shown via broken arrows in Figure 5.8b. Again, with the programmer's intervention, we can rule out some of these dependencies for exploration and inspection.

In summary, the hierarchical dynamic slicing method works as follows. Given an execution trace (corresponding to a program input) containing an observable behavior that is deemed an "error" by the programmer, we divide the trace into *phases*. This division is typically done along loop/procedure/loop-iteration boundaries so that each phase corresponds to a logical unit of program behavior. Only the interphase data and control dependencies are presented to the programmer; the intraphase dependencies are completely suppressed. The programmer then identifies a likely suspicious phase, which is then subjected to further investigation in a similar manner (dividing the phase into subphases, computing dependencies across these

```
1 void main(){
2   ...
3     x1=f1();
4     x2=f2();
5     x3=f3();
6     y=x1+x2+x3;
7 }
```

(a)

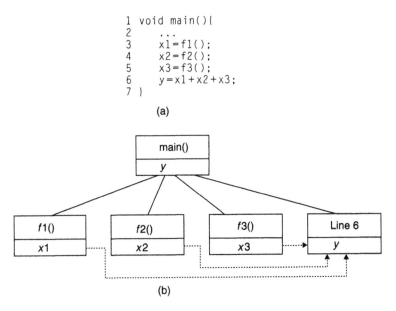

(b)

Figure 5.8

(a) A program with inherent parallelism (several dynamic dependence chains). (b) The corresponding phases. Dashed arrows represent dynamic dependencies that a programmer needs to follow for debugging.

subphases, and so on). This process continues until the error is identified. Of course, an underlying assumption here is that the programmer will be able to identify the erroneous statement once it is pointed out to him or her.

One may comment that such a hierarchical exploration of dynamic dependencies involves programmer's intervention, whereas conventional dynamic slicing is fully automatic. Here we should note that the process of error detection by using/exploring a dynamic slice involves a *huge* manual effort; the manual effort in exploring/comprehending the slice simply happens *after* the computation of the slice. In the hierarchical method, we are interleaving the computation and comprehension of dynamic dependencies. As in dynamic slicing, the computation of the dynamic dependencies is automatic in our method; only the comprehension involves the programmer. Moreover, the programmer is exposed to the complex chain(s) of program dependencies gradually, rather than all at once, thereby allowing better program comprehension.

5.1.2 Fault Localization

So far, we have presented the dynamic slicing method. This method is fully formal and requires examination of the control/data dependencies in an execution trace. The difficulties in using it include (a) time and space overheads for storing/analyzing program traces and (b) potentially large slice sizes. In the preceding, we examined methods to deal with the second problem — comprehension of large slices. However, we still have to grapple with the time and space overheads of dynamic slicing. As observed earlier, state-of-the-art dynamic slicing tools (such as [97]) employ various tricks such as online compaction of the execution trace and program dependence analysis on the compact trace (without decompressing it). Nevertheless, the time and space overheads for large real-life programs is still substantial, and the quest for lightweight methods remains. We discuss a class of such lightweight methods here. In the following we use the terms *execution trace* and *execution run* interchangeably. Indeed, the existing literature on software debugging also uses these two terms interchangeably. Before proceeding any further, let us first give an illustrative example.

Illustrative Example

Our example is a fragment of the TCAS program from the Siemens benchmark suite [33], which has been extensively used in the software engineering community for research in testing/debugging. The TCAS program is an embedded software for altitude control. In Figure 5.9, we show a fragment of the program. Note that `Climb` and `Up` are input variables of the program. There is a bug in the following program fragment, namely, lines 2 and 4 are reversed in order. In other words, line 2 should be `separation = Up + 100` and line 4 should be `separation = Up`.

```
1.  if (Climb)
2.      separation = Up;
3.  else
4.      separation = Up + 100;
5.  if (separation > 150)
6.      upward = 1;
7.  else
8.      upward = 0;
9.  if (upward > 0)
10.     ...
11.     printf("Upward");
12. else
13.     ...
14.     printf("Downward");
```

Figure 5.9

Example program fragment from Siemens benchmark suite.

Now, consider an execution of the some program fragment with the inputs `Climb = 1` and `Up = 100`. The execution will lead to "Downward" being printed. Clearly, this is unexpected, because the developer would expect "Upward" to be printed for these inputs. Thus, the trace for the inputs `Climb = 1`, `Up = 100` is a *failing run* that needs to be debugged.

We now have an example of a failing run, but what is a *successful run*? A successful run is simply one where the program output is as expected. So, if the programmer expects the output to be "Upward," the program should print "Upward," and if the programmer expects the output to be "Downward," the program should print "Downward." Consider the program execution with the inputs `Climb = 0` and `Up = 0`. The output in this case is "Downward," and this matches the developer's expectations. Hence we deem this as a successful run. Usually, the process of determining whether a given run is failed or successful cannot be fully automated. This involves matching the program output with the developer's expectation, so the task of articulating the developer's expectation remains manual.

We have now explained what we mean by failing run and successful run. Our task is to debug a given "failed" run — to explain why it failed, that is, why the program output was not as expected. We are trying to do so by comparing it with a successful run (where the program output was as expected) in order to gain insights about what went wrong in the failed run. The computed "difference" between the failed run and the chosen successful run is reported to the programmer as the *bug report*. The key questions now are:

- Given a failed run, how do we choose a successful run?
- Given a failed and a successful run, how do we compute their difference?

Both the questions have their answers in a evaluation metric for execution runs. A common (and very rough) metric is the set of statements executed in an execution run. If we have a successful run and a failed run, we can compute their difference by computing the difference of the set of statements executed. The question now is how to get a successful run? In other words, how do we choose a successful run corresponding to a given failed run σ_f? We will choose a successful run σ_s such that the set of statements executed in σ_s is "close" to the set of statements executed in σ_f. In fact, given a program P and failed execution run σ_f in P, we can do the following:

- Typically the program P will be endowed with a test suite (set of test cases) based on some coverage criteria (covering all statements or all branches in the program). We construct the execution runs for the test cases from the test suite. Let this set of execution runs be $Runs_{all}(P)$.
- From among the execution runs in $Runs_{all}(P)$, we chose those that are successful, that is, runs where the program output meets the programmer's

expectations. Let this set be $SuccRuns_{all}(P)$; clearly $SuccRuns_{all}(P) \subseteq Runs_{all}(P)$.

- We choose an execution run $\sigma_s \in SuccRuns_{all}(P)$ such that the quantity $|stmt(\sigma_f) - stmt(\sigma_s)|$ is minimized. Here $stmt(\sigma)$ is the set of statements in an execution run σ, and $|S|$ is the cardinality or the number of elements in a set S. Note that for two sets S_1 and S_2, the quantity $S_1 - S_2$ denotes the set difference, that is, elements appearing in S_1 but not in S_2.

Thus, we choose a successful execution run σ_s, such that there are only a few statements appearing in the failed run σ_f, but not in σ_s. The idea here is that if a statement appears only in the failed run but not in the successful run, it is a likely error cause.

In our running example, the inputs `Climb = 1` and `Up = 100` lead to an unexpected output. The set of statements executed in this failed execution run is $\{1,2,5,7,8,9,13,14\}$. Furthermore, the inputs `Climb = 0` and `Up = 0` lead to an expected output. The set of statements executed in this successful execution run is $\{1,3,4,5,7,8,9,13,14\}$. So, the bug report is the difference between these two sets:

$$\{1,2,5,7,8,9,13,14\} - \{1,3,4,5,7,8,9,13,14\} = \{2\}$$

Once this line is pointed out to the developer, he or she should be able to locate the error in line 2.

Note here that the choice of successful execution run is crucial. Consider an execution of the program in Figure 5.9 with the inputs `Climb = 1` and `Up = 200`. When executed with these inputs, the program will print "Upward," which is what the developer expects. So, the execution run for these inputs is deemed as a successful run. What would have happened if we chose this execution run to compare with our failed execution run (the one resulting from the inputs `Climb = 1` and `Up = 100`)? The set of statements executed for the inputs `Climb = 1` and `Up = 200` is $\{1,2,5,6,9,10,11\}$. So, in this case the bug report (the difference in executed statements between the failed run and the chosen successful run) would have been

$$\{1,2,5,7,8,9,13,14\} - \{1,2,5,6,9,10,11\} = \{7,8,13,14\}$$

The bug report in this case consists of more statements. Moreover, the statements do not pinpoint to the actual error cause in the program; they are only manifestations of the error cause. This simple example should demonstrate to the reader that the choice of successful run is crucial for the usefulness of the bug report generated by fault localization methods.

Figure 5.10 summarizes the class of trace-based debugging methods we are presenting here — commonly called *fault localization*. The aim of these methods is to find the error cause in a failed execution run (a run with unexpected behavior) in a given program. This is done by comparing the failed execution run with a successful

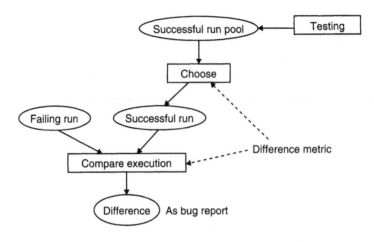

Figure 5.10

Fault localization methods.

execution run. The successful execution run is chosen from a test pool, possibly constructed by coverage-based testing. The chosen successful run is then compared with the failed execution run, and the difference is reported back to the developer as a bug report. Of course, there are many metrics by which to compare the execution traces, such as:

- Sets of statements executed,
- Sequence of branch statements executed,
- Sequence of statements executed,
- Sequence of variable values taken (for selected variables), and so on.

Trace Comparison Metric Based on Statement Sets

The simplest trace comparison metric (which is very efficient to compute) is simply: *Set of statements executed in failed run − Set of statements executed in successful run*. Given a failed run, we choose a successful run that minimizes this quantity. However, this trace comparison metric does not distinguish between runs that execute exactly the same statements but in a different order. Consider the schematic program fragment in the following, consisting of an if-then-else within a loop:

```
for (...) {
    if (...)  S1 else S2;
}
```

Consider two runs of the program ⟨S1,S2,S1,S2⟩ and ⟨S2,S1,S2,S1⟩. These two runs execute the conditional branch in the if-then-else statement differently in every iteration of the loop. Yet a trace comparison metric based on sets of statements executed cannot distinguish between these two runs. Given a failed run, say, $\langle S1, S2, S1, S2 \rangle$, suppose we choose $\langle S2, S1, S2, S1 \rangle$ as the successful run with which we compare our failed run. The result is a null bug report, which is not only useless for debugging, but also misleading to the developer.

Trace Comparison Metric Based on Branch Alignments

For the reasons mentioned in the preceding, the software debugging community has studied trace comparison metrics that compare traces of a program by finding out which branches are evaluated differently. Such a difference metric measures the difference between two execution runs π and π' of a program, by comparing behaviors of "corresponding" branch statement instances from π and π'. The branch statement instances with differing outcomes in π, π' are captured in $diff(\pi, \pi')$ — the difference between execution run π and execution run π'. In order to find out "corresponding" branch instances, a notion of *alignment* is defined, to relate statement instances of two execution runs. Typically, such a branch alignment can be based on *dynamic control dependence*. Here we illustrate the distance metric with an example. The reader can refer to related literature [32] for an in-depth understanding of the topic.

Consider the program fragment in Figure 5.11, taken from the Siemens benchmark suite [33]. This piece of code changes all substrings s_1 in string lin matching

```
1.    while (lin[i] != ENDSTR) {
2.        m= ...
3.        if (m >= 0) {
4.            ...
5.            lastm = m;
6.        }
7.        if ((m == -1) || (m == i)) {
8.            ...
9.            i = i + 1;
10.       }
11.       else
12.           i = m;
13.   }
14.   ...
```

Figure 5.11

An example program fragment from the Siemens benchmark suite. We use the example to illustrate trace comparison metrics.

a pattern to another substring s_2. Here variable i represents the index to the first unprocessed character in string lin, variable m represents the index to the end of a matched substring s_1 in string lin, and variable lastm records variable m in the last loop iteration. The bug in the code lies in the fact that the branch condition in line 3 should be if (m >= 0) && (lastm != m). At the ith iteration, if variable m is not changed at line 2, line 3 is wrongly evaluated to true, and substring s_2 is wrongly returned as output, deemed by programmer as an observable "error."

In Figure 5.12, we show some traces from the program in Figure 5.11. The difference between execution runs π and π' is: $diff(\pi, \pi') = \langle 3_3, 7_{14} \rangle$, as indicated in Figure 5.12. This is because branch instances $3_3, 7_{14}$ are aligned in runs π and π' and their outcomes are different in π, π'. If the branches at lines $3_3, 7_{14}$ are evaluated differently, we get π' from π. Similarly, the difference between execution runs π and π'' is $diff(\pi, \pi'') = \langle 7_6, 7_{14} \rangle$.

Why do we capture branch event occurrences of π that evaluate differently in π' in the difference $diff(\pi, \pi')$? Recall that we want to choose a successful run for purposes of fault localization. If π is the failing run and π' is a successful run, then $diff(\pi, \pi')$ tells us which branches in the failing run π need to be evaluated differently

Execution run			Alignment			Difference	
π	π'	π''	π π'		π π''	$diff(\pi, \pi')$	$diff(\pi, \pi'')$
1^1	1^1	1^1					
2^2	2^2	2^2					
3^3	3^3	3^3				•	
4^4		4^4					
5^5		5^5					
7^6	7^4	7^6					•
8^7	8^5						
9^8	9^6						
		12^7					
1^9	1^7	1^8					
2^{10}	2^8	2^9					
3^{11}	3^9	3^{10}					
4^{12}	4^{10}	4^{11}					
5^{13}	5^{11}	5^{12}					
7^{14}	7^{12}	7^{13}				•	•
8^{15}							
9^{16}							
	12^{13}	12^{14}					
14^{17}	14^{14}	14^{15}					

Figure 5.12

Example to illustrate alignments and difference metrics. The first three columns show the event sequences of three execution runs π, π', and π'' of the program fragment in Figure 5.11 (page 201). The next two columns show alignments of (π, π') and (π, π''), where solid lines indicate aligned statement instances and dashed lines indicate unaligned statement instances. The last two columns show the difference between execution runs — [32].

to produce the successful run π'. Clearly, if we have a choice of successful runs, we would like to make minimal changes to the failing run to produce a successful run. Thus, given a failing run π and two successful runs π', π'', we choose π' over π'' if $diff(\pi, \pi') < diff(\pi, \pi'')$. This requires us to *compare* differences. How we do so is elaborated in the following. Given a failing run π and two successful runs π', π'' we can say that $diff(\pi, \pi') < diff(\pi, \pi'')$ based on a combination of the following criteria:

- Fewer branches of π need to be evaluated differently to get π' as compared to the number of branches of π that need to be evaluated differently to get π''.
- The branches of π that need to be evaluated differently to get π' appear closer to the end of π (where the error is observed), as compared to the branches of π that need to be evaluated differently to get π''.

To illustrate our comparison of differences, consider the example in Figure 5.12. Recall that $diff(\pi, \pi') = \langle 3_3, 7_{14} \rangle$, and $diff(\pi, \pi'') = \langle 7_6, 7_{14} \rangle$, as illustrated by the "•" in the last two columns of Figure 5.12. Comparing $\langle 3_3, 7_{14} \rangle$ with $\langle 7_6, 7_{14} \rangle$, we see that $\langle 7_6, 7_{14} \rangle < \langle 3_3, 7_{14} \rangle$ because statement instance 7_6 occurs after statement instance 3_3 in execution run π.

Summary of Trace Comparison Methods

In summary, which trace comparison metric is chosen and how the traces are compared is a matter of choice. However, based on the metric, we can choose the successful run from a pool of successful runs (say, the test suite of a program). In particular, suppose we have an execution trace σ_f that is failed, meaning it shows an unexpected behavior. We want to compare it with another execution trace σ_s such that:

- σ_s does not show any unexpected behavior, that is, the program outputs in run σ_s are as per the developer's expectations, and
- σ_s is the closest to σ_f in terms of the comparison metric being used.

Thus, based on the trace comparison metric being used, we choose the successful run against which we compare a given failed execution run, and report the difference between the two runs as a bug report.

5.1.3 Directed Testing Methods

So far, we have studied different debugging methods which either (a) analyze the dependencies in a failed trace or (b) compare a failed trace with a "chosen" successful trace. These methods can be combined with testing techniques in a postmortem fashion. In other words, given a program P, we generate a test suite (set of test inputs) for P, and the traces for the test inputs in the test suite are subjected to analysis.

On the other hand, one could envision testing methods that are more directed to exposing errors. Conventional software testing methods are often driven with the sole goal of *coverage*. What do we mean by coverage in the context of test generation? Let us take the statement coverage criteria. We say that a set of test inputs S achieves statement coverage if each statement in the program appears in the trace for at least one test input in S. Similarly, one can define other coverage criteria such as branch edge coverage. The reader can refer to standard texts on software engineering [86] for details of test coverage.

Standard test coverage criteria such as statement coverage provide very weak guarantees about the software's reliability. Statement coverage merely says that each statement in the program is executed for some test input in the test suite. However, this does not mean that executing the tests in the test suite will expose the bug in a buggy statement. If a statement is buggy, its execution does not guarantee the manifestation of the bug in the statement. Of course, if a statement in the program is buggy and it is executed for some input, there is more chance of the bug in the statement being manifested in the form of an unexpected output.

Ideally, what we would like to do via systematic program testing is to expose the different paths in a program. However, enumerating all paths in a program and finding inputs that exercise these paths is not easy. The number of program paths is exponential on the number of branch instances, and the number of branch instances (individual executions of a branch statement) itself can be very large. Exhaustive testing by trying out all inputs is simply not an option with real-life embedded software, because there are too many inputs to test. Often, there are even infinitely many inputs — consider an image compression program; we cannot test it with all possible input images.

So, we are stuck between the frying pan and the fire! We cannot employ brute-force methods such as exhaustive testing of all inputs, because these methods do not scale up for real-world programs. We also cannot hope to cover all program paths by lightweight methods such as random testing; successive experimental studies have shown that random testing leads to poor coverage of program paths. Nor can we expect to cover all paths (or even a large fraction of them) simply by covering some other code artifact such as statement coverage. How do we proceed?

One answer to this problem seems to be systematic path exploration via directed testing. In this approach, we start testing our program P with a random input i. Suppose executing the program with input i goes along program path π. During the execution of program P with input i, we collect the condition under which path π is executed. This is the path condition of π and captures the set of inputs (one of which

```
1.  if (Climb)
2.      separation = Up;
3.  else
4.      separation = Up + 100;
5.  if (separation > 150)
6.      upward = 1;
7.  else
8.      upward = 0;
9.  if (upward > 0)
10.     . . .
11.     printf("Upward");
12. else
13.     . . .
14.     printf("Downward");
```

Figure 5.13

Example program fragment from Siemens benchmark suite.

is, of course, i) whose executions go along path π. We then slightly modify the path condition π to produce another path condition π', which is solved to produce another test input. This process goes on, every time modifying the current path condition, thereby getting a new path and then finding a test input that exercises this new path. This is essentially a method of systematic exploration of program paths by finding suitable inputs to exercise the paths. The hope is that, by exploring more program paths, we have a better chance of encountering errors in the program.

We now illustrate this method with an example. Consider the program fragment in Figure 5.9, reproduced here as Figure 5.13 for convenience. The inputs to this program fragment are Climb (boolean variable) and Up (integer variable). Suppose we start with a random input Climb == 0 and Up == 457. This produces the following path:

```
1.  if (Climb)

3.  else
4.      separation = Up + 100;
5.  if (separation > 150)
6.      upward = 1;

9.  if (upward > 0)
10.     . . .
11.     printf("Upward");
```

The path condition (i.e., the conditions on the input on which the foregoing path is executed) is

$$Climb == 0 \land Up + 100 > 150 \land upward > 0$$

The preceding is a conjunction of three primitive constraints. To systematically explore other paths, we can negate the last primitive constraint to get

$$Climb == 0 \land Up + 100 > 150 \land upward \leq 0$$

This path turns out to be infeasible — no program input exercising this path. So, we negate the next primitive constraint and get

$$Climb == 0 \land Up + 100 \leq 150$$

Solving this constraint we can get a sample input `Climb == 0, Up == 0`, allowing us to explore a new path given as follows.

```
1.   if (Climb)

3.   else
4.       separation = Up + 100;
5.   if (separation > 150)

7.   else
8.       upward = 0;
9.   if (upward > 0)

12. else
13.      ...
14.      printf("Downward");
```

Continuing further in this fashion, we can explore the different paths in the program and get concrete inputs that exercise these program paths. This method is called directed testing, because we modify the path constraint of the current path being explored to explore a new path. Thus, the method is *directed* toward exploring more paths in the program. It will achieve significantly more coverage than random testing, where several randomly generated inputs may exercise the same program path. One can employ such a directed testing approach for exposing more program behaviors in a systematic way, thereby hoping to encounter corner cases leading to exceptions/crashes during the testing phase.

Before concluding our discussion on directed testing, we should mention that several subtle issues in a directed testing algorithm have not been discussed here. In our example, the first path we obtained in the preceding had a path constraint

$$Climb == 0 \land Up + 100 > 150 \land upward > 0$$

Here `Climb` and `Up` are input variables. However, `upward` is a program variable whose value is related to the value of the input variable `Up`. In fact, the (boolean) value of `upward` is directly correlated to the condition `Up + 100 > 150`. Directed testing methods/tools will usually try to detect such correlations. As a result, they can avoid exploring infeasible paths, such as the path with constraint

$$Climb == 0 \land Up + 100 > 150 \land upward \leq 0$$

in our example.

Other issues in directed testing methods include search strategies for exploring paths. The method we outlined here via an example essentially employs depth-first search to explore paths. New paths are obtained from the current path being explored by backtracking (where we negate the condition corresponding to the last branch encountered). Other search strategies such as breadth-first or best-first have also been explored in various tools. The interested reader may refer to related articles such as [29] for details.

5.2 FORMAL VERIFICATION

Dynamic or trace-based checking methods are very useful for testing-oriented debugging. In other words, the software validation flow here revolves around program testing — we test a program against selected test cases, and for the failed test cases (the ones for which the program output does not match the programmer's "expectations"), we analyze the traces for these test cases using dynamic checking methods. However, program testing, by its very nature, is nonexhaustive. It is not feasible to test a program against all possible inputs.

As a result, for safety-critical software it is crucial to employ checking methods that go beyond testing-oriented debugging. Currently, many functionalities in our daily lives are software controlled — functionalities that earlier used to be controlled by electrical/mechanical devices. Two specific application domains where software is increasingly being used to control critical functionalities are automotive and avionics. Naturally, for such software it is critical to give certain *guarantees* about the software. Unfortunately, testing cannot deliver any guarantees about software behavior. Testing can only be used to show the presence of bugs; it cannot be used to guarantee the absence of bugs.

For safety-critical software, it is necessary to *formally* check properties of the software and provide guarantees about its behavior. However, this is a tall order. How do we specify the guarantees that we need? And, how do we formally check programs for such guarantees? Our first thought is to employ automated checking methods such as model checking, which we discussed earlier (Chapter 2). Recall that model checking checks a temporal logic property (a property constraining the order in which events can occur) against a finite-state transition system. Model checking is not directly applicable for software verification, because any program in a modern programming language (such as C or Java) contains variables from *infinite* domains (integers, floating-point numbers). The presence of a single integer variable in the program makes it infinite-state, because the variable may take up infinitely many values. The solution to the problem is to come up with abstractions of the variable values. That is, instead of maintaining the exact values of the program variables, we maintain only a finite abstraction of the variable values. We first give an example of the abstract representation of variable values, and then explain how the abstraction is achieved.

Consider the program fragment in Figure 5.14. This program contains only one integer variable x. Suppose we want to prove that x == 0 at the end of the program. One possibility is to exactly maintain the control flow and data variable values, and check that x is indeed zero at the end of the program. The problem with this approach is that x can, in general, acquire infinitely many values — in other words, the amount of memory required to store the value of x is unbounded. Indeed, in any implementation of integer data types, a finite number of bits (say 32 or 64 bits) will be allocated to represent an integer. In our reasoning, we do not want to be restricted by the exact implementation of integer data types, nor do we need to be. Instead, we can abstract the value of the program variables by maintaining the true/false values of certain *propositions* about the program variables. Simply put, we do not maintain the exact values of the program variables; instead we only maintain the true/false answers to certain questions on the program variable values. Thus, in the preceding example, instead of maintaining the exact value of x, we might only maintain whether x == 0. This may be denoted by a boolean variable [x == 0], which is true if x == 0 and false otherwise. With such an abstraction, building a finite-state transition system is easy. It is a graph whose nodes are the (abstracted) program states, and each edge denotes a transition between two states via the execution of a program statement. The finite-state transition system for the following program will be as shown in Figure 5.15.

```
int x;
1   x = 0;
2   x = x + 1;
3   x = x - 1;
4   ...
```

Figure 5.14

Program fragment for showing data abstraction.

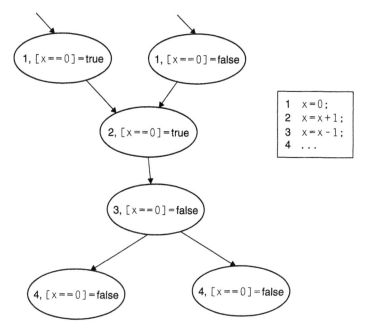

Figure 5.15

A program fragment and its abstracted transition system.

In the finite-state transition system shown in Figure 5.15, each program state (i.e., each node in the graph) corresponds to:

- The value of the program counter (i.e., where the control flow is), and
- The value of the boolean variable [x == 0].

In other words, the control flow in the program is represented exactly — we do not employ any abstraction there. On the other hand, while representing the value of the data variables, we do not maintain the exact values — we only maintain the true/false answers to certain questions on the program variables. In this case, the only program variable is x, whose exact value is not maintained — instead we only maintain whether x is equal to 0. In other words, we abstract a program P with another program P' such that

- The control flow in P and P' are identical, and
- The only data type in program P' is boolean, that is, all variables in program P' are boolean variables.

The boolean variables in program P' are, of course, related to the data variables in program P. Indeed, each boolean variable in P' denotes a true/false question about the variable values in program P. Given a set of true/false questions about the variables in P, deriving program P' from program P is automatic. Program P' really represents a finite-state transition system that can be subjected to state space exploration via model checking. The states of the transition system correspond to (a) the value of the program counter, and (b) the value of the boolean variables. Assuming that the number of possible program counter values (roughly correspond-ing to the number of lines in the program) is finite, and the number of boolean variables is finite, the number of states in the transition system is indeed finite.

Figure 5.16 shows the overall role a method such as software model checking can play in software validation. Here we assume that only the software is available for validation — we do not have a finite-state machine–like model of the software available for model checking. Naturally, this means we need to synthesize a finite-state transition system out of the software itself. This finite-state transition system is used for model checking. Given a program P, we abstract it to another program P' where all data variables in P' have the type boolean. We call P' a boolean pro-gram, and it implicitly represents a finite-state transition system whose states can be explored via model checking. The temporal logic properties verified through model checking may be provided by the programmer (where they typically denote desirable

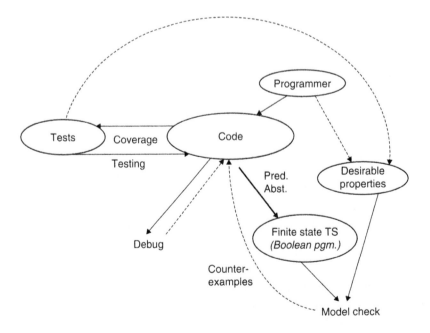

Figure 5.16

Validation flow with software model checking.

properties of the software — typically invariant properties), or they may be found by "specification mining" from the test cases. Specification mining involves finding a software specification (such as invariant properties) by running the software for different test cases and documenting the observed behavior. The Daikon tool [24], in particular, is useful for mining invariant properties from observed behavior of a program on test cases.

5.2.1 Predicate Abstraction

We now formally describe predicate abstraction — the task of generating a boolean program from an arbitrary imperative program with infinite domain variables (e.g., integers), complex data structures, and pointers to heap locations. As mentioned earlier, a boolean program is a program with all the standard control-flow constructs, but only one datatype (boolean). Thus, all variables in a boolean program are boolean variables. Thus, the main task of predicate abstraction is to abstract away the data variables in a program — the control flow is maintained exactly.

Now the question is, what do the boolean variables in the abstracted program denote? Clearly, these boolean variables need to have some connection with the variables in the original program (with complex data structures). In general, given an arbitrary C program P, the boolean variables of its corresponding boolean program P' can denote any boolean expression containing variables in P that is expressible in the C programming language. There is one important point that needs to be clarified here. The boolean program P' will not be executed. Instead, from P', we construct a finite-state transition system that represents all the behaviors of P'. Thus, while assigning a boolean variable v in P', we may assign v to true, false or unknown. If v is assigned unknown, this means that v can be either true or false. Note that if we were executing P', strictly speaking, we will be in a dilemma — is v true or false after executing the assignment `v = unknown`? However, if we are simply interested in constructing a finite-state transition system out of program P', there is no problem — we can simply allow two possible program states after the execution of `v = unknown`, one with `v == true` and the other with `v == false`.

We now explain predicate abstraction with some simple example programs. In order to simplify our presentation, we only discuss the abstraction of a single procedure. We first discuss the abstraction of assignment statements and then the abstraction of conditional branches. Note that the code for any procedure can be expressed in terms of assignments and conditional branches.

Assignment Statement

We are now talking of abstracting a statement `x = e` in the original program into one or more assignments in the abstracted program. Here `x` is a variable in the original program (whose domain is possibly infinite, say an integer variable). x could even involve pointers. Also, e is an expression involving program variables (each of which can again involve pointers, or variables over infinite domains). Thus, we might be abstracting an assignment statement *p = *p + 1. Moreover, we are abstracting it with respect to a set of predicates. Each of these predicates may again involve pointers, or variables over infinite domains. So, we might be abstracting *p = *p + 1 with respect to the single predicate *p > 0. We can abstract it as follows:

```
if ([*p>0] == true){ [*p>0] = true; } else{ [*p>0] = unknown; }
```

This is indeed what we expect: If [*p > 0] is true, by incrementing *p by 1, it continues to be true. On the other hand, if [*p > 0] is false, by incrementing *p by 1, we get *p to be 0 or greater than 0. Hence we set the predicate [*p > 0] to be unknown — meaning it can be true or false.

As another example, consider the abstraction of the assignment statement x = y w.r.t. the predicates [x == 0] and [y == 0]. In the abstracted program we can simply replace x = y with [x == 0] = [y == 0]. In effect, the abstracted assignment is saying that x is equal to zero if and only if y is equal to zero.

Now suppose we abstract *p = *q w.r.t. the predicates [*p == 0] and [*q == 0]. We want the abstracted code to say that if p and q do not point to the same memory location, the predicate [*p == 0] is true if and only if [*q == 0] is true. Otherwise, the predicate [*p == 0] is unchanged.

```
if (&p == & q) [*p == 0] = [*q == 0];
```

Note that the foregoing statement cannot be included in the abstract program, because its only data type is boolean. Thus, [*p == 0] and [*q == 0] can appear as variables in the abstract program, but not p, q. To address this issue, predicate abstraction makes use of an offline static analysis called "alias analysis." Alias analysis analyzes the program code and finds out pairs that can never alias to the same memory location (never ever during the execution of the given program!). So, if the output of such an analysis tells us that the pair p, q may never be aliases, we abstract *p = *q as [*p == 0] = [*q == 0]; otherwise *p := *q is simply abstracted as a skip statement.

In general, the method for abstracting assignment statements works as follows. Consider the abstraction of an assignment statement x = x + 1 w.r.t. two predicates [x == 2], and [x < 5] (where x is an integer variable). We find the impact of the assignment statement on each of the two predicates we are maintaining in the abstract program — [x == 2] and [x < 5]. So, we might be tempted to write the abstract program as

```
if (x == 1){[x == 2] = true;} else{[x == 2]= false;}
```

and

```
if ( x < 4){ [x < 5] = true;} else{[x < 5] = false;}
```

The trouble with this code is simple — it still contains the variable x, which is an integer variable. We want the abstracted program to contain only boolean variables so that we can synthesize a finite-state transition system out of the program. In this example, instead of maintaining the exact value of x (which is an integer), we are keen to maintain only the true/false values for the two boolean variables [x == 2] and [x < 5]. So, to achieve this effect we must replace conditions such as x == 1 in the foregoing code with boolean expressions over [x ==2] and [x < 5]. Here we show one (inefficient) method of computing these boolean expressions (the reader may refer to [9] for more details). We first consider the four possible valuations of the predicates [x == 2] and [x < 5] and check which of them imply x == 1:

$$[x ==2] \wedge [x < 5] \Rightarrow x ==1 \qquad \text{NO}$$
$$[x==2] \wedge \neg[x < 5] \Rightarrow x == 1 \qquad \text{YES}$$
$$\neg[x ==2] \wedge [x < 5] \Rightarrow x == 1 \qquad \text{NO}$$
$$\neg[x == 2] \wedge \neg[x < 5] \Rightarrow x == 1 \qquad \text{NO}$$

Thus, we infer that in the domain of the boolean variables [x ==2] and [x < 5], we can be sure that x ==1 only if [x ==2] is true and [x < 5] is false, that is, if [x ==2] $\wedge \neg$ [x < 5] holds.

Similarly, let us do the same exercise for the dual condition $x \neq 1$:

$$[x ==2] \wedge [x < 5] \Rightarrow x \neq 1 \qquad \text{YES}$$
$$[x==2] \wedge \neg [x < 5] \Rightarrow x \neq 1 \qquad \text{YES}$$
$$\neg [x ==2] \wedge [x < 5] \Rightarrow x \neq 1 \qquad \text{NO}$$
$$\neg [x == 2] \wedge \neg [x < 5] \Rightarrow x \neq 1 \qquad \text{YES}$$

Here we infer that in the domain of the boolean variables [x ==2] and [x < 5], we can be sure that $x \neq 1$ if [x == 2] $\vee \neg$ [x < 5] holds. Now instead of writing the statement

```
if (x == 1){[x == 2] = true;} else{[x == 2]= false;}
```

in the abstracted program, we may write the following:

```
if([x ==2] && ![x < 5]){ [x == 2] = true;}
else if ([x ==2 ] || ![x < 5]){ [x ==2] = false;}
else { [x ==2] = unknown;}
```

This code captures the effect of the assignment x = x +1 on the predicate [x == 2]. Note that we conservatively assigned the "unknown" value to the boolean variable [x ==2] unless we could reason (in the abstract domain) that x == 2 will hold or not hold after the assignment. In other words, if we could reason (in the abstract domain involving the boolean variables [x ==2] and [x < 5]) that x == 2 will certainly hold after the assignment, we assigned [x == 2] to true; if we could reason (in the abstract domain involving the boolean variables [x ==2] and [x < 5]) that x ==2 will certainly not hold after the assignment, we assigned x == 2 to false; in all other cases we conservatively set the boolean variable [x == 2] to unknown, meaning it can be true or false. What this means is that at this control location in the abstract program, the value of the boolean variable [x == 2] can be nondeterministically true or false — and both possibilities will be considered while constructing the finite-state transition system from the abstracted program. Once again we must clarify for the reader that the abstracted program is being used only for synthesizing a finite-state transition system out of it, and this finite-state transition system will be subjected to search-based property checking procedures such as model checking (which we described earlier in Chapter 2). In other words, the synthesized abstract program will *not* be executed; instead, it is searched for allowed behaviors.

Now, the manner in which we constructed the effect of the assignment x = x +1 on the predicate [x ==2], we can also do the same for the predicate [x < 5]. After all, our abstract domain consists of these two predicates (or boolean variables; we use the terms *predicates* and *boolean variables* rather interchangeably here) [x == 2] and [x < 5]. So, let us do it here. Recall that we want to represent the following statement as accurately as possible in the abstracted program:

```
if ( x < 4){ [x < 5] = true;} else{[x < 5] = false;}
```

So, again the trouble is that we are not allowed to write boolean expressions such as x < 4 in the abstracted program, because x is not a variable in the abstracted program, whereas [x == 2] and x < 5 are variables in the abstracted program. Again, we look at the four possible true/false valuations of [x == 2], [x < 5] and see which of them imply x < 4:

$$[x ==2] \land [x < 5] \Rightarrow x < 4 \qquad \text{YES}$$
$$[x==2] \land \neg[x < 5] \Rightarrow x < 4 \qquad \text{YES}$$
$$\neg[x ==2] \land [x < 5] \Rightarrow x < 4 \qquad \text{NO}$$
$$\neg[x == 2] \land \neg[x < 5] \Rightarrow x < 4 \qquad \text{NO}$$

So, we infer that in the domain of the boolean variables [x ==2] and [x < 5], we can be sure that x < 4 only if [x == 2] is true. Similarly, we also look at the four possible true/false valuations of [x == 2], [x < 5] and see which of them imply the dual condition ¬ x < 4:

$$[x\ ==2] \wedge [x\ <\ 5] \Rightarrow \neg x\ <\ 4 \qquad \text{NO}$$
$$[x==2] \wedge \neg[x\ <\ 5] \Rightarrow \neg x\ <\ 4 \qquad \text{NO}$$
$$\neg[x\ ==2] \wedge [x\ <\ 5] \Rightarrow \neg x\ <\ 4 \qquad \text{NO}$$
$$\neg[x\ ==\ 2] \wedge \neg[x\ <\ 5] \Rightarrow \neg x\ <\ 4 \qquad \text{YES}$$

So, we infer that in the domain of the boolean variables $[x\ ==2]$ and $[x\ <\ 5]$, we can be sure that $x < 4$ only if $\neg[x\ ==\ 2] \wedge \neg[x\ <\ 5]$ is true. Now, instead of writing the statement

```
if ( x < 4){ [x < 5] = true;} else{[x < 5] = false;}
```

we can write the following to capture the effect of $x = x + 1$ on the predicate $[x\ <\ 5]$:

```
if ([x == 2]) { [x < 5] = true;}
else if (! [ x == 2] && ![x < 5]) { [x < 5] = false;}
else {[x < 5] = unknown;}
```

In summary, if we have a C program with an integer variable x and an assignment statement $x = x+1$, and the value of x is being abstracted with only two boolean variables $[x\ ==\ 2]$, $[x\ <\ 5]$ (i.e., we just keep track of whether x is equal to 2, and x is less than 5, rather than maintaining the exact value of x), we can replace the assignment $x = x +1$ by the following block of code in the abstracted program. Note that in the abstracted program x is not a variable, but $[x==2]$, $[x\ <\ 5]$ are. Our code block tries to decide the value (true/false/unknown) for the two variables $[x\ ==\ 2]$, $[x\ <\ 5]$. The processing code for $[x\ ==\ 2]$ and $[x\ <\ 5]$ was discussed in the preceding. However, we cannot simply put these codes in sequence, because essentially we want to capture a "parallel" execution of these codes — given a value of $[x\ ==\ 2]$ and $[x\ <\ 5]$ prior to the assignment $x = x + 1$, we want to find the value of $[x\ ==\ 2]$ *and* $[x\ <\ 5]$ after the assignment.

```
tmp1 = [x == 2];  tmp2 = [x < 5];
if(tmp1 && !tmp2){ [x == 2] = true;}
else if (tmp1 || !tmp2){ [x ==2] = false;}
else { [x ==2] = unknown;}
if (tmp1) { [x < 5] = true;}
else if (!tmp1 && !tmp2) { [x < 5] = false;}
else {[x < 5] = unknown;}
```

One important point needs to be clarified here. In the unabstracted program, if a statement is an execution step, the statement $x = x + 1$ represents a step of execution. In that case, in the abstracted program, we treat the code block in the preceding as an execution step. Although we know that the abstracted program is not executed, but analyzed. Still it is important to clarify the execution steps, since it tells us at which program points we observe the program states. So, while constructing a finite-state transition system from the abstracted boolean program, the code block mentioned in the preceding will correspond to a *single transition*.

It might appear as if we are replacing a simple assignment x = x + 1 with a lot of complex code! However, note that the foregoing piece of code in the abstracted program will be generated automatically, given the C program. And, given a program with only boolean variables (which refer to conditions on the values of variables in the original C program), we can synthesize a finite-state transition system that is subject to formal validation via automated checking procedures (such as model checking).

Conditional Branches

Having described the abstraction of assignment statements in a C program into a fragment of boolean program (a C program whose only datatype is boolean), we now look at conditional branches. Conditional branches appear in if-then-else statements as well as loops. In fact, using conditional branches and assignments, we can capture the effect of any code within a single procedure of a standard imperative programming language such as C. In the following, we consider conditional branches as they appear in if-then-else statements. Loops can then be considered as conditional branch statements with one of the branches executing a go-to statement. Thus, a while-loop statement of the form

```
L: while (cond){
       ... /* Loop Body *
   }
```

can be seen as

```
L: if (cond){
       ... /* Loop Body */
     go to L;
   }
```

Our abstraction could work on the foregoing if-then statement, rather than the while loop.

Now, let us consider a conditional branch in the form of an if-then-else statement; if-then statements are simply treated as special cases of if-then-else statements. An if-then-else statement

```
if (cond) { S1 } else { S2 }
```

can also be seen as

```
if (*) { assume(cond); S1 }
    else { assume(!cond); S2 }
```

The (*) denotes a nondeterministic choice. Again, the reader need not worry about the execution of such nondeterministic choices. We recall here that we are interested in synthesizing a finite-state transition system out of our abstracted programs, rather than executing those programs.

The semantics of the `assume` statement is defined as follows. For any condition φ, `assume(`φ`)` behaves like a `skip` statement (i.e., a statement with no effect) if φ is true. Otherwise, if φ is false, the statement results in a termination of execution (without raising any exception or error). Given such a semantics of the `assume` statement, it is clear that the encoding given in the preceding is equivalent to an if-then-else statement. The question really is, why we should choose to work with such an encoding rather than directly working with an if-then-else statement. The answer to this question lies the abstraction we perform. Note that `cond` represents a boolean expression over the variables in an arbitrary C program. However, in the abstracted program, we can refer only to selected boolean variables that capture relationships among the variables in the C program. Thus, we will not be able to capture `cond` exactly in the abstracted program. In fact, our abstracted if-then-else statement will be of the following form:

```
if (*) { assume abstract(cond); abstract(S1) } else
      { assume abstract(!cond); abstract(S2) }
```

Clearly S1 and S2 will again contain assignment/conditional branch statements — so their abstraction will proceed based on our abstraction scheme for assignment and conditional branch statements. We need to explain how to compute `abstract(cond)` and `abstract(!cond)`.

Whichever way we abstract the conditions, we want to preserve the property that whenever a condition is true, its abstraction must be true. Thus, in the template code discussed before, we will have

$$\text{cond} \Rightarrow \text{abstract(cond)}$$
$$\text{!cond} \Rightarrow \text{abstract(!cond)}$$

If that is the case, for an if-then-else statement `if(cond) { S1 } else { S2 }`:

- Whenever `cond` holds, the then-part (in this case S1) is guaranteed to be executed in the abstracted boolean program, and
- Whenever `cond` does not hold, the else-part (in this case S2) is guaranteed to be executed in the abstracted boolean program.

Because of the information lost in abstraction, the reverses of the foregoing statements are not true. Thus, whenever the then-part (in this case S1) is executed in the abstracted boolean program, it is not guaranteed that `cond` holds. Similarly, whenever the else-part (in this case S2) is executed in the abstracted boolean program, we cannot guarantee that `cond` does not hold.

Other Control Constructs

In the preceding, we have left out the full details of the abstraction of conditions — that is, given a condition `cond`, the algorithm for computing `abstract(cond)` is not presented here in detail. However, whatever `abstract(cond)` we compute will satisfy the property `cond` $\Rightarrow$ `abstract(cond)`. The interested reader can refer to [9] for details.

Similarly, abstracting assignments and conditional branches tells us only how to abstract the code for a single procedure. For a program involving multiple procedures, we will abstract each procedure in the C program to a procedure in the boolean program. However, for procedure calls and returns, we need to ensure that procedures in the boolean program take parameters and return only boolean variables (the predicates w.r.t. which we are abstracting the C program). Again, the interested reader can refer to [9] for details.

5.2.2 Software Checking via Predicate Abstraction

Predicate abstraction is simply a tool, a means to an end. It is not an end in itself. Given an arbitrary program P, predicate abstraction allows us to generate a boolean program P_{bool} out of P. P_{bool} has the same control flow as that of P, the difference between the two programs being that the only datatype in P_{bool} is boolean; the boolean variables in P_{bool} refer to relationships among the variables in P. Because the number of control locations of a program is finite, this enables us to easily construct a finite-state transition system TS_P from the boolean program P_{bool}. The finite-state transition system TS_P can then be subjected to automated checking methods such as model checking.

However, because of abstraction, P_{bool} and TS_P contain more behaviors (i.e., more execution traces) than the program P. In other words, P_{bool} and TS_P contain execution traces that are not traversed by any input in P. These correspond to paths in the control flow graph of P, which are not exercised by any input — commonly called, in literature, "infeasible program paths." Let us illustrate the phenomenon via a simple example. Consider the abstraction of the program in Figure 5.17 w.r.t. the predicate [x == 0]. We have numbered the lines in the program for convenience. Thus, the program we are considering is

```
1   x = 0;
2   x = x + 1;
3   x = x - 1;
4   if (x == 1) {
5       ... /* error */}
```

We can clearly see that the error location is never reached in any concrete execution of the program. However, if we abstract the program w.r.t. the predicate

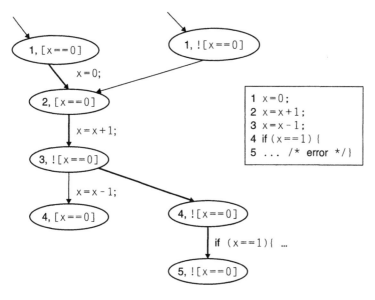

Figure 5.17

A program fragment and the finite-state transition system obtained by predicate abstraction w.r.t. the predicate [x == 0]. A path to the error location (a counterexample trace) is marked in bold.

[x == 0], we will get the finite-state transition system (via a boolean program that is automatically derived by predicate abstraction) shown in Figure 5.17. Here, line 5 (the error location) can be reached.

The results seem puzzling. What went wrong? In essence, nothing! Our abstraction is indeed intended to capture an overapproximation of the set of behaviors of the original program. Let us follow how the abstract program behaves, line by line. Before the execution of line 1 of our program (i.e., in the initial state), the variable x can be anything. Hence we allow for [x == 0] to be true or false in the initial state (refer Figure 5.17). Next we execute the assignment x = 0 and go to line 2. At this stage, the predicate [x == 0] must be true. Then we execute x = x + 1 and go to line 3. At this stage, in line 3 we know only that [x == 0] must be false. Notice the subtle loss of information we have suffered! If we were following a concrete execution, we would have known that x is equal to 1 at this stage. However, because of our abstraction, we only know that [x == 0] is false, that is, x is not equal to zero. As a result, when we go from line 3 to line 4 (by executing x = x - 1), we can only conclude that [x == 0] can be both true/false in line 4. This makes us conclude that the error location in line 5 is reachable.

The preceding explanation certainly looks like bad news! Let us take stock of the situation. Given an arbitrary C program P, and a set of predicates to track, we can automatically obtain a finite-state transition system TS_P that can be subjected to model checking. However, there is a small catch here. The finite-state transition system TS_P that we construct is not exactly equivalent to the original program P. Rather, the set of execution traces in the constructed transition system TS_P is a superset of the execution traces of the program P. Now, suppose the finite-state transition system is subjected to model checking of a linear-time temporal logic (LTL) property (refer to Chapter 2). Recall that a finite-state transition system satisfies an LTL property φ if and only if *all* its execution traces satisfy φ. Thus, on model checking an LTL property φ against TS_P, if we observe that TS_P satisfies φ, we can be certain that program P also satisfies φ. However, if TS_P does not satisfy φ and returns a counterexample trace violating φ, we cannot be certain that TS_P does not satisfy φ. Because TS_P has more execution traces than the program P, the counterexample trace may come from these additional spurious traces, as in the case of Figure 5.17.

Figure 5.18 summarizes the basic design flow in software model checking. Given a program P and a LTL property φ, we first convert P into a finite-state transition system TS_P via predicate abstraction. We then check TS_P against φ using a model-checking tool. If TS_P satisifies φ, because of the nature of our predicate abstraction, we know that program P satisifies φ. However, if TS_P does not satisfy φ and a counterexample trace is produced by the model-checking tool, we cannot be sure whether the counterexample trace results from a real error in P, or it is an additional

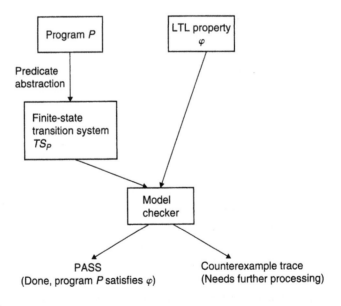

Figure 5.18

Overall flow in software model checking.

spurious behavior that is introduced owing to the overapproximation of behavior in predicate abstraction. In other words, the counterexample trace requires further processing.

Let us now revisit the example of Figure 5.17. Here the counterexample trace (a path to the error location) that we obtained is as follows:

$$(1, [x == 0]) \xrightarrow{x=0} (2, [x == 0]) \xrightarrow{x=x+1} (3, ![x == 0])$$
$$\xrightarrow{x=x-1} (4, ![x == 0]) \xrightarrow{if(x==1)} (5, ![x == 0])$$

Now, let us try to check whether this path can be exercised by any concrete input. In trying to do so, we calculate a constraint representing the conditions under this path can be executed. If such a constraint is found to have no solutions, we can infer that the path is infeasible. The constraint accumulated for the foregoing path will be

$x0 == 0 \wedge$	// from the initial state
$x1 == 0 \wedge$	// from the assignment $x = 0$
$x2 == x1 + 1 \wedge$	// from the assignment $x=x+1$
$x3 == x2 - 1 \wedge$	// from the assignment $x=x-1$
$x3 == 1$	// from the condition $(x == 1)$

This constraint, when simplified, leads to $x0 == x1 == 0 \wedge x2 == 1 \wedge x3 == 0 \wedge x3 == 1$, which is unsatisfiable. In other words, the constraint is saying that the value of variable x at some point has to be both 0 and 1, which is impossible. Hence the constraint is unsatisfiable and the counterexample trace we found out is spurious or infeasible (i.e., not exercised by any concrete input).

Having found out that the counterexample trace is infeasible, what should we do? Recall that we abstracted the program in Figure 5.17 w.r.t. the predicate [x == 0]. On model checking the resultant finite-state transition system against the property that an error location cannot be reached, we found a counterexample trace (a path to an error location). When we tried to find out the set of inputs that can exercise the given counterexample trace, it was found that no concrete input can exercise the counterexample trace, that is, it is infeasible. *So, our counterexample trace is an additional spurious behavior that is introduced owing to the overapproximation of behavior in predicate abstraction.*

How do we proceed now? It seems that the only way out is to *refine* our abstraction. By abstracting our program w.r.t. only the predicate [x == 0], in effect, we are only keeping track of whether x is equal to zero. No other information about the value of variable x is kept track of in the abstracted program. This is what is causing the additional, spurious traces, one of which is our counterexample trace. So, we need to keep track of more information about the variable values. In effect, we need to abstract our program w.r.t. a *bigger* set of predicates. This is what constitutes the refinement step. Before proceeding further, let us clarify why abstraction w.r.t. a bigger set of predicates should be seen as a *refinement*. If we abstract a program w.r.t. a null set of predicates, we deem every path in the program's control flow graph as feasible. This is the coarsest possible abstraction. If we now abstract the program w.r.t. some predicate [x == 0], where x is a program variable, we are refining the abstraction, because we at least keep track of whether x is zero. Then, if we abstract the program w.r.t. a bigger set — say, [x == 0] and [x == 1] — our abstraction becomes more fine-grained, because we now keep track of whether x is 0, and whether it is 1.

So, in predicate abstraction, we maintain an abstract view of the memory state of a program. Instead of maintaining the exact values of the program variables, we are only allowed to ask true/false questions about the program variable values — these questions are the predicates w.r.t. which we abstract the program. Naturally, the more questions we allow ourselves to ask, the more refined is our abstraction of the memory state!

It is clear now, that the way to refine our abstractions is to add to the set of predicates. The issue now is, which predicates to add? We can try to find the additional predicates from the spurious counterexample trace we found. For this reason, software model-checking approaches often go by the acronym *CEGAR — counterexample guided abstraction refinement*. In particular, given a spurious counterexample trace, we inspect the *reason* why it is infeasible, and add predicates based on this intuition. It should be noted that this process of refinement via adding predicates is a collection of heuristics and thus can be tackled in many ways. Thus, in our example in Figure 5.17, we can find the reason for our counterexample trace being infeasible by analyzing its path constraint (note that the variables $x0, x1, x2, x3$ in the constraint refer to values of the varible x at different points in the program execution):

$$x0 == 0 \land x1 == 0 \land x2 == x1 + 1 \land x3 == x2 - 1 \land x3 == 1$$

which is simplified to

$$x0 == 0 \land x1 == 0 \land x2 == 1 \land x3 == 0 \land x3 == 1$$

The "unsatisfiable core" of this constraint (the minimal part of the constraint which is still unsatisfiable) is

$$x3 == 0 \land x3 == 1$$

Thus, we can observe from the preceding that it is important to keep track of whether x is 0 and whether x is 1. Because we previously abstracted the program w.r.t. the predicate [x == 0], we can now refine our abstraction as abstracting w.r.t the predicate set { [x == 0], [x ==1] }. In other words, we add the predicate [x == 1] — instead of simply monitoring whether x == 0, our abstracted program will now also monitor whether x == 1. The resultant finite-state transition system

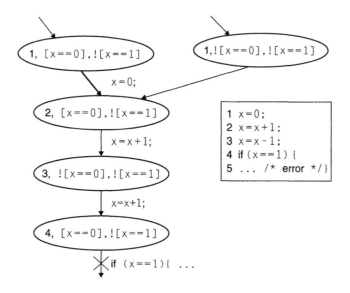

Figure 5.19

A program fragment and the finite-state transition system obtained by predicate abstraction w.r.t. the predicates [x == 0] and [x==1]. No paths to the error location exist in the abstracted program.

is shown in Figure 5.19. From Figure 5.19, we can see that no path to the error location exists. In other words, by refinining the abstraction, we have been able to prove the following property: The error location is not reachable from initial state. In LTL, this property would be stated as $G\neg error$, where the proposition *error* is true only in the error location of the program (refer to Figure 5.19) and is false otherwise.

In summary, software model checking via predicate abstraction involves choosing an initial set of predicates and then refining this set based on the counterexample traces obtained. The flow of the entire procedure appears in Figure 5.20. If the user does not have a good idea about what the initial set of predicates may be, he or she can start with the null set of predicates. This the coarsest possible abstraction. We can subject the resultant finite-state transition system (which captures only the control flow of the program, and no data flow) to model checking. If no counterexamples are found, the program already satisfies the property being verified. If a counterexample trace π is found, we subject it to a spuriousness check. This is done by constructing a constraint representing the set of inputs which can execute π, and then solving this constraint. If the constraint is satisfiable, then π points to a real error in the program; if the constraint is unsatisfiable, this means that π is a spurious counterexample, an additional behavior resulting from the coarse nature of our abstraction. In this case, we inspect the unsatisfiable path constraint corresponding to π to get a *refinement*— additional predicates that need to kept track of. In this way, starting from a possibly

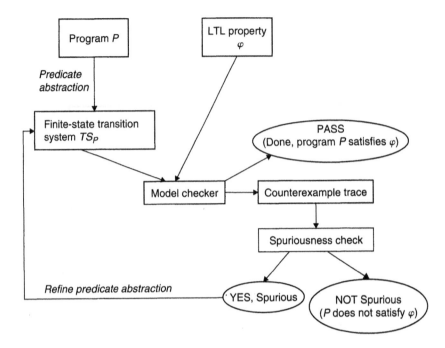

Figure 5.20

Detailed flow of software model checking.

null set of predicates, we can build up a set of predicates w.r.t. which we abstract the program being verified. In effect, we are running a loop involving the following steps:

$$Abstract \rightarrow Model\ Check \rightarrow Refine$$

At any iteration of this loop, we have can three possible outcomes from a model checking run.

1. Model checking produces no counterexamples.
2. Model checking produces a counterexample that is found to be not spurious.
3. Model checking produces a counterexample that is found to be spurious.

In the case of outcome (1), we stop, because our property has been proved. In case of outcome (2), we again stop, because our property has been disproved — the counterexample points to a real property violation in the program. However, in the case of outcome (3), our property has been neither proved nor disproved. So, in this case we refine our abstraction and model check the refined transition system with the hope of proving or disproving the property being verified.

What the framework of Figure 5.19 does is to provide a pragmatic handle on a very hard problem, namely software verification. The general problem is undecidable, so fully automated verification is out of the question. The usual solution then is to *abstract* the program behaviors and employ automated checking methods on the abstracted program. However, the task of abstraction involves tremendous human ingenuity. How do we abstract the program? Which variables do we keep track of ? If we are keeping track of a variable x with an unbounded domain (say, an integer variable), how do we develop a finite abstraction of the unbounded domain?

Predicate abstraction and abstraction refinement provide pragmatic answers to such questions. They free the user from having to construct a difficult abstraction for the sake of formally verifying his or her program.

Instead the user may start with a null abstraction, and then gradually refine the abstraction based on the counterexamples encountered in successive runs of model checking. In other words, abstraction refinement is a verification methodology or verification framework, rather than a verification technique. By employing this methodology, the user is freed from the burden of having to invent abstractions for verifying his or her program.

It should be noted that verifying temporal properties of arbitrary programs is an undecidable problem. So, clearly the *Abstract* → *Model Check* → *Refine* loop in Figure 5.19 cannot be guaranteed to terminate. The user can employ such an abstraction refinement framework with a possible bound on the maximum number of refinement steps. In practice, lot of experimental studies on real-life embedded software show very promising results with abstraction refinement based verification. Here, the abstraction refinement methodology allows the user to gradually build an abstraction (based on the counterexamples encountered), rather than having to guess it. Moreover, the verification is found to terminate within a few iterations of abstraction refinement in these case studies. The interested reader may refer to [4] for reports on real-life case studies with Windows device drivers.

5.2.3 Combining Formal Verification with Testing

Testing and formal verification are two complementary techniques for validating functionality. Testing exposes few program behaviors, but any wrong behavior thereby exposed is truly a wrong behavior — there are no false alarms reported by testing. On the other hand, formal verification exposes *all* program behaviors, albeit at an abstract level. However, because of the abstractions involved, "bugs" reported by formal verification can be false alarms. In other words, testing and formal verification have complementary strengths and weaknesses.

Testing methods work at the concrete level: They execute the program with concrete inputs. Naturally, they cannot cover all program behaviors — exhaustively covering all concrete inputs of any real-life program is an impossibility! Directed testing methods (Chapter 5.1.3) alleviate this concern somewhat — they are trying to cover all program paths, rather than all concrete inputs. Thus, one may say that directed testing methods partition the input space of a program, such that two inputs i, i' are in the same partition if and only if inputs i, i' exercise the same program path. Given such a partitioning of the input space, directed testing methods are trying to expose one concrete input per partition. However, the number of program paths in any real-life program is also huge — even for a program without loops, b branches can lead to anywhere between $b + 1$ to 2^b paths depending on the control flow (see Figure 5.21). Clearly, if we have b branches containing 2^b acyclic paths within a loop with L iterations (where L is large), we will have $(2^b)^L$ paths — a huge number! Hence, covering all program paths simply via testing is also not feasible for much real-life software.

Formal verification methods, on the other hand, abstract the behaviors of a program. One example of such an abstraction is predicate abstraction (Section 5.2.1) where we abstract the memory store of a program while leaving the control flow unabstracted. Formal verification methods achieve full coverage of program behaviors in the abstract state space. However, because of the information (about program

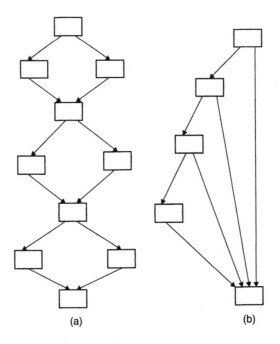

(a)   (b)

Figure 5.21

An acyclic program with 3 branches having (a) 2^3 program paths and (b) $3 + 1$ program paths.

variable values) lost in the abstraction, the errors reported by covering the abstract state space might not correspond to actual errors in a concrete program. We saw an example in Section 5.2.2, reproduced here for convenience:

```
1   x = 0;
2   x = x + 1;
3   x = x - 1;
4   if (x == 1) {
5       ... /* error */}
```

Here, by abstracting the program only w.r.t. the predicate [x == 0] and model checking the abstracted program, we are unable to infer that the error location is unreachable. Thus, we report a false bug, a path to the error location as follows:

$$(1,[x == 0]),2,[x==0]),(3, ![x==0]),(4,![x==0]),(5, ...)$$

This is what we mean by a false positive or a false alarm: a reported bug that does not correspond to any program error. Such a false alarm appears because of the information loss in abstraction and will show up during model checking of the abstract state space.

Because formal verification (such as model checking) and testing methods have complementary strengths and weaknesses, there have been attempts to combine them and reap the benefits of both. One possibility that has been studied is to use model checking for systematic generation of tests. Yet another possibility is to use tests (and the observations resulting from running these tests) for learning about the program model, when the program is a black box [71]. Usually these methods can be thought of as model checking helping testing, or vice versa.

In the recent past, software validation methods where testing and model checking simultaneously help each other have also been studied. To discuss the inner workings of such methods, we modify the example program in the preceding and introduce a program loop that does not modify variable x:

```
1   x = 0;
2   x = x + 1;
3   x = x - 1;
4   for (i=0; i<100; i++){
5              ... /* x is not modified in the loop */
6   }
7   if (x == 0) {
8       ... /* error */ }
9   ...  /* end of program */
```

Suppose we want to check whether the error location is reachable. How do we start? We can perform predicate abstraction of the program and perform model checking of the abstracted program. The property we want to verify states that the error location is never reached — specified as

$$G(pc \neq 8)$$

in linear-time temporal logic (LTL). The foregoing property states that the program counter (pc) never goes to line 8 (the error location). A violation of the property will be a counterexample trace that reaches line 8.

To perform predicate abstraction, we need a set of predicates w.r.t. which we abstract. What set of predicates do we choose? As discussed earlier, we can simply start with the *null* set of predicates. This the coarsest possible predicate abstraction, which treats each path in a program's control-flow graph as feasible (i.e., the abstraction assumes that for each path π in the control flow graph of a program, there is some program input exercising the path π). Model checking finds the shortest counterexample trace:

$$1, 2, 3, 4, 7, 8$$

Because we did predicate abstraction w.r.t. a null set of predicates, we are not keeping track of the program variable values at all in the abstracted finite-state transition system. We only keep track of the program-counter value (also called the control location). We can now analyze this counterexample trace by collecting its path constraint, as mentioned in Section 5.2.2. This will show that the foregoing is a spurious counterexample, because there is no concrete execution $1, 2, 3, 4, 7, 8$ — the loop needs to be iterated 100 times!!

According to the abstraction refinement methodology, we need to abstract our program w.r.t. a new predicate and run model checking again. The trouble with this approach is that whatever predicates we abstract our program with, model checking will successively uncover longer and longer paths to line 8 (all of which are spurious, that is, do not correspond to any concrete program execution). These paths correspond to the number of times we iterate through the loop.

$$1, 2, 3, 4, 7, 8$$
$$1, 2, 3, 4, 5, 6, 4, 7, 8$$
$$1, 2, 3, 4, 5, 6, 4, 5, 6, 4, 7, 8$$
$$\dots$$

This is clearly inefficient. In our program, we will then need 100 refinement steps to show that the error location is indeed not reachable. If we had a loop iterating 1 million times, we would have required 1 million refinement steps!

Fortunately, testing methods can be combined with model checking to solve our problem. Here, we first abstract the program w.r.t. the null set of predicates and run model checking. This produces (as before), the counterexample trace:

$$1, 2, 3, 4, 7, 8$$

We can now use directed testing to attempt a concrete test trace that goes through this path (or as long a prefix of the path as possible). We find a concrete trace that visits lines 1, 2, 3, but not line 8. The trace is

$$1, 2, 3, (4, 5, 6)^{100}, 4, 7, 8$$

Note that this is a concrete path which can be exercised by *executing* the program. Thus, our concrete test trace straightaway shows that the error location is reachable, because it visits the error location (line 8). So, we completely avoided the 100 refinement steps necessary to show this error via pure abstraction refinement-oriented verification.

In summary, testing methods try to find witnesses of errors, whereas formal verification methods prove the absence of errors. Both have their unique plus and minus points. By judiciously combining them, we can develop powerful software validation methods that rely on testing to show presence of bugs, and on verification to show absence of them. The interested reader is referred to [28] for an advanced treatment of this topic.

5.3 REFERENCES

The area of software debugging has seen substantial growth in the past 10 to 15 years. Some of the works are based on static analysis to locate common bug patterns in code (e.g., [39]), whereas others espouse a combination of static and dynamic analysis to find test cases that expose errors (e.g., [20]). Another section of works addresses the problem of software fault localization (typically via dynamic analysis) — given a program and an observable error for a given failing program input, these works try to find the root cause of the observable error. The works on software fault localization proceed by either (a) dynamic dependence analysis of the failing program execution (e.g., [80, 99, 100, 104, 105]), or (b) comparison of the failing program execution with one chosen program execution that does not manifest the observable error in question (e.g., [32, 76, 103]). These works go hand-in-hand with testing, because testing locates observable errors, and debugging seeks to explain them. There are also related efforts on directed software testing [29], where paths of the program are systematically explored to find offending test cases. The PEX tool [89] uses similar techniques for unit test generation of Java programs.

Application of formal verification methods such as model checking has also been a topic of intense research over the past two decades. One of the first points of reference in this area is the SPIN model checker [38], which we discussed in Chapter 2. The SPIN checker was originally used for protocol modeling and verification. Subsequently, it was adapted for software verification via added features, such as embedding C code into a modeling language description. Around 2000–01, the idea of abstraction refinement–based checking of software was developed. Checkers built around this philosophy include SLAM [12], BLAST [7], and Magic [16]. A recent work [28] discusses the combination of abstraction refinement based checking with testing.

5.4 EXERCISES

5.1. Suppose you want to use a model checker (such as the SPIN tool discussed in Section 2.9) to generate test cases of a terminating sequential program written in a C-style imperative language. What are the temporal properties you can feed in to meet the *statement coverage* criterion for test generation (a test suite such that all program statements are covered)?

5.2. In this chapter, we discussed the role of dynamic slices for program debugging. Based on slices, we can define the notion of a "dice" where $dice(x,y) = slice(x) - slice(y)$ for two slicing criterion x,y. Comment on the role of dices in software debugging: Under what circumstances might you use them for debugging?

5.3. One method of software testing for inputs with large domains is called "equivalence partitioning." In this method, the domain of an input variable is *partitioned* into equivalence classes, so that from each equivalence class only one test input will be tried out. Now, there is a wide choice of when we define two test inputs to be "equivalent" and put them into an equivalence class. Suppose we define two test inputs to be equivalent when they produce the same path in the program.

- Give an example program where such an equivalence partitioning will lead to efficient testing, that is, only a few test cases to try.
- Give an example program where such an equivalence partitioning will lead to inefficient testing, that is, too many test cases to try.

5.4. Consider the following program:

```
if (x > 2) {y = x + z;} else {y = x - z;}
if (y > 0) {return 0;} else {return 1;}
```

- Give one sample test input for which the foregoing code will return the value 0.
- Characterize the set of all test inputs that cause the foregoing code to return the value 0. Explain your answer.

5.5. Consider the following program with two threads, which are composed asynchronously. Assume that initially A = 0, and each assignment is executed atomically. What are the possible contents of the array X when the program terminates? Explain your answer, without constructing the finite-state machine corresponding to the asynchronous composition.

```
Thread 1:   (A := 1; A := 2; A := 3; A:= 4;) composed with
Thread 2: (X[1] := A; X[2] := A; X[3] := A; X[4] := A;)
```

5.6. Consider the program fragment

```
x = 5; x = x +1; x = x - 1; y = x
```

Suppose we want to prove that $y == 5$ at the end of the program. Show that the predicate abstraction {y==5} is insufficient to prove this property. Also construct a predicate abstraction that is sufficient to prove the property. You are only allowed to abstract the data store of the program via predicates, but the control flow should not be abstracted.

5.7. Consider the following program fragment:

```
x = 0; while (x < 100){ x = x + 1 }
```

Suppose we want to prove that $(x == 100)$ at the end of the program. What is the initial abstract transition system we start with if we follow the abstract model-check refine methodology? What are the abstractions of the memory store (predicate abstractions) that we will encounter if we prove the property by abstraction refinement? Justify your answer *in detail*.

5.8. Consider a multithreaded program where n threads running on a single processor are trying to access a shared object using a round-robin scheme. We want to prove mutual exclusion of access of the shared object for any n. Can we employ the abstraction refinement based software verification discussed in this chapter? Justify your answer. If your answer is yes, explain how. If your answer is no, can you suggest any alternative verification methods?

Bibliography

[1] R. Alur and D. L. Dill. A theory of timed automata. *Theoretical Computer Science*, 126:183–235, 1994.

[2] J. Akella and K. McMillan. Synthesizing converters between finite state protocols. In *International Conference on Computer Design*, 1991.

[3] R. Alur and M. Yannakakis. Model checking of message sequence charts. In *International Conference on Concurrency Theory (CONCUR)*, 1999.

[4] T. Ball, et al. Thorough static analysis of device drivers. In *EuroSys*, 2006.

[5] D. Burger and T. Austin. The SimpleScalar Tool Set, Version 2.0. Technical Report CS-TR-1997-1342, University of Wisconsin, Madison, June 1997.

[6] A. Biere, E. M. Clarke, R. Raimi, and Y. Zhu. Verifying properties of a PowerPC microprocessor using symbolic model checking without BDDs. In *Computer Aided Verification (CAV)*, 1999.

[7] D. Beyer, T. A. Henzinger, R. Jhala, and R. Majumdar. The Software Model Checker BLAST: Applications to Software Engineering. *International Journal on Software Tools for Technology Transfer*, 2007.

[8] M. Broy, B. Jonsson, J.-P. Katoen, M. Leucker, and A. Prestchner. *Model-Based Testing of Reactive Systems*. Springer, 2005.

[9] T. Ball, R. Majumdar, T. Millstein, and S. K. Rajamani. Automatic predicate abstraction of C programs. In *International Conference on Programming Language Design and Implementation (PLDI)*, 2001.

[10] G. Borriello. *A New Interface Specification Methodology and its Applications to Transducer Synthesis*. PhD thesis, University of California, Berkeley, 1988.

[11] D. Brylow and J. Palsberg. Deadline analysis of interrupt-driven software. In *ACM SIGSOFT Symposium on the Foundations of Software Engineering (FSE)*, held jointly with European Software Engineering Conference (ESEC-FSE), 2003.

[12] T. Ball and S. K. Rajamani. The SLAM project: Debugging system software via static analysis. In *ACM Symposium on Principles of Programming Languages (POPL)*, 2002.

[13] G. Buttazzo. *Hard Real-time Computing Systems: Predictable Scheduling Algorithms and Applications*, 2nd ed. Springer, 2005.

[14] E. M. Clarke et al. Verification of the futurebus+ cache coherence protocol. *Formal Methods in System Design*, 6, 1995.

[15] P. Cousot and R. Cousot. Abstract interpretation: A unified lattice model for static analysis of programs by construction or approximation of fixpoints. In *Proceedings of the Fourth Annual ACM Symposium on Principles of Programming Languages (POPL)*, pp. 238–252, January 1977.

[16] S. Chaki, E. Clarke, A. Groce, S. Jha, and H. Veith. Modular verification of software components in C. In *International Conference on Software Engineering (ICSE)*, 2003.

[17] E. M. Clarke and E. A. Emerson. Synthesis of synchronization skeletons for branching time temporal logic. In *Logic of Programs: Workshop, Yorktown Heights, LNCS* Vol. 131, 1981.

[18] E. Clarke, O. Grumberg, and D. Peled. *Model Checking*. MIT Press, 1999.

[19] CPLEX. The ILOG CPLEX Optimizer v7.5, 2002. Commercial software, `http://www.ilog.com`.

[20] C. Csallner and Y. Smaragdakis. DSD-Crasher: A hybrid analysis tool for bug finding. In *ISSTA*, 2006.

[21] CTAS. Center TRACON automation system. NASA, `http://www.ctas.arc.nasa.gov`.

[22] W. Damm and D. Harel. LSCs: Breathing life into message sequence charts. *Formal Methods in System Design*, 19(1), 2001.

[23] L. de Alfaro and T. A. Henzinger. Interface automata. In *Joint 8th European Software Engineering Conference and 9th ACM SIGSOFT International Symposium on the Foundations of Software Engineering (ESEC-FSE)*, 2001.

[24] Michael D. Ernst, Jake Cockrell, William G. Griswold, and David Notkin. Dynamically discovering likely program invariants to support program evolution. *IEEE Transactions on Software Engineering*, 27, 2001.

[25] J. Engblom and A. Ermedahl. Modeling complex flows for worst-case execution time analysis. In *Proceedings of IEEE Real-time Systems Symposium (RTSS)*, December 2000.

[26] J. Edmison, D. I. Lehn, M. Jones, and T. Martin. E-textile based automatic activity diary for medical annotation and analysis. In *International Workshop on Wearable and Implantable Body Sensor Networks (BSN)*, 2006.

[27] The FlexRay Communications System Specifications, ver. 2.1, 2005. `www.flexray.com`.

[28] B. S. Gulavani, T. A. Henzinger, Y. Kannan, A. V. Nori, and S. K. Rajamani. SYNERGY: A new algorithm for property checking. In *ACM SIGSOFT Symposium on the Foundations of Software Engineering (FSE)*, 2006.

[29] P. Godefroid, N. Klarlund, and K. Sen. DART: Directed automated random testing. In *ACM SIGPLAN International Conference on Programming Language Design and Implementation (PLDI)*, 2005.

[30] AbsInt Angewandte Informatik GmbH. aiT: Worst case execution time analyzer, 2005. `http://www.absint.com/ait/`.

[31] A. Goel, S. Meng, A. Roychoudhury, and P. S. Thiagarajan. Interacting process classes. In *International Conference on Software Engineering (ICSE)*, 2006.

[32] L. Guo, A. Roychoudhury, and T. Wang. Accurately choosing execution runs for software fault localization. In *International Conference on Compiler Construction (CC)*, 2006.

[33] M. Hutchins et al. Experiments on the effectiveness of dataflow- and controlflow-based test adequacy criteria. In *ACM/IEEE International Conference on Software Engineering (ICSE)*, 1994.

[34] D. Harel. Statecharts: A visual formalism for complex systems. *Science of Computrer Programming*, 8(3):231–274, 1987.

[35] D. Harel and O. Kupferman. On object systems and behavioral inheritance. *IEEE Transactions on Software Engineering*, 2002.

[36] D. Harel and R. Marelly. *Come, Let's Play: Scenario-Based Programming Using LSCs and the Play-Engine*. Springer-Verlag, 2003.

[37] G. Holzmann. SPIN Model Checker, Bell Laboratories, 1991.

[38] G. Holzmann. *The SPIN Model Checker*. Addison-Wesley, 2004.

[39] D. Hovemeyer and W. Pugh. Finding bugs is easy. In *OOPSLA Onward Session*, 2004.

[40] C. Healy and D. Whalley. Automatic detection and exploitation of branch constraints for timing analysis. *IEEE Transactions on Software Engineering*, 28(8), 2002.

[41] C. Jard. Synthesis of distributed testers from true-concurrency models of reactive systems. *Information and Software Technology*, 45(12):805–814, 2003.

[42] L. Ju, S. Chakraborty, and A. Roychoudhury. Accounting for cache-related preemption delay in dynamic priority schedulability analysis. In *Design Automation and Test in Europe (DATE)*, 2007.

[43] R. Jayaseelan, T. Mitra, and X. Li. Estimating the worst-case energy consumption of embedded software. In *IEEE Real-Time and Embedded Technology and Applications Symposium (RTAS)*, 2006.

[44] L. Ju, A. Roychoudhury, and S. Chakraborty. Schedulability analysis of MSC-based system models. In *IEEE Real-Time and Embedded Technology and Applications Symposium (RTAS)*, 2008.

[45] H. Kopetz and G. Bauer. The time-triggered architecture. *Proceedings of IEEE, Special Issue on Modeling and Design of Embedded Software*, 91(1):112–126, 2003.

[46] H. Kopetz and G. Grunsteidl. TTP—a protocol for fault-tolerant real-time systems. *IEEE Computer*, 27(1), 1994.

[47] J.-C. Kao and R. Marculescu. On optimization of e-textile systems using redundancy and energy-aware routing. *IEEE Transactions on Computers*, 55(6):745–756, 2006.

[48] C.-G. Lee et al. Analysis of cache-related preemption delay in fixed-priority preemtive scheduling. *IEEE Transactions on Computers*, 47(6), 1998.

[49] E. A. Lee. Building unreliable systems out of reliable components: The real time story. Technical Report UCB/EECS-2005-5, University of California at Berkeley, 2005.

[50] Edward A. Lee. The problem with threads. Technical Report UCB/EECS-2006-1, EECS Department, University of California, Berkeley, Jan. 2006; *IEEE Computer* 39(5):33–42, May 2006.

[51] Y. Liang, L. Ju, S. Chakraborty, T. Mitra, and A. Roychoudhury. Cache-aware optimization of BAN applications. In *International Conference on Hardware-Software Codesign and System Synthesis (CODES+ISSS)*, 2008.

[52] C. L. Liu and J. W. Layland. Scheduling algorithms for multiprogramming in a hard-real-time environment. *Journal of the ACM*, 20(1):46–61, 1973.

[53] X. Li, Y. Liang, T. Mitra, and A. Roychoudhury. Chronos: A Timing Analyzer for Embedded Software, 2005. `http://www.comp.nus.edu.sg/~rpembed/chronos/`.

[54] L. Lavagno, G. Martin, and B. Selic. *UML for Real: Design of Embedded Real-time Systems*. Kluwer Academic Publishers, 2003.

[55] Y.-T. S. Li, S. Malik, and A. Wolfe. Performance estimation of embedded software with instruction cache modeling. *ACM Transactions on Design Automation of Electronic Systems*, 4(3):257–279, 1999.

[56] K. G. Larsen, P. Pettersson, and W. Yi. UPPAAL in a nutshell. *International Journal on Software Tools for Technology Transfer*, 1, 1997.

[57] K. Lahiri, A. Raghunathan, and S. Dey. Fast performance analysis of bus-based system-on-chip communication architectures. In *IEEE/ACM International Conference on Computer-aided Design (ICCAD)*, 1999.

[58] X. Li, A. Roychoudhury, and T. Mitra. Modeling out-of-order processors for software timing analysis. In *IEEE Real-Time Systems Symposium (RTSS)*, pp. 92–103, December 2004.

[59] T. Lundqvist and P. Stenström. Timing anomalies in dynamically scheduled microprocessors. In *Proceedings of the 20th IEEE Real-Time Systems Symposium (RTSS)*, pp. 12–21, December 1999.

[60] J. Lehoczky, L. Sha, and Y. Ding. The rate monotonic scheduling algorithm: Exact characterization and average case behavior. In *IEEE Real-time Systems Symposium*, 1989.

[61] T. Mitra and A. Roychoudhury. Worst-case execution time and energy analysis. In *The Compiler Design Handbook: Optimizations and Machine Code Generation*, 2nd ed. CRC Press, 2007.

[62] S. Narayan and D. D. Gajski. Interfacing incompatible protocols using interface process generation. In *Design Automation Conference (DAC)*, 1995.

[63] H. S. Negi, T. Mitra, and A. Roychoudhury. Accurate estimation of cache-related preemption delay. In *International Conference on Hardware-Software Codesign and System Synthesis (CODES+ISSS)*, 2003.

[64] R. Passerone, L. de Alfaro, T. A. Henzinger, and A. Sangiovanni-Vincentelli. Convertibility verification and converter synthesis: Two faces of the same coin. In *International Conference on Computer Aided Design (ICCAD)*, 2002.

[65] P. R. Panda, N. D. Dutt, and A. Nicolau. On-chip vs. off-chip memory: The data partitioning problem in embedded processor-based systems. *ACM Transactions on Design Automation of Electronic Systems (TODAES)*, 5(3), 2000.

[66] S. Park, K. Mackenzie, and S. Jayaraman. The wearable motherboard: A framework for personalized mobile information processing (PMIP). In *DAC*, 2002.

[67] A. Pnueli. The temporal logic of programs. In *IEEE Symposium on Foundations of Computer Science (FOCS)*, 1977.

[68] R. Passerone, J. A. Rowson, and A. Sangiovanni-Vincentelli. Automatic synthesis of interfaces between incompatible protocols. In *Design Automation Conference (DAC)*, 1998.

[69] P. Puschner and A. Schedl. Computing maximum task execution times — a graph based approach. *Real-Time Systems*, 13(1), 1997.

[70] PSL. Property Specification Language. Accellera, `http://www.eda.org/vfv/docs/PSL-v1.1.pdf`.

[71] D. Peled, M. Y. Vardi, and M. Yannakakis. Black box checking. In *FORTE/PSTV*, 1999.

[72] J. P. Queille and J. Sifakis. Specification and verification of concurrent systems in CESAR. In *International Symposium on Programming, LNCS*. Vol. 137, 1982.

[73] M. A. Reniers. *Message Sequence Chart: Syntax and Semantics*. PhD Thesis, TU/e, 1999.

[74] Rhapsody. I-logix, inc. website: `http://www.ilogix.com`.

[75] A. Roychoudhury, T. Mitra, and S. R. Karri. Using formal techniques to debug the AMBA system-on-chip bus protocol. In *Design Automation and Test in Europe (DATE)*, 2003.

[76] M. Renieris and S. P. Reiss. Fault localization with nearest neighbor queries. In *Automated Software Engineering (ASE)*, 2003.

[77] A. Roychoudhury and P. S. Thiagarajan. Communicating transaction processes. In *IEEE Intl. Conf. on Applications of Concurrency in System Design (ACSD)*, 2003.

[78] A. Roychoudhury, P. S. Thiagarajan, T.-A. Tran, and V. Zvereva. Automatic generation of protocol converters from scenario-based specifications. In *IEEE Real-time Systems Symposium (RTSS)*, 2004.

[79] S. Schliecker et al. Reliable performance analysis of a multicore multithreaded system-on-chip. In *International Conference on Hardware Software Codesign and System Synthesis (CODES-ISSS)*, 2008.

[80] M. Sridharan, S. J. Fink, and R. Bodik. Thin slicing. In *PLDI*, 2007.

[81] A. C. Shaw. Reasoning about time in higher-level language software. *IEEE Transactions on Software Engineering*, 1(2):875–889, July 1989.

[82] V. Suhendra, T. Mitra, A. Roychoudhury, and T. Chen. WCET centric data allocation to scratchpad memory. In *IEEE Real-time Systems Symposium (RTSS)*, 2005.

[83] V. Suhendra, T. Mitra, A. Roychoudhury, and T. Chen. Efficient detection and exploitation of infeasible paths for software timing analysis. In *Proceedings of the 43rd ACM/IEEE Design Automation Conference (DAC)*, pp. 358–363, July 2006.

[84] Carnegie Mellon University, `http://www.cs.cmu.edu/~modelcheck/smv.html`. *The CMU SMV Model Checker*, 1998.

[85] Cadence Berkeley Laboratories, Free download from `http://www-cad.eecs.berkeley.edu/~kenmcmil/smv/`, California, USA. *The Cadence SMV Model Checker*, 1999.

[86] I. Sommerville. *Software Engineering*, seventh ed. Addison-Wesley, 2004.

[87] L. Sha, R. Rajkumar, and S. S. Sathaye. Generalized rate-monotonic scheduling theory: A framework for developing real-time systems. *Proceedings of IEEE*, 82(1), 1994.

[88] Stateflow. The MathWorks, inc. website: `http://www.mathworks.com`.

[89] N. Tillman and J. de Halleux. Pexwhite box test generation for .NET. In *Tests and Proofs, LNCS 4966*, Springer, 2008.

[90] H. Theiling, C. Ferdinand, and R. Wilhelm. Fast and precise WCET prediction by separated cache and path analyses. *Real-Time Systems*, 18(2/3):157–179, May 2000.

[91] L. Thiele, E. Wandeler, and S. Chakraborty. A stream-oriented component model for performance analysis of multiprocessor dsps. *IEEE Signal Processing Magazine*, 22(3), 2005.

[92] UBET. Ubet. `http://cm.bell-labs.com/cm/cs/what/ubet/`.

[93] S. Uchitel, J. Kramer, and J. Magee. Synthesis of behavioral models from scenarios. *IEEE Transactions on Software Engineering*, 29, 2003.

[94] M.Y. Vardi and P. Wolper. An automata-theoretic approach to automatic program verification. In *IEEE International Symposium on Logic in Computer Science (LICS)*, 1986.

[95] R. Wilhelm et al. The worst-case execution-time problem — overview of methods and survey of tools. *ACM Transactions on Embedded Computing Systems (TECS)*, 7(3), 2008.

[96] R. Wilhelm. Determing bounds on execution times. In *Handbook on Embedded Systems*. CRC Press, 2005.

[97] T. Wang and A. Roychoudhury. *Jslice*: A dynamic slicing tool for Java programs. National University of Singapore, `http://jslice.sourceforge.net`.

[98] T. Wang and A. Roychoudhury. Using compressed bytecode traces for slicing Java programs. In *ACM/IEEE International Conference on Software Engineering (ICSE)*, 2004.

[99] T. Wang and A. Roychoudhury. Hierarchical dynamic slicing. In *International Symposium on Software Testing and Analysis (ISSTA)*, 2007.

[100] T. Wang and A. Roychoudhury. Dynamic slicing on Java byte-code traces. *ACM Transactions on Programming Languages and Systems (TOPLAS)*, 30(2), 2008.

[101] T.-Y. Yen and W. Wolf. Performance estimation for real-time distributed embedded systems. *IEEE Transactions on Parallel and Distributed Systems*, 9(11), 1998.

[102] Z.120. Message Sequence Charts (MSC'96), 1996.

[103] A. Zeller. Isolating cause-effect chains from computer programs. In *ACM SIGSOFT Symposium on the Foundations of Software Engineering (FSE)*, 2002.

[104] X. Zhang, N. Gupta, and R. Gupta. Pruning dynamic slices with confidence. In *PLDI*, 2006.

[105] X. Zhang, S. Tallam, N. Gupta, and R. Gupta. Towards locating execution omission errors. In *PLDI*, 2007.

Index

Printed and bound by CPI Group (UK) Ltd, Croydon, CR0 4YY

03/10/2024

01040301-0008